A CONCISE
HISTORY OF MUSIC

BY

WILLIAM LOVELOCK, D.Mus.

with drawings by
EDGAR HOLLOWAY

BELL & HYMAN
LONDON

Published by
BELL & HYMAN LIMITED
Denmark House
37–39 Queen Elizabeth Street
London SE1 2QB

First published in 1953 by
G. Bell & Sons Ltd.
Reprinted 1955, 1959 (revised),
1962, 1964, 1966 (revised), 1968, 1969,
1972 (revised), 1974, 1979, 1980 (revised), 1981, 1984

ISBN: 0 7135 0678 4

Printed and bound in Great Britain by
Cox & Wyman Ltd, Reading

CONTENTS

FOREWORD

IN writing this book I have tried to trace not only how
the main stream of music developed, but also, to some
limited extent, the underlying causes of that development. The growth of an art does not take place in a
vacuum; it is inevitably affected by many external factors,
and these cannot be overlooked or underestimated. A book
of this length can be no more than a bare outline, and
much that is of interest has had to be omitted, to keep to
the main line of development. I have not attempted to
mention every possible composer, but have rather referred
to those who appear to be the more important. In any
case, a history which consists mainly of lists of composers
and their works is of but little value. What matters is the
way in which music grew, the development of styles
and forms.

In the case of many of the earlier composers there is
often some divergence of opinion as to the dates of their
births and deaths. I have given those sanctioned by the
more recent research, though even here there is at times
some lack of agreement among authorities.

I must record my gratitude to Dr. Wilfrid Dunwell,
B.A., B.Mus., for his patience in reading my drafts chapter
by chapter. His comments and criticisms have invariably
been both helpful and stimulating.

W. L.

ACKNOWLEDGEMENT

The record lists for the 1972 printing have
been revised by Mr Roy Emmerson

SUGGESTIONS FOR STUDY

SINCE this is a book for the beginner, not for the specialist, it is not proposed to include a detailed bibliography. It is suggested, however, that the student should supplement his reading by the books mentioned below; also that relevant chapters of any or all in List 1, and any other comparable books on the general history of music, should be read in conjunction with the individual chapters of the present work. From experience both in his student days and as a teacher, the writer has found that a surer grasp of facts is to be gained by reading what several writers have to say about a given matter or period, rather than by constantly rereading a single book. Moreover, each writer deals with his subject from his own angle; one will tend to stress one aspect, while another will adopt a different approach. So that by the time the student has been through three or four different books he should have a fairly all-round grasp of the basic facts.

Constant reference to relevant articles in such compilations as Scholes' *Oxford Companion to Music*, Grove's *Dictionary of Music*, Collins' *Music Encyclopedia* and the *Harvard Dictionary of Music* is invaluable to supplement the inevitably condensed information given in the chapters which follow.

It cannot be too strongly stressed that reference to the music itself, studying the printed copy and listening to performances, is essential for anything like a full understanding. (It may be pointed out to the prospective examination candidate that the days are long past when a pass in history could be achieved by writing about what one had merely read about. Examiners expect some knowledge of the music itself, not just of other people's opinions of it.) For the period up to Bach, a brief but useful book, which every student should possess, is *Masterpieces of Music before 1750*, by Parrish and Ohl (Faber), containing examples of the chief types of composition from the days of plainsong onwards. More comprehensive, and invaluable to the earnest student, is the unique *Historical Anthology of Music*, by Davison and Apel (2 vols., Oxford University Press), available in any reputable library. For the period since 1750 sufficient music is available, including miniature scores, for the student to make his own selection with some guidance from a teacher.

The record lists to each chapter do not pretend to be in any way comprehensive, but they should be especially useful in the earlier period.

List 1.   General Outlines

Einstein: *A Short History of Music* (Cassell).
Finney: *History of Music* (Harrap).
Sachs: *Short History of Music* (Dobson).
Colles: *The Growth of Music* (Oxford University Press).
Parry: *The Art of Music* (Kegan Paul).
Stanford and Forsyth: *History of Music* (Macmillan).
Westrup: *An Introduction to Musical History* (Hutchinson's University Library).

The last-named deals in an illuminating manner with the background against which music was composed during various periods.

List 2.   For More Detailed and Comprehensive Study

The Oxford History of Music (Oxford University Press).
Reese: *Music in the Middle Ages* (Dent).
Bukofzer: *Music in the Baroque Era* (Norton).
Einstein: *Music in the Romantic Era* (Norton).
Lang: *Music in Western Civilisation* (Norton).
Strunk: *Source Readings in Music History* (Faber).
Walker: *History of Music in England* (Oxford University Press).
Dent: *Opera* (Pelican Books).
Abraham: *A Hundred Years of Music* (Duckworth).
Man and his Music: 4 vols. (Rockcliffe).

The writings of Sir Donald Tovey—Essays and Lectures on Music, the six volumes of Essays in Critical Analysis (Oxford University Press), and his articles on music in the *Encyclopaedia Britannica* are not only informative, but stimulating.

Those who wish to delve into the processes of contemporary music are referred to:

Abraham: *This Modern Stuff* (Citadel Press).
Maine: *New Paths in Music* (Nelson).
Dyson: *The New Music* (Oxford University Press).
Lambert: *Music Ho!* (Faber).
Carner: *A Study of 20th-century Harmony* (Williams).
Křenek: *Studies in Counterpoint* (Schirmer).
Bauer: *20th-century Music* (Putnam).
Dunwell: *Evolution of 20th-century Harmony* (Novello).
Spink: *An Historical Approach to Musical Form* (Bell).
Mitchell: *The Language of Modern Music* (Faber).

The lives of most of the great composers, with consideration of their works and styles, are usefully dealt with in Dent's 'Master Musicians' series of books.

Records

For the earlier periods the H.M.V. *History of Music in Sound,* and the German *Archiv* series are invaluable and it is hardly necessary to look elsewhere.   The lists from the time of Bach onwards are the merest suggestions, and can be supplemented *ad lib.* by reference to the various catalogues. All records mentioned are available at the time of writing, but current catalogues should be consulted since frequent changes are made.

N.B.   All records for Chapters 1 to 6 are available in Mono only.

CHAPTER ONE

ON THE STUDY
OF MUSICAL HISTORY

WE may well begin with a question: What are the object and the value of the study of the history of music? It should be obvious that to undertake the study of any subject without some definite aim, merely to load the mind with a host of facts which may never be put to any use, is a waste of time, interesting as it may be. The object of our study of musical history should be to increase our understanding of the art; its value is that it can give us a greater appreciation of and insight into the works of the various composers. Not only can it augment our understanding and appreciation, but it can broaden them so that, given the receptiveness which comes by deliberately trying to keep an open mind, we can follow intelligently and gain enjoyment, in the highest sense, from the music of all periods, not confining our liking and listening to that which makes the most immediate appeal. We can achieve some understanding of and sympathy with a composer whose work may at first seem unattractive, by knowing why he wrote in his particular style. Admittedly, everyone has personal preferences. One type of mind is, for example, more strongly attracted by the style of Mozart or Beethoven than by that of Bach or Handel; while another may instinctively prefer the latter to the former. But there is no reason why both minds should not appreciate the greatness of all four composers, this appreciation being fostered and deepened by the thoughtful study of history. The person who says, 'I don't like Bach's music, therefore it is no good,' is simply adopting the attitude of the fond mother who remarked, when watching a platoon on the

march, 'Our Jack's the only one in step'; he betrays a total
lack of historical background. Also, be it said, of common
sense. Whether we personally 'like' the music of Bach or
of any other great composer, or whether we find it lacking
in appeal, we must still admit its greatness, since it is
attested by the general consent of educated musical opinion.

There are a number of ways of approaching the study
of musical history. Of these the least useful is the method
of memorising the dates of the births and deaths of composers. Not that such knowledge is to be deprecated; but
the fact that Bach was born on March 21st, 1685, and died
on July 28th, 1750, is relatively immaterial. What does
matter is the fact that his active life as a composer lay in
the first half of the 18th century.

The personal circumstances of a composer's life are important in so far as they affected his output of composition.
In some cases, e.g. a large number of the composers of the
17th and 18th centuries, the effect was considerable; in
others, and especially since the beginning of the 19th century, it was far less so. More generally important are the
influences which went to the formation of a composer's
style, and the way in which he may have influenced his
successors.

The effect which the course of a composer's life may have
had on his output is well illustrated by reference to the
chief appointments which Bach held. Leaving aside his
short year of service as organist at St. Blasius' Church in
Mulhausen, his first important post was that of organist at
the Ducal Court of Weimar, to which he was appointed
in 1708. His duties necessitated the provision of works for
performance on the instrument in the castle chapel, hence
a large number of preludes and fugues, the toccatas, the
Little Organ Book, etc. After his promotion to the position of *konzertmeister* in 1714, he was obliged to furnish
a 'new piece monthly' for the chapel; hence many cantatas. From 1717 to 1723 Bach was *kapellmeister* to
Prince Leopold of Anhalt-Cöthen, *i.e.* he was responsible

for the court music which, in this instance, was of a secular nature. 'The Cöthen court', to quote Prof. C. S. Terry,* 'was "reformed", its chapel an unlovely vault in which only stern Calvinist psalm tunes were heard.' Bach was concerned with the provision of instrumental music, in some of which the Prince himself took part. Hence such works as the orchestral suites, the concertos, and the sonatas and suites for violin. For the time being he had no need to write choral music, and therefore gave it no attention.

On his appointment, in 1723, as Cantor at St. Thomas's Church in Leipzig, Bach was faced with the task, among other things, of providing some fifty-nine cantatas annually, and although he indulged in a good deal of 'borrowing' from one work to another, adapting older movements to fresh words, his extant cantatas number over 200. Besides these, the Leipzig period also saw the birth of the Passions and other great choral works, written under the obligations of his appointment. It is a solemn thought that had Bach remained at Cöthen until he died, we might never have had the experience of being enthralled by the *St. Matthew Passion*, the motet *Sing Ye to the Lord*, or the *Mass in B Minor*, to name no others.

Returning now to the question of the study of musical history. Another method of approach is the study of the growth of the various forms, *i.e.* the structural principles, which have emerged in the course of the centuries. But this is to some extent a limited aspect, and is in any case bound up with the development of the various styles. It is the study of the origins and development of these styles which is perhaps the most useful and generalised approach, since the nature of a style is determined by all possible factors—melody, harmony, texture, formal structure, etc. —as well as the actual aim and object of the compositions. We shall therefore try to trace, admittedly only in brief outline, the growth of musical styles.

In the past 1,000 years, which is the approximate period

* *Bach, a Biography.*

to be covered by our study, a number of differing styles have originated, developed to a climax, and then more or less gradually declined. Up to about the year 1600, composers were chiefly concerned with mastering the technique of polyphony—that is, the satisfactory combination of two or more simultaneous melodies and rhythms. A number of peaks were scaled *en route*, and the polyphonic summit was reached in the latter part of the 16th century. In the years immediately before 1600, however, new ideas, based on a more harmonic approach, were in the air. These were exploited in many directions and led, in the first half of the 18th century, to the twin summits of Handel and Bach. Before these two men had completed their life-work further new ideas began to emerge, leading, by way of the 'classical' sonata and symphony, through Haydn and Mozart to Beethoven. Beethoven himself was the bridge into the next period, the 'Age of Romanticism', with which are associated the names of such men as Weber, Schumann, Liszt and Wagner. And so we move into the present century, with its many conflicting currents.

It must be realised that there is no clear dividing line between the various periods and styles; they merge, the culmination of one style being overlapped by the beginnings of a new one. This may be clearly seen in reference to Bach, some of whose own sons were among the progenitors of what developed into the 'classical' style, and who were inclined to look upon their great father as old-fashioned, irreverently referring to him as 'the Old Wig'. Neither must it be thought that a new style of writing makes, as it were, an entirely fresh start; it is a gradual development from its predecessor, in due course reaching its culmination, and germinating in its life the seeds of its successor.

Such labels as 'classic' and 'romantic' must not be taken too literally. 'Romanticism', for example, is assumed to imply, among other things, the expression of personal emotion in music and a tendency to subordinate other matters to this expression. It is applied particularly to music of the 19th century. But composers of this period were not the first to give their music this personal expressiveness; the Elizabethan madrigalists had done so over 200 years earlier, while some would claim that, at least in this connection, the greatest of all romantics was Bach. Similarly with the term 'modernism'. It is common to speak of 'modern' music and a 'modern' style as if they were inventions of the 20th century. But there have always been modernists. Bach's sons were modernists in that they thought and wrote in what was in their time a 'modern', *i.e.* a new idiom. Schumann writes of Beethoven as one of the 'moderns'. Possibly the greatest and most influential of all modernists were those unknown pioneers who, some time before the year 1000, first gave system and order to singing at intervals other than the octave and unison, for instance the 4ths or 5ths which separate the tenor and bass voices; from which conception derives all music written since their day.

The history of the development of an art cannot be dealt with in isolation. Music, like painting, sculpture or architecture, has been continuously affected by external factors, in particular ecclesiastical and social conditions and changes. In a relatively brief study of musical history it is obviously impossible to deal with the effects of such factors in any detail; all that can be done is to indicate some of the more outstanding influences and to show their outcome.

In medieval times the majority of musicians, whether composers or executants or both, were in the service of the Church; many, indeed, were in holy orders. Their chief duty was to provide and perform music for the church services, though this did not mean that they necessarily confined their attention and labours solely to such music. Up to the time of the reformers—Luther, Calvin and the English Protestants—church music developed on certain lines, generally conformable to the (Catholic) religious outlook of the times, and calculated, especially in the 16th century, to enhance the devotional impulses of the worshippers. The congregation, however, took little or no part in the musical side of the services. The Reformers, despite certain differences in method and achievement, had many aims in common, among these being a more actual and personal participation by the congregation in the act of worship. To this end the use of the Latin tongue, customary in the Western Church from its very beginning, was discarded, the services being conducted in the vernacular, and some, at least, of the music being congregational. This had an immediate effect on the style of music composed for use in the Reformed Churches, an effect which was rapidly felt in other directions. Most notable, to cite a specific example, was Luther's introduction of the *chorale*. From this arose the *Chorale Prelude*, a form of composition brought to the ultimate peak of perfection by Bach, many of whose works in this *genre* are of unsurpassable beauty. Yet had Luther never begun his fight against abuses in the Church, Bach's chorale preludes, and his cantatas and Passions, might never have been written.

In the later Middle Ages the changing social conditions and the wider spread of culture provided opportunities for large numbers of musicians to take service in the households of wealthy rulers and noblemen, who, either from natural inclination or in conformity with the prevailing fashion, posed as patrons of the arts. The composer, however employed, was expected to provide music acceptable to the taste of his employer, this taste being largely dictated by the fashion of the moment. This is not to imply that the only music written in, say, the 18th century, was such as might satisfy the palate of the wealthy but possibly untutored layman. Musicians have always been ready to experiment, and much has depended on the employer. A patron such as the great Prince Nicholas Esterhazy, Haydn's employer for many years, may be said to have been indirectly responsible for a great amount of progress and development in music by his encouragement of his great musician-servant (who, incidentally, was expected to wear a livery like any other employee), and by his great personal interest in the art. Haydn, possibly more than any other musician of this period, the 'Age of Patronage', was in a position to give rein to his inventive genius in every direction, to the lasting benefit of music.

It is only by experiment that progress is possible; it is the man with the forward-looking type of mind, be he musician, painter or designer of aeroplanes, who forces man out of the rut of 'what was good enough for my father is good enough for me'. Experiment may at times have been wild—at one point it reached such a pitch that the authority of a papal Bull was needed to curb its exuberance—but even the wildest experiments may have in them the seeds of future developments of real value. (Not so many years ago there were those who laughed at the Wright brothers' attempts to fly in a heavier-than-air machine.) The 'man with a mission' may be a fanatic with a large bee buzzing in his bonnet, but his aims and ideas, however fantastic they may seem to his contemporaries, may be based on principles which can lead his successors steadily forward to a goal which he himself could only dimly envisage.

The reader should not misinterpret the preceding paragraphs. Music has not 'progressed' in the sense that it has continually 'got better and better'. To say that the science of medicine has progressed by 'getting better' between the Middle Ages and the present day is an obvious truism. But who is to say whether, for example, the *9th Symphony* of Beethoven is intrinsically 'better' than the *St. Matthew Passion* of Bach or *Messiah* of Handel, both of which were written before Beethoven was born? It is only in comparatively recent times that a clear realisation of the value of much of the older music has come about, due largely to the work of musicians who had the interest to study the works of earlier ages. The musician-servant of the 18th century, for example, provided only contemporary music for the delectation of his employer, and had to be prepared

to compose what was required for any given occasion.*
Composing to order was largely the rule, whatever post
the musician held, and 'revivals' of older works were unheard of. What the audience wanted was the music of
their own time, this being presumably considered 'better'
than that of preceding generations. At the present day
this would be comparable to performing, say, the symphonies of Sibelius, Vaughan Williams and Walton, but
neglecting entirely those of Haydn, Mozart and Beethoven.
In the case of medicine we are dealing with concrete facts.
We can say categorically that penicillin is a better curative
agent than some horrible medieval compound of frogs' eyes
and bats' blood. But music is of all things the least concrete and tangible, and while personal preference may give
the listener a bias towards the music of one period rather
than another, it is essential to realise that there has never
been a time when works of real artistic value were not being
written.

In the writings of the 17th and 18th centuries we find
continual reference to the contemporary 'perfection' of
music. In 1647, Heinrich Schütz, in the Preface to the
second part of his *Symphoniae Sacrae*, refers to 'the modern
Italian manner . . . by means of which music is thought to
have at length attained its final perfection'. Nearly a hundred years later, Jean Philippe Rameau implies that the
music of his time is 'more perfect than that of the ancients'.
While in 1752 Joachim Quantz states that 'it took a long
time to bring music to that approximation of perfection
in which it stands to-day'. Possibly the first to realise
the fallacy of this attitude was the Belgian musicologist

* The Italian violinist Vivaldi furnishes an excellent example of the
working of this system. In 1709 he was appointed professor of the violin
at the *Ospedale della Pieta* in Venice, becoming *Maestro dei Concerti* (concert director) in 1716. A condition of his appointment was that he
should provide two concertos a month for performance by the orchestra,
so that the total of his works in this form, all more or less written to
order, is immense. And this before 'mass production' was heard of.
See also the mention above of Bach's various posts and the types of
composition resulting therefrom.

François-Joseph Fétis (1784 to 1871), who writes: 'One of the greatest obstacles to the fairness of judgments on the value of musical works is found in the doctrine of progress applied to the arts. I have long striven against it, and I had to endure lively altercations when I maintained that music changes, and that it progresses only in material elements.'

We may agree that perfection has been achieved within a given style, as in, for example, the work of a Palestrina, a Bach or a Mozart, but personal taste cannot be set aside. If beauty, as it has been said, is in the eye of the beholder, we may perhaps also say that perfection in music lies in the ear of the listener. For one, perfection may be represented by the *St. Matthew Passion* of Bach; for another by the *Jupiter Symphony* of Mozart (which Schumann included among the things in this world of which 'there is nothing to be said at all'); while yet another may find the unsurpassable in Beethoven's *Choral Symphony*.

Not every composer has been a Bach, a Mozart or a Beethoven; not every poet can be a Shakespeare or a Milton. Nevertheless, the work of the lesser men has its value, and that not merely because it points towards that of the giants. We may admit, for example, that Bach's study of the works of Pachelbel and Buxtehude helped greatly to form his own style; it is certain that he learned much from them, and we can see, at this distance of time, that they were, so to speak, only part of the way up the mountain whose summit he ultimately attained. But while they did not achieve the stature of their great successor, they produced much music which is itself of far from negligible value.

Finally, the need to hear music of all periods and styles must be stressed most strongly. All our study of history, of style, of form or of anything else is so much wasted effort unless it is applied to improve our understanding and appreciation of music itself; and music has no real existence except in sound. Which brings us, full circle, back to the opening of this chapter.

CHAPTER TWO

THE BEGINNINGS
OF WESTERN EUROPEAN MUSIC

IN early times the chief, if not the only patron of the arts was the Church, and it is in the music for the various services—the Mass and the other 'Offices'—that the first developments which have led to the music of the present day are to be traced. Folk-song is the oldest form of music, but although its style has varied from century to century and from country to country, it can hardly be said to have developed. Similarly, the secular callings of minstrel and *jongleur* are of great antiquity, but their art developed only up to a certain point. (The French *jongleur* derives from the Latin *joculator*, whose function in Roman times had obviously some connection with the lighter side of musical entertainment.) Possibly the only 20th-century survivals of the minstrels in the British Isles are the strolling fiddlers sometimes encountered in parts of Ireland.

All music is based on some kind of scale, and an account of the origins of our music must begin with some consideration of the derivation of its scale-system.* The scales which were the basis of the early church music derive from those of the ancient Greeks and are known as *modes*. A mode consists essentially of a series of sounds proceeding by steps from a note to its octave, and its name and character are determined by the order of the tones and semitones (and sometimes other intervals) within that series. It is important to realise that mode and key are two entirely different things; key depends on pitch; mode does not. The actual pitch of a mode is immaterial; provided that the

---

* But let it not be thought that the scale is invented before the music is composed. Music, at first in the form of melody, gradually evolved and from it a scale-system was ultimately derived. In other words, practice came before theory. See also page 31.

set order of tones and semitones is maintained, the mode remains unchanged, whatever the pitch. The difference between the keys of C major and G major lies in the fact that the latter begins a perfect 5th higher (or a perfect 4th lower) than the former; but their mode is identical. In both, as in all major scales, there are semitones between the 3rd and 4th and the 7th and 8th degrees above the tonic, the other degrees being separated by whole tones. In any harmonic minor scale there are semitones between the 2nd and 3rd, the 5th and 6th and the 7th and 8th degrees, while there is an augmented 2nd between the 6th and 7th; the other degrees lie a tone apart. Thus, whatever its pitch or 'key', the mode of any minor scale is the same as that of any other one, but differs from that of any major scale.

The modal system of the ancient Greeks was highly organised and complex, the scales being classified as diatonic, chromatic and enharmonic. The medieval scale-system, which served as a basis for composition until the 16th century, arose from a misunderstanding of the Greek diatonic system. To describe in detail how this misunderstanding came about would require far more space than can be spared. Briefly, the differences between the two systems are as follows. The Greeks recognised four principal modes, the *Dorian, Phrygian, Lydian* and *Mixolydian*, beginning respectively on E, D, C and B, and consisting, in modern terminology, of 'white notes' only. Their characters were distinguished, as has already been mentioned, by the positions of the semitones in relation to the lowest notes. To these were added four subordinate modes, the *Hypodorian, Hypophrygian, Hypolydian* and *Hypomixolydian*, beginning a 5th below their respective principals. There would seem to be little doubt that the earliest music of the Christian Church had strong affinities with that of the Jewish rite, but writers on music throughout the Middle Ages based their work on such garbled versions of Greek theory as were passed on from the ancient world to the Dark Ages. This was so even in the Byzantine (Eastern)

Church, which was, at least geographically, the most likely inheritor of the ancient Greek tradition. The Byzantines formulated four 'chief' modes and four subordinate ones which began a 4th below their respective chiefs. The subordinate modes were called 'plagal' and corresponded to the 'hypo' modes of the Greeks. But error had crept into the conception of the system, since the four 'chief' modes of the Byzantines began respectively on D, E, F and G, *i.e.* in ascending order as opposed to the descending

Ex. 1.   The Medieval Modes

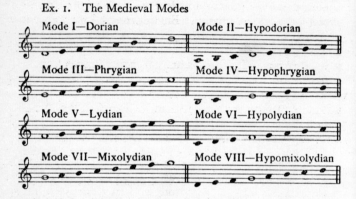

order of the Greeks.   Further, the first mode was that on D as against the Greek *Dorian*, which began on E.   It is impossible to say exactly how or why these errors arose in the Byzantine theory. They were accepted by such western writers as Boethius (approx. 475 to 520) and Alcuin (735 to 804).

Later writers, misunderstanding the explanations of the 2nd-century author, Ptolemy, failed to perceive the true Greek theory, but adopted the Greek names, applying them wrongly. The ultimate outcome was a series of modes known as *Dorian, Phrygian, Lydian* and *Mixolydian*, beginning respectively on D, E, F and G, and known as *Authentic* modes, with their respective plagal versions beginning a 4th lower called and *Hypodorian, Hypophrygian*, etc.

At a later period two more modes, with their plagal attendants, were admitted, the *Aeolian* (A to A) and the *Ionian* (C to C). This gave a series of twelve modes of which the complete theory was ultimately expounded by the Swiss writer Henricus Glareanus in his *Dodecachordon* in 1547. The *Aeolian* mode is practically our minor scale, and the *Ionian* our major. They were hardly new inventions, but their incorporation into the official system did provide theoretical justification for the current practice of composers. The *Ionian* mode was far from uncommon in secular music—the famous English round *Sumer is icumen in*

Ex. 2. Aeolian and Ionian Modes

(13th or early 14th century) is as clearly in the major scale as anything ever written—but it was frowned upon by the Church for this very reason, and was dubbed *Modus Lascivus*, the 'wanton' mode.

Examination of Exx. 1 and 2 shows that some modes with different names, *e.g. Dorian* and *Hypomixolydian*, *Hypodorian* and *Aeolian*, are superficially identical. This identity is, however, apparent rather than actual. A mode was distinguished by its *Final*, that is, the lowest note of its 'authentic' version. Thus, the final of both *Dorian* and *Hypodorian* is D, that of the *Mixolydian* and *Hypomixolydian* is G, and that of the *Aeolian* and *Hypoaeolian* is A. A melody in the authentic *Dorian* mode would lie fundamentally between D and its octave, circling round the dominant A, and would end on the lower D. In the *Hypodorian* mode the melody would lie between A and its octave, but would end on D, not on A. An authentic *Aeolian* melody would also lie between A and its octave, but would end on the final A. It must be remembered that a 'final' is not a 'tonic'. A final is the note on which a (modal) melody ends—the lowest note of its authentic mode. A tonic is the note which gives its name to a key, and it has already been pointed out that the term 'key' is inapplicable in modal music.

The difference between authentic and plagal melodies may perhaps be further clarified by reference to two well-known tunes of later date. The melody of 'Drink to me only with thine eyes', if written in G major, lies between G and its octave. It might be said to be in the 'authentic' key of G major. The melody of 'You Gentlemen of England', in the same key, lies within the octave above D, but uses only the notes of the scale of G major and ends on G. It might therefore be said to be in the 'plagal' form of G major.*

It is sometimes stated that St. Ambrose (333 to 397) was responsible for the arrangement of the four authentic modes, and that St. Gregory the Great, who was Pope from 590 to 604, added the plagal versions. It is far from certain that this is so, though both undertook or initiated some systematisation of the church music of their time. It is doubtful whether either had anything to do with the theoretical basis of music or, indeed, composed at all. Ambrose, apart from insisting on a more restrained and devout style of performance than that prevailing, was the author of a number of Latin hymns which are still in use, and was responsible for an *Antiphonary* which was later replaced by that of Gregory. Gregory was responsible for reforms in both ritual and music. His name is most commonly associated with 'Gregorian chant', a method of rendering the psalms which is still the standard in the Roman Church and also in many English churches.

The origins of our present system of musical notation

---

[1] These two melodies are to be found in the *New National Song Book* (Boosey and Hawkes).

were remarkably humble. The Greeks had a notation based on their alphabet, but this method, although it appeared in western Europe, using Roman characters, about the 10th century, never gained any great hold there. As long as the body of church music remained but small, it is possible, though by no means certain, that it may have been passed on orally, probably undergoing frequent modification in the process. But even if oral transmission ever did exist, the increased use of music in the services, and the undesirability of variation, made some system of notation obviously essential. The earliest attempts were vague, consisting of *neumes*. These were a kind of directional signs placed above the Latin text, and were at first little more than mnemonics for one who was already familiar with the music. They indicated, roughly, whether the tune rose, fell, or remained on the same note, *i.e.* its general curve, and may be compared with the cabalistic signs used by some teachers of elocution to indicate the rise and fall of the voice.

In course of time the number of neumes grew quite large, and their shapes and meanings became increasingly definite. Even so, a large element of vagueness remained, the interpretation of any given neume, or group of neumes, depending too much on the individual singer. In the 9th and 10th centuries there were numerous attempts to devise a really definite and satisfactory method of pitch-notation, and some time before the year 1000 one writer—it will never be known who—decided to draw above the text a single red line representing the note F, with neumes above, across, or below it. This, the origin of our present stave, was an enormous step forward, since it clearly indicated one definite note from which others could be more or less accurately calculated. Even so, strict accuracy was certain only within the immediate vicinity of the line, *i.e.* within a range of four or five notes. The complete solution was eventually reached in two further stages. A yellow line, representing C, was added above the red one for F, giving still greater exactness; and finally two black lines were added, one on each side of the

F line. This produced a complete stave of four lines, which was sufficient for the notation of a very large number of the traditional melodies.

The addition of the yellow and black lines to the original red F is sometimes attributed to the Benedictine monk Guido d'Arezzo (*c.* 990 to 1050), but it seems more likely that he merely advocated and helped to popularise a method which was already to some extent in use.* Guido's chief works are *Micrologus*, in which he expounds his methods of teaching, and *De Ignoto Cantu*, a treatise on sight-singing which opens with the caustic statement that 'the most fatuous of all men of our times are the singers'! It is certain that Guido simplified and clarified neumatic notation, his reforms leading in the direction of our present note shapes. He also made systematic use of the first seven letters of the alphabet for naming notes, and invented a system of 'Solmisation', in which the degrees of the scale are designated by syllables rather than by letters, as in Tonic Solfa. Rather surprisingly, his method was based not on one of the officially acceptable modes, but on the 'wanton' Ionian. Whether this was due to secular influence or to prophetic genius is debatable. The fact is that he noticed that the lines of a well-known hymn to St. John Baptist began successively on the notes C, D, E, F, G and A, and it was from the initial syllables of the lines of this hymn, used as mnemonics—*ut-re-mi-fa-sol-la*—that he formed his system. These names, with the addition of *si* for B, are still used in France and Italy, though in the latter country the more singable *do* is substituted for *ut*.

* It must be realised that the writings of this early period, long before the invention of printing, are scarce and their authorship often uncertain. The authors, moreover, were not writing for posterity but for their contemporaries who, in all probability, already had some idea of the subject with which any given treatise was dealing. Many early writers seem almost to have been constitutionally incapable of expressing themselves with any clarity, and difficulties are increased by the fact that for centuries the language used was ecclesiastical Latin, which is at times almost incomprehensible. There are therefore a number of matters on which even the most erudite of musicologists cannot be certain.

It was stated above that the four-line stave was adequate for the notation of a large number of melodies. It must, however, be noted that absolute pitch was not then fixed as it is, by general agreement, nowadays. The relative pitch of the notes of a scale was quite definite, but the absolute pitch of a melody would vary according to the singer and according to the mode. Thus, the authentic *Dorian* mode and any melody in that mode could be noted with no trouble within the limits of the four-line stave:

Ex. 3

D E F G A B C D

But as long as the second line represented F, a *Hypodorian* melody (A to A) would lie partly above or partly below the stave, and leger lines were as yet far in the future. The solution to this difficulty was found in clefs (a clef is literally a 'key') which could be moved up or down the stave in the same way as the C clef moves on our present five-line stave according to whether the part is being read by, for example, a viola player (middle line) or a tenor trombonist (4th line).* For a *Hypodorian* melody, therefore, the clef would need to be placed higher on the stave so as to make available more lines and spaces below the note it indicated. See Ex. 4, overleaf.

* The so-called 'Great Stave' of eleven lines, with the C clef always on the 6th line, so beloved of writers of books on the rudiments of music, is merely a theoretical abstraction. In the course of the centuries the number of lines in the stave has varied, often according to the caprice of the individual composer, and also according to the type of composition. There are examples of staves of fifteen lines with three clefs at different levels, and the maximum would seem to be one of no fewer than twenty-five lines for a five-part composition. The eleven-line stave, as one authority says (C. F. Abdy Williams, *Notation*), 'was never in practical use except by accident'. The medieval composer shifted his clefs about to suit himself, a practice which, in combination with an unwieldy stave, at times produces results alarming to the 20th-century eye.

The earliest clefs were F and C, and were originally formed simply as capital letters. In the course of time, and probably owing to the desire of scribes to embellish them, they have assumed their present shapes. The G (treble) clef appeared first in the 13th century, but was only rarely used before the rise of instrumental music in the 16th century.

Ex. 4. Hypodorian Mode

A B C D E F G A

Before leaving this very rough outline of early notation, one other point must be mentioned. The Greek diatonic system, although largely based on the 'white-note' scale, admitted what would now be called B flat in certain cases, and this carried over into the medieval system. One reason for this was the dislike of the augmented 4th F to B (the medieval theorist's *Diabolus in Musica* or 'Devil in music'), which could be 'softened' into the perfect interval by flattening the upper note. Two kinds of B were therefore recognised, 'hard' and 'soft'. The hard B—B *durum*—was indicated when necessary by the sign ♮, also known as B *quadratum* or 'square' B; the soft B—B *mollis*—was shown by ♭, B *rotundum* or 'round' B. These two signs are respectively the origins of our ♮ and ♭. The sharp sign ♯ was a later invention, and was at first used equally with ♮ to indicate a contradiction of ♭.

So far only the theoretical aspects of the early music have been considered; what was the music itself? The answer to this question is 'pure melody'. Deliberate singing or playing in two or more parts seems to have been unheard of, though it is hardly possible that it cannot at times have occurred accidentally. The ancient Greeks understood 'magadizing', *i.e.* playing or singing in octaves; indeed, this was hardly avoidable if women and men, or boys and men, were performing together. But the mere duplication of a melody at the octave is not part-singing or playing. It must be realised that misunderstandings of ancient Greek theory, and the lack of clear and definite notation, had little if any effect on the composers themselves during the centuries when the body of 'Plainsong' was being built up. Who were the men who wrote much of the music will never be known. Even if Ambrose and Gregory actually composed, their contribution, as compared with the enormous amount of such music still extant and still in regular use in the Catholic Church, much of which dates from very early times, could be but small. It is worth remembering that practice always precedes theory; the composer writes as he feels impelled to write, and then the theorist comes along and explains what he has done and how he has done it.

Many people find plainsong an acquired taste, and it must be admitted that the lack of harmony and the use of unfamiliar scales may be some slight bar to its immediate understanding and appreciation. Nevertheless, to those who will take the trouble to familiarise themselves with it, plainsong is as rewarding as any other style of music. The first essentials, as in approaching any music which may need some effort for appreciation, are an open mind and an acceptance of the fact that, since educated musical opinion agrees that it is a highly-developed branch of musical art, there must be something of value in it which is worth searching for. It is most strongly urged that those to whom plainsong is unfamiliar should take every opportunity of hearing it as it is performed in the bigger Catholic churches and cathedrals. Merely humming it over to oneself, or playing it on the piano, conveys nothing of its dignity and beauty; it is music for use under certain conditions and must be heard in the surroundings for which it is intended.

Plainsong can only be correctly understood and interpreted when sung unaccompanied. It is more than doubtful whether instruments were used in churches at all before about the 9th century, and the only instrument which has never been considered unacceptable is the organ. In the Middle Ages there was continual warfare between the musicians, who tried to introduce into the church instruments other than the organ, and the ecclesiastical authorities, who disapproved of their use on account of secular associations. (Later, however, the authorities modified their attitude considerably; hence, among other things, the orchestrally accompanied Masses of Mozart and Schubert.) The earliest organs, in any case, could hardly do more than duplicate the melody; even had such a thing as 'Harmony' been evolved (it had not), the crude instruments of the time could not have attempted it.* The use of organ accompaniment to plainsong, although common enough nowadays, is strictly speaking an anachronism, and is only to be tolerated if of the most simple and restrained character.

The music of the Church, then, at least up to the 10th century, was purely melodic, any melody being normally limited to the compass of one octave—the octave of its mode. It was, moreover, not bound by any rigid metrical rhythm. Definite note values were not thought of until the 12th century, when 'measurable music' first made its appearance. Authorities differ considerably on the rhythmic treatment of plainsong; all that can be said with any certainty is that there was no organised system of relative note values comparable to minim, crotchet, etc.

The types of composition embodied in plainsong are those applicable to the various services of the Church, the melodic style varying from simple to highly ornate. The hymns which occur in services such as Vespers and Compline are frequently of a very straightforward kind, often using mainly one note to each syllable, and exhibiting a minimum of ornamentation. An example is the Advent hymn, of which

* The 'keys' were actually 'sliders', pulled out or pushed in to admit or prevent the admission of air into the pipes. The invention of keys to be depressed dates from the 12th century, and the earliest were of a size to be struck by the clenched fist; hence the term *pulsator organorum* —organ-beater—for the organist.

the words are attributed to St. Ambrose, *Conditor alme siderum*. The usual English version begins: 'Creator of the stars and light.'

Ex. 5.   Conditor alme siderum

Of the more ornate kind we may quote the Passion Sunday hymn *Vexilla Regis* ('The Royal banners forward go'). It dates from the end of the 6th century.

Ex. 6.   Vexilla Regis

This is one of the great melodies of all time, as will be readily agreed by all who have heard it sung in its proper surroundings.

The most highly ornate melodies are found in some of the music for the Mass. Much of this is of great beauty, with an amazingly complex melodic outline, classified as 'melismatic' plainsong. *Melisma* is a Greek word literally meaning 'song'. The term 'melismatic' is applied to passages where several notes are taken to one syllable.

The most important body of plainsong is that for the Mass. It is divided into two categories, the *Ordinary* and the *Proper*. The Ordinary consists of those portions of which the words are invariable, *viz. Kyrie Eleison* ('Lord have mercy'), the *Gloria*, the *Credo*, the *Sanctus* ('Holy, holy, holy') and *Benedictus* ('Blessed is He that cometh in the name of the Lord') and the *Agnus Dei* ('O Lamb of God'). The setting of these sections comprises a 'Mass' in the musical sense. The *Graduale Romanum*, which is the official book of music for both the Ordinary and the Proper, contains a number of plainsong settings of the Ordinary, thus permitting a certain amount of variety.

The Proper of the Mass comprises those portions of which the words vary according to the occasion, and although every passage has its own music, there is only one setting of each; there are no alternatives as in the Ordinary. The Proper consists of four sections—*Introit*, *Gradual*, *Offertory* and *Communion*. These are always sung to plainsong, having been 'set' by composers only very rarely.

RECORDS

H.M.S. Vol. 2, HLP 3

CHAPTER THREE

THE EARLY DEVELOPMENT OF COUNTERPOINT

IN the latter part of the 10th century was written a work called *Musica Enchiriadis*. The authorship, as is the case with so many of the early writings, is doubtful, but is now generally attributed to a certain Abbot Otger.* This book, whoever its author, is a landmark in the history of music, since it gives the first account of a method of singing in anything but unisons or octaves. It expounds the principles of *Organum* or *Diaphony* (the two terms are synonymous—medieval writers are always careful to insist on this), of which the essential basis is the duplication of a melody in parallel 4ths or 5ths. The author of *Musica Enchiriadis* did not invent organum. It seems to have arisen some time in the 9th century, so that Otger, like Guido d'Arezzo in his later writings on notation, merely explained a practice which was already in common use.

In its simplest form organum involved the straightforward doubling of a plainsong melody at the perfect 4th or 5th below. The plainsong was then known as the *Vox Principalis* or Principal Voice, and the doubling part as the *Vox Organalis* or Organal Voice. Thus, the simple fragment at Ex. 7 (*a*) could have an organal part added as at either (*b*) or (*c*).

Ex. 7

* It was formerly attributed to a Flemish monk named Hucbald.

Further, the principal voice could be doubled at the octave below, and the organal voice at the octave above, giving four-part parallel movement:

Ex. 8

Absolute parallelism of the voices was, however, modified at times because of a rule that the organal voice might not descend below tenor C. (The reasons for this rule were logical enough to the musicians of the time, but are far too complicated to be elucidated here.) Thus, if the principal voice dropped below F, oblique motion—one part moving while the other is stationary—came about.

Ex. 9

Principal voice

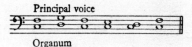

Organum

By the time of Guido d'Arezzo organum at the 4th below was the only accepted procedure; that at the 5th had fallen into disuse, and in his *Micrologus* Guido states clearly that it is 'not allowed'. Rules, more or less complex, for the adding of the organum had been worked out in detail, to allow for all kinds of possibilities, and the employment of oblique movement was normal in the appropriate circumstances. Much thought had also been given to the *occursus*, the 'coming together' of the voices at the end of a passage so that they ended on a unison, forming what we should now call a cadence.

Ex. 10

Ex. 10, quoted from Guido, shows that in certain cases a step beyond oblique motion was taken, *viz.* contrary motion. This at first would only occur in approaching a cadence, but the fact that by Guido's time (he died in 1050) it was accepted as 'correct' procedure, under however limited conditions, proves that there had been some progress since the time of Otger. More important, however, is the fact that the occasional use of contrary motion led musicians to explore and exploit its possibilities apart from the *occursus*.

The kind of writing so far dealt with is known as the *Old Organum*; that based on contrary motion, which is generally accepted as dating from about 1050, is called the *New Organum*. Unfortunately, there is here a gap in our knowledge. Guido deals with the old organum, and the Englishman John Cotton, in his *Musica*, written about 1100, deals to some extent with the new. There is also an anonymous treatise of about the same date, *Ad Organum Faciendum* ('On the Making of Organum'), which explains the new procedures. But writers between Guido and Cotton simply ignore new organum, and the fact that it now came into existence is attested only by a few examples of the music itself, composed for performance and not merely to illustrate theoretical principles. The most important and illuminating of these examples are found in an English MS. called the 'Winchester Troper', which dates from not later than 1080, and which proves that contrary motion was rapidly being combined with the old parallel and oblique procedures.

Ex. 11

This shows both similar and contrary motion, and includes the 3rd as well as the perfect concords. Although to us the major and minor 3rd are entirely consonant, to the early medieval musician they were discords. The major and minor 6th were felt to be even more dissonant, and it was some time before they were freely accepted as concords. The earliest examples of the new organum still rely mainly on the unison, 4th, 5th and octave, but within the next century 3rds and, gradually, 6ths make more frequent appearance. In later examples of the new organum more and more prominence is given to movement in contrary motion; some, indeed, employ it almost exclusively. By this time, it is to be noted, the octave doubling of principal and organal voices had dropped out of use. Simple two-part writing was the rule.

At this point it may be well to digress and to trace briefly the manner in which composers' attitude to concord and discord has developed. Scientifically, *i.e.* in accordance with the laws of acoustics, concord and discord are classified and distinguished in exact terms. The perfect 4th, 5th and octave are perfect concords, the major and minor 3rd and 6th are imperfect. All other intervals are discords, and all combinations of three or more notes containing within themselves one or more dissonant intervals are also discords. Aurally, however, a concord is any combination of sounds which the ear is willing to accept as such, and in the course of time this 'aural tolerance', regardless of scientific authority, has increased more and more.

By the 16th century what may be called the traditional academic attitude to discord was fairly fully developed, but such procedures as the unprepared appoggiatura were still outside the composer's vocabulary. Discords were taken either as passing notes, or were prepared and resolved as suspensions. It is often stated that Claudio Monteverdi (1567 to 1643) was the first to take the 7th of a chord without preparation, but he seems to have been anticipated by the Englishman William Byrd in his four-part Mass. In the course of the 17th century composers began to exploit the emotional possibilities of new methods of dissonance— unprepared 7ths, appoggiaturas, etc.—to a considerable degree, though to some extent the English madrigalists of the late 16th century had pointed the way. By the end of the 17th century the attitude to the handling of dissonance had developed enormously, and in the work of Henry Purcell, for example, we find some really surprising procedures. But it is to be noted that his most startling combinations of notes always resolve logically and, what is more important, *sound* logical.

Throughout the 18th and much of the 19th centuries composers continued to hold an orthodox and traditional attitude to the treatment and use of discord. The treatment, it is true, had become gradually less rigid, but a discord, in the traditional sense, was still a discord and must be resolved. In this respect the most forward-looking composer of the 18th century was Bach, whose freedom is at times astounding. In the latter half of this century there was a tendency to greater restraint, composers being on the whole content with a more restricted vocabulary. In the work of Liszt (1811 to 1886) and Wagner (1813 to 1883) a change of attitude begins to emerge. The 'norm of consonance' of both these composers was a good deal in advance of that of their predecessors, and also of many of their contemporaries. (By 'norm of consonance' is meant what the ear will accept as a concord, not requiring resolution.) To Wagner, at least in his later works, a 7th chord did not necessarily need to be resolved in the traditional way; he frequently used a series of more or less unrelated discords for some specific emotional or illustrative purpose, regardless of 'orthodox' rules. But all his harmonies, however astringent or unexpected, have a traditional basis; they can be 'explained' in traditional terms.

Since Wagner's time composers have delved deeper and deeper into the possibilities of dissonance, and the ear has come to accept as concords combinations of sounds which were formerly considered to be discords. So that in the case of some of the more 'advanced' composers, *e.g.* Schönberg and Bartók, any distinction between concord and discord in the traditional sense has completely broken down. The principle is rather that of tension *versus* relaxation, the more astringent combinations contrasting with those which are less so. Not that this principle is new; it is almost as old as harmonised music itself. The distinction, too, depends largely on such matters as context and the prevailing style. The emotional or psychological effect of any given dissonant combination is far greater, far more pungent, if it occurs in the course of a passage which is fundamentally consonant, than if its surroundings are almost entirely dissonant. But whereas the older composers used discord (in the traditional sense) as a relief from uninterrupted concord, the more advanced present-day writers do not admit the old distinction at all. They use the less tense combinations as a relief, where desirable, from the more tense ones. And the musical ear is able to move with them, and can now accept, quite easily, sounds which a century ago would have been considered excruciating.

Returning now to the 12th century. Despite the addition of an organal voice, of whatever style, to the plainsong, the rhythm of the music still remained that of the words to which it was sung. In the latter part of the 12th century musicians began to turn their attention to the possibility of 'measure' in music—that is, to find some system whereby musical sounds could be of definite length regardless of the words. Here again the origin of the initial impulse is obscure; we have to accept the fact that from about the middle of the century works appeared dealing with the principles of *musica mensurabilis* or 'measurable music'. It is possible that the impulse came from a desire to sing two different sets of words simultaneously, in which case some method was needed of fitting them together, so that not only would they start and finish at the same time, but that the laws of organum could also be complied with *en route*. This, however, is by no means certain. It may also be possible that, despite the Church's traditional lack of sympathy with secular music, there may have been some influence from the dance. Any dance necessarily involves regular pulsation, and it is exactly this idea of the *even beat* which is the basis of measurable music.

Practically all the earliest examples of measurable music depend on the subdivision of a basic long note into three, *i.e.* the time is triple. It has been claimed that from 1150 to about 1300 all music was in triple time, but this may be an overstatement since the oldest extant treatise, *Discantus Positio Vulgaris*, seems to suggest duple possibilities. Dance tunes of this period were not infrequently in duple time. There is, however, no doubt that any leaning to such time in sacred music disappeared very quickly, and that triple time became not merely the normal but the only kind of measure. The basic fact of triple time was that the long note could be subdivided in three ways—two beats plus one, one plus two, or one plus one plus one; and as long as the time taken over the long note remained invariable these subdivisions could be combined with each other, and with the basic note, in a variety of ways. The fragment on p. 42 shows some of the possible combinations in a three-voice passage.

Extending the basic idea of the triple subdivision of the long note, series of such subdivisions, with or without the inclusion of the long note itself, were organised into *Rhythmic Modes*, a complicated system in which, among other things, the value of a written note might depend on that of the note preceding, or sometimes following, it. The merest outline of this system would require many pages of explanation, and its intelligibility, without numerous examples, would be questionable. Broadly speaking, it involved the setting out of a voice part in one or other of some six metrical arrangements of note-values, the one 'mode' persisting throughout the whole of the part. This obviously induced a great deal of rhythmical rigidity, and the whole method was undoubtedly mechanical in its application. Its value, as we can now see, lay in the fact that it helped musicians

Ex. 12

to the understanding and management of metrical rhythm as opposed to the free, verbal rhythm of earlier times. The use of the rhythmic modes persisted until about the end of the 13th century, when with the advent of new and freer ideas, they fell into disuse.

It must be understood that although musicians had now arrived at an understanding of the even beat and exact note-values based on triple rhythm, they did not divide their music into bars of equal length. A mark similar to a barline might be used at the end of a phrase, but barlines in the modern sense, dividing up the music into portions each containing the same number of beats, determined by a time-signature, did not come into regular use until the rise of instrumental music in the 16th century. Time-signatures, indeed, lay still in the future, and the earliest ones, in any case, had an entirely different signification from those of the present day, as will be seen in due course.

The most important work dealing with measurable music is the *Ars Cantus Mensurabilis* ('The Art of Measurable Song'), by Franco of Cologne, late 12th century. Franco's importance is shown by the name sometimes given to this period—the 'Age of Franconian Discant'. Other works of later date than *Discantus Positio Vulgaris* are (*a*) an anonymous MS. in the British Museum, (*b*) John Garland's *De Musica Mensurabilis Positio* (early 13th century), and (*c*) Walter Odington's *De Speculatione Musicae* (late 13th to early 14th centuries). As will be seen later, the principal composers of whom record exists were French, but it is worth noting that two of the above theoretical works were by Englishmen.

The advent of measurable music necessarily brought about changes and developments in notation. It was mentioned in Chapter 2 that Guido d'Arezzo's simplification of the old neumatic notation tended towards our present-day note-shapes. This tendency was intensified in measurable music, though a number of the old specifically neumatic signs lingered on in use to some extent, becoming gradually rarer. Even as late as the 18th century the Italian Martini refers to one kind in a book printed in 1774. The basic note of measurable music was the Breve (Latin *brevis*—short), which was also known as a 'Time'. Longer than this were the Long (Latin *longa*) and the Maxim (*maxima*—greatest); shorter were the Semibreve (*semibrevis*—half-short) and the Minim (*minima*—least). There were, however, complications unknown in our modern, exact system of notation. A long, for example, might be worth either two or three breves, and a breve two or three semibreves; the idea of placing a dot after a note to show that it was divisible into three equal parts had not yet been thought of. Different writers, moreover, held varying opinions on such matters. Petrus de Cruce, one of the few definitely known composers of the period, seems to have had individual ideas on the relative values of notes, requiring sometimes as many as seven semibreves to be sung to a breve. It was not until the 14th century that universal clarity and agreement were achieved.

The principal styles of composition in the Age of Franconian Discant were the *Cantilena*, the *Motet*, the *Conductus* and *Organum*. *Cantilenae* included various kinds of dance-songs—*virelais* and *ballades*—and many come under the heading of *rondels* or *rondeaux*. The *rondel* varied in length from a few bars to something quite extensive, and the same words were used for all the voices. It seems to have had some affinity with the later *round*, in that each of its voice parts (usually three) was taken by each singer in turn; but the voices did not begin one after another as in a true round. All began together, interchanging at the end of each phrase. There is some doubt, however, as to the exact construction of a *rondel*, since contemporary writings, *e.g.* those of Odington, are somewhat obscure. The most notable composer of *rondels* was Adam de la Hale (*c.* 1230 to 1287), a *trouvère* (see Chapter 4).

The most famous of all compositions of the *rondel* type is the English *Rota* (the term is the composer's), *Sumer is icumen in.* Unlike other extant *rondels*, it is a true round, in which the four upper voices enter in turn, in canon, over a two-part independent bass which is also canonic. Apart from its remarkable beauty, it is exceptional in being for six voices, and the management of the part-writing is much in advance of other works of the period. It was formerly supposed to have been written about 1226, but more recent research places its date at 1280 or later.* Even so, it is an astounding piece of work. Musicologists have argued for years on how it could have been written in the 13th century, without coming to any definite conclusion; we do not know, and probably never shall know, whether its composer was a freak genius, or whether it is the only surviving example of an English school which was far in advance of all others. But it exists, and we may be proud of the fact that it is English.†

* Willi Apel places it *c.* 1310.

† Giraldus Cambrensis (1147 to 1220) has some interesting things to say about part singing in Wales in the 12th century. A useful and instructive condensation is to be found on p. 128 of *Music in Western Civilisation*, by P. H. Lang.

The *cantilena* was a true 'composition' in that its writer composed the whole thing. In the *motet*, however (not to be confused with that of later times, *e.g.* the 16th century), the object was the fitting of one or more known melodies above the tenor, which part itself was most frequently derived from a fragment of plainsong; so that it was not so much composition as musical carpentry. It is to be noted that in the Middle Ages there was a distinction between the 'inventor' of a melody, who was known as *phonascus*, and he who worked with already-existing material, the *symphonetes*. The tendency was, oddly enough to us, to rate the *symphonetes* higher than the *phonascus*. In such a work as a motet the aim of the *symphonetes* was to fit together known melodies, merely, to quote Sir Hubert Parry,* 'easing off the corners and adapting the points where the cacophony was too intolerable to be endured'.

In the motet the lowest voice, the tenor, took a melody, normally in long notes, against which the upper voice or voices 'discanted'. These discants were, as stated above, known melodies. The tenor part was known as the *cantus firmus* or 'fixed song', the tenor being he who 'held' this *cantus firmus*, from the Latin *tenere*, to hold.† Tenors were at first taken from plainsong, and contemporary MSS. frequently give them single syllables of fantastic length. An example quoted in the *Oxford History of Music* consists, in modern notation, of some 87 bars of 3/2 time, the tenor having the one word *latus*. The syllable *la* endures for 86 bars, being broken up by rests, so that from the verbal point of view a mere vocalisation on 'ah' would be equally effective. Later motets sometimes used instrumental dance tunes for their tenors, and recent research suggests that these, as well as those from plainsong, were probably played on instruments. The upper parts of a motet were not only

* *The Art of Music.*

† The use of the term 'bass' for the lowest part came later, as an addition below the tenor. In the period with which we are dealing the tenor was the lowest part in the score.

carpentered out of known melodies, but also retained their
original words, hence the peculiarity of 'polytextuality',
different words to each voice. In an example in the *Oxford
History* the two discanting voices each sing different verses
addressed to the Blessed Virgin.* It was a common enough
practice for one or more of the added parts to take a secular
song, as in an example in *Discantus Positio Vulgaris*, where
the *duplum* sings a Latin hymn to the Blessed Virgin and
the *triplum* a French love-song. The result of such unseemly
practices will be seen in due course.

In *Organa* (plural of *organum*) both measured and unmeasured music appeared in the course of the same piece.
Organum purum ('pure organum') seems to have designated
the sections which were unmeasured, and was applied solely
to music in two parts. The tenor took a fragment of plainsong in long notes while the *duplum* discanted freely above it.

The *Conductus* avoided the use of ultra-long notes or syllables in the tenor, and tended to be more homophonic in
style than the motet or organum. It appears that some
portions were performed with words and some without
them. The conductus was distinguished by having a tenor
not based on plainsong, though Franco and Odington differ
as to whether it should be made up by the composer or
adapted from some other source.

Mention may also be made of the *Hocket*, which term
may possibly be derived from 'hiccough'. It was an extraordinary system in which the notes of a melody were alternated between two voices. The reader may care to imagine
the effect of the National Anthem sung as illustrated in Ex. 13.
Hocketing has been described by one writer as 'a cruel
medieval stratagem'. The epithet seems apt!

In the Church services use was made not only of written
works (*contrapunctus a penna*) but also of improvised discant
(*contrapunctus a mente* or *discantus supra librum*). (It may perhaps be mentioned that the latter practice still survives,

* The part next above the tenor was called *duplum* or *motetus*. A third
part was the *triplum*, and a fourth the *quadruplum*.

though with a secular connotation, in the 'jam sessions' of certain dance musicians.)   The choirman who improvised his discant above the plainsong *cantus firmus* was supposed to follow out certain definite rules, but it would seem that singers had changed but little since Guido voiced his bitter complaint in *De Ignoto Cantu* (see p. 28).   The theorist Jacob of Liége inveighs similarly in his *Speculum Musicae*

Ex. 13

God   our   - cious   *etc.*

save   gra -   Queen

(1321).*   He begins by referring mildly to the 'impudence' of singers who know nothing of the nature of consonance, goes on to castigate 'mutilation, curtailment and corruption' of the song, and finally boils over with the statement that the singers 'howl, shriek and bark like a dog'.   Even in the 12th century, in the early days of discant, John of Salisbury (*c.* 1115 to 1180) states categorically that 'music defiles the service of religion', and many other writers deplore, often in unmeasured terms, the practices which had arisen.†   For a time the musicians persisted in their unseemly conduct, but by the beginning of the 14th century the patience of the Church authorities was exhausted, and in 1324/25 Pope John XXII promulgated a Bull calculated to bring them to their senses.   The essential substance of this pronouncement was: 'Stop desecrating the plainsong.' Without being quite so outspoken as John of Salisbury or Jacob of Liége, the Pope made it quite clear that florid discanting above the plainsong was to cease, under pain

   * Until recently this work was attributed to the Norman Johannes de Muris.

   † Singers seem to have tended to get out of hand from the earliest times; see the remark on Ambrose's reforms, p. 26.

of 'suspension from office of eight days', and that the only permissible discant was the old parallel organum of the time of Otger. So potent was this prohibition that even in 1408, over eighty years later, florid discant on plainsong was still forbidden at Notre Dame in Paris, where it had first flourished.

The outcome of all this will be dealt with in Chapter 5, but it may be well to mention here a theory which has been current for long enough, but of which the authenticity is more than doubtful. According to this theory, the singers, having perforce returned to parallel organum, resorted to what has been called 'an artifice of the most ingenious and subtle kind'. Between the two parallel lines of organum at the 5th were inserted 3rds, making complete triads, though we are not told who was responsible for this innovation, nor exactly when it first appeared. To avoid a mere series of parallel triads in root position the plainsong, written *below* the organal parts, was assigned to the highest voice, who automatically sang it an octave above its written pitch, producing *fauxbourdon*, or 'false bass'. Thus a series of pleasant-sounding first inversions resulted, as opposed to the allegedly crude progression of root positions. One writer calls this 'a picturesque story of uncertain origin', which would seem to be an apt description, since there are extant examples of parallel first inversions dating from about 1300, *i.e.* before the appearance of the famous Bull. In any case, no real proof of this theory of the origin of *fauxbourdon* has ever been produced. It has already been made clear that in compositions based on plainsong, that plainsong—the basic foundational melody—was in the lowest part. But composers eventually discovered the pleasing effect of putting the melody in the highest part, so that the lowest, the 'bourdon' or bass, thus became 'false'.

The principal known composers of the period with which we have been dealing, as apart from the theorists, are Adam de la Hale, Léonin, Pérotin and Petrus de Cruce. Adam de la Hale has already been mentioned. Léonin, also known by the Latinised form of his name, Leoninus, lived in the 12th century and officiated at the cathedral of Notre Dame in Paris.* He was succeeded by Pérotin (*c.* 1183 to 1236), who, apart from his compositions, was instrumental in improving notation. He is also known as Perotinus Magnus (Pérotin the Great), and is especially noteworthy as being, apparently, the first to write for three or four voices, *i.e.* adding two or three organal parts to a *cantus firmus*. Léonin, in his *Magnus Liber Organi* ('Great Book of Organum'), undertook the composition of polyphonic settings of the Mass 'Propers' (see p. 34) for the liturgical year, which were later revised and supplemented by Pérotin.† Petrus de Cruce is a somewhat shadowy figure born at Amiens in the second half of the 13th century.

Besides the work of these men, a certain amount of music survives of which the composers are unknown, and whose approximate dates can only be fixed by the style of composition and the notation and writing in the manuscripts. A composer would write, say, a motet simply for use in the church at which he officiated. He would not necessarily sign it, and it would not be published, since the art of printing had not yet been invented. So the music, written for purely local use, would quite possibly remain buried in the library of the church concerned, and having fallen into disuse might never see the light of day until some hundreds of years later, when unearthed by a 19th-century musicologist.

As to the effect of the music itself, it is unfortunate that

* The writer of an anonymous MS. of the time calls him *optimus organista*, from which it has been deduced that he was renowned as an organist. This is incorrect. An *organista* was a writer of *organa*, while an organ player seems to have been known as *organator*. Léonin's fame therefore rests on his compositions. Organs were still in a very rudimentary state.

† The only other composer to undertake such a huge task was Heinrich Isaac, some three centuries later, in his *Choralis Constantinus*, though he consistently omits certain sections. William Byrd (1543 to 1623) also set a number of movements in his *Gradualia* (1605 to 1607).

opportunities of hearing it performed are extremely rare, though recordings are available. The mere silent reading of it conveys no true impression, while playing examples on the piano is equally unilluminating. On paper it tends to appear crude and experimental, but in actual performance it has an odd attractiveness and beauty of its own, quite unlike the music of any other period. It well repays any effort made to hear it sung.

Attention was drawn above to the fact that some of the most noted theorists of the time were Englishmen. Little, however, is known of English composers, and the most important school of composition was centred on Paris. During the 12th to the 15th centuries the influence of the University of Paris was supreme in Europe, on both intellectual and artistic development. Of the Parisians, Léonin and Pérotin are the most important representatives. We shall see in later chapters how the leadership in music passed, at various times, from one nation to another. It is, perhaps, worth remembering that the Germans, who produced most of the greatest musicians in the 18th and 19th centuries, were actually the last to enter the field.

RECORDS
H.M.S. Vol. 2, HLP 4

CHAPTER FOUR

EARLY SECULAR MUSIC

OUR study so far has dealt almost entirely with music used in the Church, for the reasons already stated, that since so little of the secular music survives, it is mainly in sacred music that we can trace growth and development. But as in any other age, songs and dance tunes abounded, though the composers are rarely known.

Dances of the 13th and 14th centuries are generically known as *Estampies*. They are sectional in construction, each section being immediately repeated, but with a different ending. There is, naturally, strongly marked metrical rhythm, and the use of duple time is not uncommon. Phrase lengths vary considerably, mixtures of three, four and six bars being frequent. Cadence points are clearly defined and there is a feeling for shape and design, in some cases even suggesting the idea of a rondo.

Mention has already been made of the antiquity of the term *jongleur*. Anglicised into 'juggler' it came to imply a body of public entertainers which included conjurers, acrobats, etc., and as early as the 10th century *jongleurs* were divided into two classes, the 'jugglers', who were looked upon with disfavour by the Church, and the *jongleurs de gestes*. These latter came from Provence and Picardy; they sang, or rather chanted, narrative poems (*gestes*) recounting heroic deeds, which seem to have been long and musically dull. Their love songs, however, were often of considerable poetic and musical value.

At the end of the 11th century began the age of the *Troubadours*. These were southern French poet-musicians, and with them may be associated their central and northern French counterparts the *Trouvères*, who appeared rather later. Both died out as the age of chivalry decayed towards the beginning of the 14th century. The names 'troubadour' and 'trouvère' have identical meanings, *i.e.* the 'finder' or inventor of a melody. The etymological root of both is the French verb *trouver*, to find. There is a clear connection here with the distinction between *phonascus* and *symphonetes* mentioned on p. 45. The troubadour or trouvère was of the phonascus or inventing variety. Many of their poems survive, but only a much smaller proportion of the music. (Grove states that the words of over 2,500 troubadours' songs are extant, but only 259 of their melodies.) Both troubadours and trouvères were notable for the cultivation of lyric poetry, which they developed to a high pitch of beauty and refinement, many of the poems being devoted to a rather mannered idealisation of woman.

The social standing of the troubadour and trouvère was above that of the *jongleur*. The latter was in any case a professional entertainer, and might be a welcome guest in court or monastery. The troubadour or trouvère might himself be of noble birth, exercising his art not as a professional but rather as a gifted amateur. Richard I of England was a troubadour, and Thibaut, King of Navarre, a trouvère. The *jongleur*, whatever his standing, was found in all parts of Europe; troubadours and trouvères were confined to those parts where the Provençale tongue was spoken, *i.e.* France, northern Spain and northern Italy.

One of the most notable trouvères was Adam de la Hale. Besides composing such works as those mentioned in Chapter 3, he also wrote some entertainments which are sometimes stated to be the precursors of the French *opéra-comique*. Of these, the most important is *Le Jeu de Robin et Marion*, a 'dramatic pastoral'. It is divided into scenes like a play, and its anticipation of *opéra-comique* is seen in the way in which the dialogue is interspersed with airs, etc.

Such music of troubadours and trouvères as has survived is purely melodic, and the manuscripts do not indicate the method of accompaniment, though it seems certain that some kind of instrumental support was improvised on the *vielle* or *fiedel*. This was a crude kind of fiddle (which term obviously derives from the old name) with a flat bridge, so that the player could hardly avoid sounding at least two notes simultaneously. From which it may be deduced that the accompaniments were of a harmonic character; they were certainly not polyphonic. While some of the melodies are modal in character, others are clearly based on the major scale—the 'wanton' mode so disliked by the Church. They are written in the contemporary plainsong notation on a four-line stave. The rhythm of some of the songs is as free as that of plainsong, but in others there is clear metrical accentuation, duple time being used as well as triple.

Almost contemporary with the troubadours were the German *Minnesingers*, who flourished in the 12th and 13th centuries. They, too, were mostly of noble birth and their songs dealt chiefly with love. Their art died about the same time as that of the troubadours. It is perhaps worth mentioning that their influence reached forward, though somewhat indirectly, into the 19th century, since Wagner's opera *Tannhäuser* includes a contest of song in which the protagonists—Wolfram von Eschenbach and Tannhäuser himself—were minnesingers and historical figures. The plot of *Tristan and Isolda* is largely based on the story as told by the minnesinger Godfrey of Strasburg, and that of *Parsifal* on Wolfram von Eschenbach's version of that legend. The songs of the minnesingers, like those of their French counterparts, show the use of the major scale and duple time.

The art of the troubadours, trouvères and minnesingers covered a relatively brief period of history, and was very limited in its range. As has already been noted, it co-incided with the age of chivalry and ceased when that age came to an end. In a limited way it is an example of the effect of a purely social condition on music. But for the rise of chivalry and all that it implied, the art of these men would not have arisen and flourished.

Before returning to the development of the main stream of music, it may be well to add a sketch of the work of the German *Meistersingers*. They were a kind of middle-class parallel to the noble minnesingers, and functioned as a guild, comparable in its structure to the various trade guilds of the late Middle Ages, members passing through the usual stages of apprentice, journeyman and master. The first of these guilds was founded in 1311 at Mainz by Heinrich von Meissen, and the movement flourished from the 14th to the 17th centuries. Unlike those of the minnesingers, the songs of the meistersingers were mostly on Biblical themes, and their construction was subject to an accepted code of rigid rules. The most famous meistersinger was Hans Sachs, who lived in the 16th century. He is introduced as one of the principal characters in Wagner's music drama *The Mastersingers of Nuremberg*, the well-known 'dawn song' in the third act being a setting of one of his poems.

RECORDS
H.M.S. Vol. 2, HLP 3/4

CHAPTER FIVE

THE 'NEW ART'
AND ITS DEVELOPMENT

IN the same way as the year 1050 forms a rough dividing line between the old and the new organum, so also the year 1300 approximately separates an old style from a new one. By the end of the 13th century the principles of measurable music were fully established, but the whole conception of the system was too rigid to last. Real development was not possible within the constricting influence of the rhythmic modes, and papal interdiction regarding the treatment of plainsong could not restrain musicians from further experiment. We find, therefore, that from about 1300 the rhythmic modes tend to fall into disuse and a far freer attitude to rhythm begins to appear. There is also improved shapeliness of melodic line and greater independence in the part-writing.

There can be little doubt that the work of the troubadours and trouvères had some effect on polyphonic music, as regards both melodic style and freedom of rhythm. We have seen that the troubadours did not confine themselves to triple measure, and it is from about 1300 that duple time appears in polyphonic compositions. It is first mentioned in a treatise by Odington about 1280, and its introduction was inevitably the beginning of the end of the rhythmic modes which were essentially based on triple time and nothing else. Composition in accordance with these new ideas became known as *Ars Nova*—the 'New Art'—in contrast to *Ars Antiqua*—the 'Old Art'. *Ars Nova*, despite its name, was not, however, an actual 'invention', but rather a development from *Ars Antiqua* which, as stated above, had reached a point where changes and modifications were inevitable.

The first theorist to expound the principles of the New Art was Philippe de Vitry (c. 1285 to 1361), whose work *Ars Nova* gives detailed instructions on the new rhythmic ideas. He deals with the use of binary rhythms and their notation, treating them as accepted facts rather than as mere theoretical possibilities. So that, like Guido and Franco, he explained what was already more or less common practice among composers. Very briefly the rhythmic system may be described as follows. In *Ars Antiqua* the long was worth three breves, the breve three semibreves, and the semibreve three minims. In *Ars Nova* the long in 'Perfect Mode' was worth three breves, but in 'Imperfect Mode' only two. In 'Perfect Time' the breve was worth three semibreves and in 'Imperfect Time' two. Similarly, in 'Perfect Prolation' the semibreve divided into three minims, and in 'Imperfect Prolation' into two. Perfection or imperfection of mode, time and prolation were indicated by a complex system of signs of which two still remain in occasional use, *viz.* C and ₵, though their original meanings no longer hold good. It is at this time, too, that the dot, indicating subdivisibility into three, first appears. A note divisible into three equal parts was 'perfect' and the dot was therefore sometimes called the 'point of perfection'. But such a dot appeared in the time-signature, not after the note as nowadays. Time-signatures were inevitably complicated, since they had to show mode, time and prolation, and whether each was perfect or imperfect, with a series of separate signs. Thus, if mode and time were perfect and prolation imperfect, the composer would place after the clef the signs ▥, O and ₵. The first indicated perfect mode, the long dividing into three breves; the second perfect time, each of these breves dividing into three semibreves; and the third imperfect prolation, each semibreve dividing into *two* minims. This is comparable, allowing for the difference in the names of the notes, to 9/8 time. The whole-bar sound:

divides into three:

Each of these also divides into three:

and each of these into two:

A further notational complication was the use of different coloured notes to show temporary changes from perfect to imperfect mode, etc., or *vice versa*, red being the most usual. To the singer who was accustomed to it, this system may have been logical and simple enough, but unfortunately the red notes might indicate something entirely unconnected with time. De Vitry states that 'another use of red notes is to enjoin singing at the octave in the passages in which they occur', citing some specific examples. Singers may at one time have been 'the most fatuous of all men', but they certainly needed to have their wits about them in the 14th century!

Of other contemporary theorists mention may be made of the Franciscan Simon Tunsted (d. *c.* 1369), who wrote a treatise codifying the principles of *Ars Nova*, De Muris (*Ars Novae Musicae*), and Jacob of Liége, who, apart from his strictures on singers, tended to oppose the new methods in his *Speculum Musicae*. Jacob seems to have looked back to the 'good old days' of Franconian discant and although neither he nor anyone else could halt the progress of the new ideas, he may perhaps have exerted some restraining influence.

The outstanding composer in France during this period was Guillaume de Machaut (*c.* 1300 to 1377), who has been described as the first practical exponent of the *Ars Nova* of de Vitry. He wrote a large number of secular works, generically known as *cantilenae*, as well as some twenty-three motets. Especially notable is his four and five voice setting of the Ordinary of the Mass—the oldest existing setting apart from the anonymous three-part *Messe de Tournai*. Duple measure is common in his work, and within it he is apt to indulge in remarkably complex rhythmic combinations. In his setting of the Mass, as in the motets, Machaut seems to have paid scant attention to the papal Bull mentioned in Chapter 3. In the Mass the tenor takes a plainsong part in notes of variable but strictly moderate length, while the upper voices discant more or less freely. Especially notable is the use of a basic motive, appearing in 'one guise or another in all the sections, binding the whole work together. In the motets Machaut adopts a severely conservative attitude, even to the use of secular songs for the discants above the long-note plainsong tenor.*

The *cantilenae* include *ballades*, *rondeaux*, *chansons* and *lais*. Each of these had its own peculiarities of construction, and it is in them that we see not only the freer rhythmic methods of *Ars Nova*, but also the more shapely melodic style which gradually developed, replacing the angularity of *Ars Antiqua*. It may be said that as a *symphonetes* Machaut was ingenious and technically competent; as a *phonascus* he showed his genuine inventiveness and musicianship. Some of his 'monophonic' *lais*—simple unharmonised songs—have all the freshness and attractiveness of French folk-song at its best. In his polyphonic compositions there is notably greater ease in the management of the part-writing. The use of discord

---

* Polytextuality died hard. A hundred years after Machaut composers were indulging in the practice of 'telescoping' the words of Mass movements, so that different sentences were being sung simultaneously, sometimes in canon. For that matter, the first movement of Bach's *St. Matthew Passion* is to some extent polytextual, and there are plenty of later examples.

is much better controlled, and there is often real expressiveness to the 20th-century ear. The old tendency to mere mechanical 'note-spinning' in accordance with the accepted rules is fast vanishing; his music begins to have some real meaning, in contrast to the artificialities of the immediately preceding period.

It is in the 14th century that we find the rise of an important body of composers in Italy. There had been an Italian school since the time of Guido, but little if anything survives which was written before about the middle of the century with which we are dealing. The main centre of the Italian school was Florence, and the work seems to have been, at least to some extent, a development of the art of the troubadours, since it reached a high level of accomplishment in accompanied song. Polyphonic writing was, of course, cultivated, a notable feature of it being the frequent use of canonic, or at least imitative writing. Neither imitation nor canon were new inventions; occasional instances of the former appear, rather casually, in works of the 13th century, while *Sumer is icumen in* is, as we have already seen, strictly canonic. However, in the works of the 14th-century Italians both devices begin to assume more and more importance as unifying factors of construction. Passages in imitation are introduced with evident intention rather than haphazardly, while strict canon is sometimes employed for a whole section of a movement. It is in the madrigals,* secular polyphonic songs, that canon and imitation chiefly appear, and it is noteworthy that in them the melody is in the upper part —a characteristic which distinguishes them very markedly from other works, both Italian and French, with the melody in the tenor. Madrigals were mostly written for two voices and, like many other Italian forms, were not based on a

---

* The madrigals have no connection with those of the 16th century. In the 15th century the use of the term *madrigal* for a musical composition fell into disuse; it survived, with its variants *madriale* and *mandriale*, in connection with lyric poetry, coming back into musical use early in the 16th century.

pre-selected *cantus firmus*. They were, that is to say, true compositions; the day of the *symphonetes* was beginning to draw to a close. The possibility of some instrumental accompaniment to the madrigal was not excluded.

The use of duple measure as well as triple was general, and is sometimes attributed to the influence of Italian folk-music. It is also possible that such types of composition as the *Ballata*, for simultaneous singing and dancing, had not inconsiderable influence, its rhythmic scheme, as compared with that of the madrigal, being simpler and more obviously of a metrically regular kind.

It has been suggested by some that the introduction of duple time into France may have been due to the transference of the papal see to Avignon in 1309, since Italian musicians would naturally be among the staff of the papal court; but this cannot be stated with any certainty, and in any case we know that as early as 1280 Odington refers to duple measure.

The most notable Florentine composer was Francesco di Landini (*c.* 1325 to 1397), who, though blind, had a high reputation as organist and lutenist. Others were Jacopo da Bologna and Giovanni da Ciscia.

Little is known of English compositions of the 14th century. Music in this country has evolved in a distinctly spasmodic fashion, and after the surprising eruption of *Sumer is icumen in*, whether it is an isolated phenomenon or the sole surviving work of a flourishing school, a period of relative stagnation set in. Manuscripts of the period are, unfortunately, scarce, but it would seem that while composers in France and Italy were achieving mastery of the methods of *Ars Nova*, English musicians were content to pay homage to the traditions of the 13th century. Another sudden eruption, in the person of John Dunstable, took place in the first half of the 15th century, after which there was another period when the lead passed to other countries. The second half of the 16th century saw the swift and amazing rise of the English madrigalists—possibly the greatest period in the whole story of our music—followed by a decline which was broken by the solitary and unpredictable genius Henry Purcell in the latter part of the 17th century. After Purcell, almost complete decay until almost the beginning of the present century. Other countries in Europe have passed through peak periods and periods of decline, but in none, perhaps, have the former been so brief and the latter so long and dismal.

Before dealing with the work of Dunstable and his successors, some mention must be made of what is known as *Musica Ficta* or 'False Music'. We have seen, in Chapter 2, that to avoid the unacceptable tritone F to B the 'soft B', B flat, was admitted. The practice of the chromatic alteration of notes gradually extended, and as early as the first quarter of the 13th century the Englishman John Garland refers to it under the heading of *Error tertii soni*—error of the third sound. The exact meaning of this term is obscure, and Garland's explanations and examples are not altogether enlightening.* It is nevertheless clear that in his time there were certain rules regarding the sharpening and flattening of notes, both in plainsong and in discants. Nothing was, however, indicated in the written music, and it was left to the performer to apply the system according to the rules with which he was supposed to be familiar. In the treatise *Ars Contrapuncti* ('The Art of Counterpoint'), ascribed to de Vitry, chromatic alteration is accepted and explained as common practice under the title of *musica ficta*, and de Muris, in his *Ars Discantus*, formulates simple and exact rules for its application. By 1320 chromatic alteration of any note of the scale was admitted. It has already been explained that the character of a mode depended on the position of the semitones in relation to the final; with *musica ficta* semitones might appear almost anywhere in a

* It is a rather peculiar fact that the early theorists, even as late as the 16th century, seem continuously to have had great difficulty in expressing themselves with ease and clarity, at least according to 20th-century ideas.

melody, so that the individual characteristics of its mode tended gradually to disappear. The modes eventually condensed into two main types—those with a major 3rd above the final, and those with a minor 3rd. Hence, ultimately, our major and minor scales, whose use as the normal basis for composition became finally stabilised about the beginning of the 18th century.

We now return to the general development of music. The work of the composers of the late 14th century shows increasing ease and fluency of treatment. Discord is used in a less casual fashion, and there are fewer corners which seem to need 'easing off'. It is in the 15th century, how-ever, that we feel more rapid and definite progress, and the first outstanding figure is the Englishman John Dun-stable (c. 1370 to 1453). He is sometimes credited with the 'invention' of composition, apparently implying that he was the first to dispense with the use of a *cantus firmus*, but this suggestion is highly debatable. Leaving aside such things as the monophonic *lais* of Machaut, and the early dance tunes, we have already seen that the polyphonic madrigals of the 14th-century Italians were true composi-tions not depending on the weaving of discants against some pre-selected melody.

Dunstable was the acknowledged leader of a school of English composers who flourished in the first half of the 15th century, his most important contemporary being Lionel Power. The work of this school seems to have been done mainly on the Continent, where their reputation stood high and where, in various important libraries, their composi-tions have mostly been found. Dunstable's name, in par-ticular, was highly honoured among continental musicians, and the poet Martin le Franc, writing before 1450, claims that the excellence of the contemporary French composers Dufay (1400 to 1474) and Binchois (c. 1400 to 1467) is due to their having followed Dunstable's lead. A little later, the theorist Tinctoris refers to 'a new art . . . whose fount and origin is held to be among the English, of whom

Dunstable stood forth as chief'. The principal characteristics of Dunstable's style were suavity and shapeliness of
melodic line, easily singable phrases, and harmonisation
largely based on triads. While passing discord is still used
at times with some freedom, there are far fewer awkward
clashes than in the work of his predecessors. The traditional method of the voices pursuing almost entirely independent melodic paths between initial and final concords,
which still survived in Machaut, had begun to disappear
rapidly in the madrigals of Landini and his school, and in
Dunstable but little of it remains. Although the ideas of
chords as such, and of chord-progression, had not yet
entered the minds of composers, such a work as Dunstable's
accompanied song *O Rosa Bella* shows quite clearly that
some such conceptions lay in the not far distant future.

Apart from his facility in writing mellifluous music,
Dunstable was far from deficient in mechanical ingenuity.
He made occasional use of points of imitation, and was
one of the first to indulge in the concoction of musical
puzzles, an occupation which was taken to extremes by
some of his continental successors. Such puzzles—various
methods of devising canons—often had but little musical
value, but the practice of them certainly increased composers' technique and helped them to an assured and
confident management of contrapuntal devices.

Dunstable's compositions include both sacred and secular
works, and he is noteworthy as being the first to cultivate
the motet as a free composition to a liturgical text. He
discarded both the old long-note *cantus firmus* and the mixed
text, giving the same words to all the voices, and laying the
foundations of a form which reached its peak in the works
of such composers as Palestrina and Victoria a century later.

With the death of Dunstable in 1453 the lead in music
passed to the Burgundian school, of which the principal
representatives are Gulielmus Dufay and Gilles Binchois.
These men began by writing in the style of the preceding
generation, with a good deal of not particularly attractive

melody and arbitrary and uncontrolled discord. But the
influence of Dunstable was strongly felt, and in the later
works of Dufay especially 'we recognise, unmistakably, the
suave and flowing melody in the separate parts, the pure
harmony of the whole, the agreeable phrasing, the propriety in the sequence of the continued sounds, which we
noticed as characteristic of the compositions of our own
countrymen in the foreign collections during this period'.*
Dufay, possibly earlier than anyone else, realised clearly
the possibilities of canon as a unifying device, and in his
Masses he made considerable use of it. He was also a
deviser of 'puzzle canons', introducing them at times into
Mass movements. His fondness for fauxbourdon—movement in parallel first inversions—may also be mentioned
as suggesting the dawning of a feeling for harmonic progression. It is from Dufay's time that the use of secular
cantus firmi for Masses begins. The tune, or part of it,
would be given to the tenor, not necessarily in its original
note-values, and possibly decorated, while the other voices
wove counterpoints against it. This practice sounds rather
like a return to the unseemliness of the 13th-century motets,
but was not really so. The melodies used as *cantus firmi*
were usually old and the words no longer in use. Moreover, they were so covered up by the surrounding counterpoint as to be almost, if not entirely, unidentifiable by the
ear. They served, in fact, merely as a framework on which
the composer could build. Possibly the most famous of
secular *cantus firmi* was the song *L'homme armé*.

Compositions of the 14th and 15th centuries are often
regarded as having been written purely for unaccompanied
vocal performance, but this is an error. Missing voice-
parts might well be supplied by instruments, and the purely
instrumental performance of works written for voices was
accepted as a regular practice. The incorporation of independent instrumental parts into vocal works was common,
as in Dufay's great motet *Ecclesiae Militantis*, which includes

* Wooldridge, in the *Oxford History of Music.*

two such instrumental lines, with symbolic meanings. It is not until we reach the 16th century that we encounter the pure *a cappella, i.e.* the essentially unaccompanied vocal style.

It is in the time of Dufay that we find the rise of what is called choral polyphony. Until about the middle of the 15th century it was customary for polyphonic movements —motets, mass movements, etc.—to be sung by a group of soloists, the full choir taking part only in the plainsong. But various manuscripts from about 1440 onwards clearly distinguish passages of polyphony to be sung by soloists from others to be taken by the chorus.

In the work of the Burgundians, as in those of the 14th-century Italians, there was considerable emphasis on secular compositions—*ballades, rondeaux, chansons*—but there is no particular distinction between sacred and secular styles. Dufay, especially, achieves a balance between the two, so that on the whole music set for secular words might serve equally well for sacred ones and *vice versa*. In the ensuing generation, which saw the foundation of the Netherlands school of composers, the emphasis is rather on sacred music. This change of attitude may possibly be due to the ending of the papal exile at Avignon and the consequent healthier state of the Church. Whatever the underlying cause, the Netherlanders' best work is, on the whole, that written for liturgical use.

The first important names of the Flemish (Netherlands) school are Johannes Okeghem (*c.* 1430 to *c.* 1495), Jacob Obrecht (1430 to 1505) and Anton Busnois (d. 1492). The great theorist of the time was Joannes Tinctoris (*c.* 1446 to 1511), whose writings, while of no great originality, explain the current technical methods. Okeghem for long had a reputation for almost fiendish contrapuntal ingenuity, and there is no doubt that he explored the possibilities of complicated canonic writing to an extent hitherto undreamed of. But study of his works reveals that his technique was really only a means to an end, that end being musical expressiveness. Among his outstanding technical feats may be mentioned a canon for thirty-six voices. Like so many of his contemporaries, he wrote a Mass on *L'homme armé*.

Obrecht's style is on the whole rather less florid than that of Okeghem, employing shorter phrases and more clearly defined cadence points. He was one of the real founders of the technique of imitative counterpoint, which was the basis of the style of the 16th century, and was also a writer of instrumental pieces. The serious cultivation of purely instrumental works dates from his time, and his output of them was considerable. Busnois learned from his teacher Okeghem the technique of imitation and, like Obrecht, may be considered as one of the founders of the 16th-century style.

A generation later appeared Heinrich Isaac (*c.* 1450 to 1517), one of the first of the Flemish school to seek a livelihood in Italy. The brilliant courts of the Florentine princes in this, the Renaissance period, offered far greater opportunities to any artist than did those in the Low Countries, and for the next hundred years there was a continual move from the Netherlands of musicians in search of wealthy patrons farther south. Isaac's career is typical. In Florence he served Lorenzo dei Medici; in 1496 he entered the service of the Emperor Maximilian, being appointed court composer at Innsbruck. In 1502 he returned to Florence, where most of the rest of his life was spent. His greatest work, the *Choralis Constantinus* (see p. 49), occupied him for many years, and shows that the imitative style was rapidly becoming the fundamental basis of choral composition. Although much of Isaac's work is of a relatively straightforward character, he occasionally indulges in extraordinarily complicated rhythmic combinations, which would tax the capabilities of even the most reliable of performers. More than Obrecht and Busnois, his use of discord is strictly controlled. Traces of the old 14th-century traditions are rare, and there are evident signs of the formation of what might be called an early academic outlook. His style shows, too, an increasing tendency to harmonic approach through the triad, already noted as traceable in the work of Dunstable; and four-part writing, established as normal by Okeghem and Obrecht, is usual.

Almost exactly contemporary with Isaac is Josquin des Prés (1450 to 1521). He was Okeghem's greatest pupil, and was in many ways the finest musician of his generation. Like Isaac, he travelled southwards, serving a number of different masters. From Okeghem he learned, with Busnois, the artifices of contrapuntal technique, even surpassing his teacher in his ability to invent and solve the most complex problems. The exercise of this mechanical ingenuity gave him a complete command of his material, a command which he used in both sacred and secular compositions to 'bring off' contrapuntal feats in a natural and convincing manner. With Josquin more than with his predecessors technique was a means to an end, and while some of his most musically interesting works are also exceedingly complex, in later secular pieces he often writes in a simpler style and achieves really amazing expressiveness. He was equally great as a composer of both sacred and secular music, and was described by the German musicologist Ambros as 'the first musician who impresses us as having genius'.

Another contemporary of Isaac was Pierre de la Rue (d. 1518). Although the greater part of his work still remains in manuscript, he appears to have attained very considerable technical mastery of the intricacies of canon. A little later is Jean Mouton (c. 1475 to 1522), an eminent pupil of Josquin, and himself possibly the teacher of Adrian Willaert, one of the great figures of the next generation. Mouton had great ability and was highly esteemed in his time.

In England after the death of Dunstable music tended to languish, but around the turn of the century we find a school of composers who seem to have deliberately held apart from the methods prevailing on the continent, in a rather reactionary manner. Although the effect of their music is agreeable enough, and the arbitrary use of discord is rare, interest in contrapuntal devices is lacking; there is smooth and equable flow of the parts, but little more. The principal composers of this school were Robert Fayrfax (d. 1521), Richard Davy (end of 15th to early 16th centuries), William Cornyshe (c. 1465 to 1523) and Richard Sampson (c. 1470 to 1554). Davy is notable as being the first Englishman definitely known to have set the 'Passion' of Christ in harmonised form. The traditional recitation of the Passion in Holy Week dates from as far back as the 4th century, and by the 12th it was sung with a fairly complex ritual. Obrecht is sometimes said to have produced a four-part setting, but the authorship is doubtful.

RECORDS

H.M.S. Vol. 3, HLP 5/6

CHAPTER SIX

VOCAL MUSIC
IN THE SIXTEENTH CENTURY

THE outstanding features of the 16th century are (a) the culmination of polyphonic sacred music, (b) the rise and development of the madrigal in Italy, (c) the brief but brilliant work of the English madrigalists, (d) the effects of the Reformation, and (e) the rise of instrumental music. The first four of these will be dealt with in the order given; instrumental music will be considered in a separate chapter.

In the work of such composers as Isaac and Josquin the contrapuntal technique of the Flemish school had reached a high level of competence, and was applied to the production of music of real expressiveness. The great writers of the 16th century attained still greater competence and expressiveness in their Masses and motets, the highest achievements being in the works of Palestrina, Victoria, Lassus and Byrd.

The motet, of which the post-Machaut foundations had been laid by Dunstable, and strengthened by Dufay and his successors, now assumed very great importance. In the truly polyphonic motet the general structural principles are as follows. Each successive phrase of words is introduced by a 'point of imitation' or 'fugue',* the voices entering one after another with the same melodic figure, though not necessarily at the same pitch. This figure is used, generally with a good deal of word repetition, to build up a complete 'section'. Each section concludes with a cadence,

---

* See Ex. 16 for an illustration. Note also that this technique of imitation is important not only as a structural method of the 16th century, but also as the ultimate origin of the fugue, which reached its climax of perfection in the hands of Bach.

and as a rule the figure for the ensuing point of imitation arises within that cadence, so that the sections are interlocked. Thus a continuous contrapuntal web of sound is created. Motets were written for from three to eight voices, though there are occasional freak examples such as Thomas Tallis's *Spem in alium* for forty voices, arranged in eight five-part choirs. Tallis was not the only 16th-century composer to attempt a task of such magnitude and complexity, but he was the only one to succeed in producing real music under such conditions.

Motets were not, however, always and entirely contrapuntal in texture; there were two other common methods of procedure. One is almost entirely chordal, with little, if any, really independent movement of the voices. Victoria's *Ave Verum Corpus* and Palestrina's *O Bone Jesu* are good examples. The other kind lies between the purely polyphonic and the chordal. It is based not so much on imitative technique as on the contrasting of varying groups of voices within the choir, which would consist of not fewer than five voices. There is relatively little use of the full choir, but variation in the combinations used is exploited to the limit—a kind of vocal orchestration. Palestrina's *Tu es Petrus* is an example of this type of motet, and the same method is used with great effectiveness in Byrd's five-part Mass. In longer motets the three styles may be found used for different sections. A noteworthy point about the chordal type of motet is that it shows an increasing feeling for chords and chord-progression *as such*. In the polyphonic works of the period it may be said that the chords arise from the interweaving of simultaneous melodic and rhythmic lines; the texture is conceived horizontally and the chord-progressions are, as it were, incidental. But in such a work as *Ave Verum Corpus* it seems evident that Victoria must have been thinking in terms of chords as chords, an attitude of mind which from now on assumes increasingly great importance. The same attitude is clearly evident in such a passage as the opening of Palestrina's *Stabat Mater*:

Ex. 14

The basic material for Masses and motets was often taken
from plainsong. The use of the secular *cantus firmus* for
masses was rapidly dying out. Early in his career, Palestrina
wrote some Masses on secular *cantus firmi*, including two on
L'homme armé, but of his total of ninety-three, only a very
few are based on such material. The Council of Trent, in
1563, severely criticised the use of the secular *cantus firmus*,
as well as the undue complexity and length of Masses, and
composers found it expedient to follow the lead given by
Palestrina in his *Missa Papae Marcelli*, written after the
Council's decree and in accordance with its views. The
method of using a *cantus firmus* had changed since the time
of Dufay. Instead of being employed primarily as a melodic
line around which counterpoints were woven, it was now
broken up into its constituent phrases, and points of imitation were worked out based on these phrases. Undue repetition of words was generally avoided. A simple example of
this method of writing is provided in Palestrina's *Missa
Regina Coeli*. The melody from which it takes its title is:

Ex. 15

Re - gi - na cae - li lae - ta - re,   Al - le - lu - ia;   Qui - a quem me -

- min - i - sti por - ta - re,   Al - le - lu - ia;   Re - sur - rex - it, si - cut

dix - it,   Al - le - lu - ia: O - ra pro no - bis De - um;   Al - le - lu - ia.

The brackets show the various sections which are used as
themes in the mass.   The opening of the *Sanctus* is based
on the first phrase:

Ex. 16

Other movements are also based on this phrase and on
the others marked in Ex. 15, thus giving thematic unity
to the whole work.

Another source of material was used in what is usually
known as the 'parody Mass' (*Missa Parodia*).   In this the
musical themes were borrowed from other compositions,
such as madrigals, motets and chansons, often by other
composers.   There seems to have been a sort of musical
freemasonry among composers, thematic inventions being
treated largely as common property.   When entirely original
material was used, a Mass was often known as *Missa Sine
Nomine*, 'Mass without a name', but some unity was often
achieved by the use of the same material for at least the
openings of some, if not all, of the movements—a kind of
'motto-theme' procedure.*

* Pietro Cerone (b. *c.* 1560), in his huge compilation *El melopeo y
maestro*, goes so far as to insist on some such method, and goes into
considerable detail. 'In composing a Mass, it is perforce necessary and
obligatory that the inventions (*i.e.* the themes) at the beginnings of the
first *Kyrie*, the *Gloria*, the *Credo*, the *Sanctus* and the *Agnus Dei* should be
one and the same.'   Not every contemporary composer seems to have
agreed with him.

The *cantus firmus* method outlined above was sometimes used in motets. Palestrina's *Veni Sponsa Christi* is a setting of a verse which the composer splits into four phrases. Each of the four interlocked sections of the motet is based on imitative treatment of the relevant phrase of the plainsong tune associated with the words.

Giovanni Pierluigi da Palestrina (1525 to 1594) was the greatest of the Italians, and spent most of his life in Rome. His technical mastery was consummate, and his music attains a pitch of serenity which is unsurpassed by any of his contemporaries. Of the Netherlanders—a long list could be given—Orlande de Lassus (1532 to 1594) and Adrian Willaert (c. 1485 to 1562) are the most important. Lassus (also known by the Latinised and Italianised versions of his name—Orlandus Lassus and Orlando di Lasso) was the greatest of them all, with a European reputation and an enormous output of music of all kinds. Like so many of his countrymen he travelled widely, and he was noted for his use of *musica reservata*—the art of giving dramatic expression to the words. He is also notable for his use of chromaticism, a strongly marked characteristic of the English school in the latter part of the century. One of his greatest and best-known works is the setting of the *Seven Penitential Psalms*.

Willaert was the founder of the Venetian school associated with the cathedral of St. Mark in Venice. St. Mark's possessed two organs and two choirs, and these resources gave rise to the composition of works on a grand scale for double chorus, the two sections acting either antiphonally or in combination. This type of writing was continued, on an even grander scale, by Willaert's successors Cipriano da Rore (1516 to 1565), Andrea Gabrieli (c. 1510 to 1586) and his nephew Giovanni (1557 to 1612).

It is at this time that Spain first comes clearly into the musical picture. The long occupation by the Moors had tended to isolate this country from the rest of Europe, but their final expulsion in the 16th century, and the union of the crowns of the Netherlands and Spain under Charles V, brought about contact and exchange of ideas between Spanish and Flemish musicians. Works by Josquin were in the library of Seville Cathedral, and from about 1500 we find a school of Spanish composers who were basing their work on the ideas of the Netherlanders. Nicholas Gombert (*c.* 1495 to 1560), a Fleming attached to the court of Charles V, spent a good deal of time in Spain, and strongly influenced the Spaniards in the adoption of the northern technical methods. The two most important members of the Spanish school were Cristobal Morales (*c.* 1500 to 1553) and Tomàs Luis de Victoria* (*c.* 1535 to 1611). Morales spent part of his life in Rome, and despite his adherence to Flemish methods managed to retain a good deal of personal idiom, with an occasional distinctively Spanish flavour. Of the musicians working in Italy, Victoria is possibly second only to Palestrina. He lacks the latter's serenity, but achieves a remarkable degree of mystic fervour. Many of the Spanish musicians wrote but little secular music; Victoria, possibly rather narrowly religious, wrote none at all.

We have seen that in England the school of Fayrfax was but little affected by current continental methods, but early in the 16th century these methods begin to appear, in the works of Christopher Tye (*c.* 1497 to *c.* 1572), Thomas Tallis (*c.* 1505 to 1585) and Robert Whyte (*c.* 1535 to 1574). All three showed great competence in the handling of the imitative style. We may note especially Tye's Mass on the popular tune *Westron Wynde* and his six-part one on *Euge Bone*. Tallis, like Tye, began by writing in the style of the preceding generation, but gradually acquired the Flemish technique, his mastery being shown in such motets as *Audivi media nocte* and *O Bone Jesu*.

The greatest name in English music of this period—one of the greatest of all time—is that of William Byrd, a

* There seems to be no particular reason for the use of the Italianised form of his name—Vittoria.

remarkably versatile genius who lived from 1543 to 1623.
He excelled in all forms of composition, sacred or secular,
vocal or instrumental. Unlike many of his countrymen, he
did not change his religion at the Reformation, thereby
causing himself a certain amount of inconvenience at various
times in his life. Although he produced a certain quantity
of music for the Reformed Church, he continued to compose
for the old rite as late as the publication of his two books
of *Gradualia* in 1605 and 1607. These were collections of
Latin motets which also included a three-part setting of
the 'crowd' parts of the Passion—a rather rare production
for an English composer. Byrd's technique was at least
equal to that of any of his continental contemporaries, and
he surpassed them all in intensity of emotional expressiveness. His three Masses, for three, four and five voices respectively, are outstanding among the sacred music of the
century, and his reputation was such that one writer dubbed
him 'the Parent of British Music'.

Turning now to the Italian madrigal, we have seen (p. 59)
that compositions with this title were produced in the 14th
century. After the time of Landini the term fell into disuse,
being revived in the early 16th century. By then the technique of choral composition had developed enormously, and
composers were ready and able to apply the latest methods
to the setting of suitable poems. Such poems were chiefly
of a pastoral or amorous character, with occasional excur-
sions into the unseemly.

In the first quarter of the century the *Frottola* was a
common Italian form. It was usually a popular song
treated with some amount of ingenuity, and was often
vulgar and frivolous. The madrigal seems to have been
to some extent a reaction against the *frottola*, of which the
last collection appeared in 1531. The great Italian *littéra-
teur* Bembo was the leader of a school which cultivated an
aristocratic and rather affected style of poetry, with the
deliberate aim of getting away from the more 'popular'
types. Since composers were attached to courts for which

this new poetry was written, they naturally began to set it to music, and the *frottola* and similar 'vulgar' forms fell into disuse. The earliest madrigals—the first collection of twenty was published in 1533 under the title *Madrigali novi de diversi excellentissimi musici* ('New Madrigals by various excellent musicians')—were for four unaccompanied voices, the melody being always in the topmost part, and the texture showing but little contrapuntal ingenuity. Instrumental accompaniment, whether to the top part as a solo, or in combination with all the voices, was, however, an accepted practice. It should be understood that the madrigal was for domestic music-making; public concerts were still far in the future. The most notable of the earliest composers were the Roman Constanzo Festa (d. 1545) and the expatriate Fleming Phillippe Verdelot (d. before 1567).

In the ensuing generations, which saw the rapid development and culmination of the form, greater use was made of contrapuntal artifice, and five-part work is typical; six voices were also often used. The general plan of construction became similar to that of the polyphonic motet, a series of interlocked sections based on imitations of a melodic figure. The poems set were generally not longer than twelve lines, and although the subjects remained chiefly amorous or pastoral, madrigals were also written dealing with such matters as children's games and the chatter of washerwomen—Bembo notwithstanding. Great care was taken over apt setting of the words and, to quote the writer of the article in Grove's *Dictionary*, 'both words and music acquire a marvellously skilful technique of deliberate voluptuousness'.

The list of madrigalists is extensive. Willaert, Jacob Arcadelt (c. 1514 to c. 1570), Hubert Waelrant (c. 1518 to 1595), Philippe de Monte (c. 1521 to 1603) and Lassus are notable among the Netherlanders. Waelrant was exceptional in that he seems to have spent his life in his native country. De Monte was among the most prolific, pro-

ducing over 600 madrigals as well as numerous sacred
works. Of the Italians we may mention Cipriano da Rore
and Luca Marenzio (c. 1560 to 1599). Palestrina's output
of madrigals was small, and in his later years he seems to
have been rather ashamed of having written them. In the
Preface to his fourth book of motets he says: 'There exists
a vast mass of love-songs of the poets. . . . They are the
songs of men ruled by passion, and a great number of
musicians, corrupters of youth, make them the concern of
their art. . . . I blush and grieve to think that once I was
of their number.' Palestrina must have developed much
the same kind of outlook as Victoria.

With the advent of new ideas and a new outlook at the
beginning of the 17th century, the madrigal underwent
rapid modification, which will be briefly considered in
Chapter 8, and then went quickly, almost suddenly, out
of fashion.

The principal stimulus to the writing of madrigals in
England was the publication by Nicholas Yonge, in 1588,
of *Musica Transalpina*, a collection of Italian madrigals with
the words translated into English. Not that the form was
unknown here before this. Leaving aside a collection of
secular songs published in 1530 by Wynkyn de Worde, there
is Richard Edwards' *In going to my naked bed*, not later than
1564. The first publication containing a number of pieces
approximating in style to the Italian (or Flemish) madrigal
was Byrd's *Psalmes, Sonnets and Songs of Sadness and Pietie*
which appeared in 1588, but earlier in the year than *Musica
Transalpina*. After the publication of the Italian work, however, a great flood of madrigals appeared, no fewer than
forty-three sets being brought out before the final one by
John Hilton in 1627.

The English madrigal falls into three classes, (a) the
madrigal proper, whose normal style and structure have
already been mentioned, (b) the *Ballett*, and (c) the *Ayre*.
The ballett was a descendant of the Italian *ballata*, which
originated in the 14th century, and was for simultaneous

singing and dancing.* The 16th-century English form
retained much of the traditional dance-like rhythm, was
strongly metrical and rarely contrapuntal. It was also
characterised by the use of a 'fa-la' refrain, some sets being
entitled 'Balletts or Fa-las'. It was usually strophic, *i.e.*
the same music was used for two or more verses of words,
word repetition being avoided. It thus differed strongly
from the madrigal proper which was 'through-composed'
and inevitably employed much repetition of words. The
Ayre (=Air) was in the nature of an accompanied solo
song, the accompaniment being either vocal or instrumental,
generally on the lute. Like the ballett, it was strophic and
simple in texture. The term *Canzonet* was sometimes used
as an alternative to madrigal, especially by Thomas Morley,
whose attempted explanation of it does not always match
the works which he designates as such.

Most notable in the works of the English madrigalists is
the exceedingly apt and subtle way in which the music
illustrates the words; any word or phrase that suggests the
possibility of musical illustration is seized upon with avidity
and dealt with vividly. Still more notable, perhaps, is the
degree of emotional intensity which is achieved in settings
of the sadder poems, an intensity unmatched by any of
the Italians or Flemings. We have only to read through
such a work as Thomas Weelkes' *O Care, thou wilt despatch me*
to realise the truth of the statement in Chapter 1 that the
Elizabethans were romanticists.

On the technical side there appears an increasing feeling
for chord-progression and key (as opposed to mode).
Although the madrigal proper was generally of polyphonic
texture, purely homophonic, *i.e.* chordal passages are often
met with, and it is in these that the composers exploit what
they were learning about the emotional possibilities of
chords and chord-progression. Weelkes' *O Care* provides
a magnificent example.

* Even late in the 16th century Giovanni Gastoldi (*c.* 1556 to 1622)
published balletts 'for singing, playing and dancing'.

Ex. 17

We have to look forward to Purcell and Bach before again finding such poignancy.

Possibly the greatest of our madrigalists were Weelkes (c. 1575 to 1623) and John Wilbye (1574 to 1638), but the work of Orlando Gibbons (1583 to 1625) must not be overlooked. Gibbons specialised in what has been called the 'ethical' madrigal, of which the words have a moral rather than an amorous tone. From this point of view his madrigals lie, as it were, between the normal type and the motet—serious, but not sacred. One of his finest examples is *What is our life*, a meditation on human weakness.

Of the writers of balletts, Thomas Morley (1557 to 1603) is unsurpassed for delicacy and lightness of touch. He is notable also as the author of *A Plaine and Easie Introduction to Practicall Music*, which was a standard instructional work for two centuries, and is an invaluable source of information on the contemporary methods of composition.

The Ayre, a peculiarly English form of composition, often attained, like the madrigal, remarkable intensity of expression. John Dowland (1562 to 1626) and Thomas Campion (1567 to 1620) are perhaps the two greatest composers in this form. Dowland was one of the best-known musicians in the whole of Europe, and spent part of his life in Paris and in Italy. He has rightly been described as one of the world's greatest song-writers, and was not only a superb melodist, but also a harmonic innovator of great originality. He was probably the finest lutenist of his time. Campian was both poet and musician, his settings of his own lyric poems, with lute accompaniment, being second in value only to the work of Dowland.

Of the 16th-century French musicians, apart from those to be considered in succeeding paragraphs, mention may be made of Clément Jannequin (1485 to c. 1560). His work lay chiefly in the direction of secular chansons, mostly for four voices, and he is notable for his attempts at illustrative setting of words, e.g. The Song of the Nightingale. He was also the composer of a (vocal) battle-piece, possibly the first of a long line of such pieces, which are generally more notable for naïveté than for musical value.

We have now to consider the effects of the Reformation on music. Apart from purely doctrinal matters, the musical aims of all the reformers, in England (Cranmer), in Germany (Luther) or in Geneva (Calvin) were much the same, viz. that the words, in the vernacular, should be heard and understood by the congregation, and that the congregation themselves should take some part in the singing. The Calvinists were in some ways the most radical, permitting only metrical versions of the psalms. Hymns, being 'man-made' and not biblical, were considered unacceptable. The important musicians here are the French Huguenots Claude Goudimel (c. 1505 to 1572), who died in the Massacre of St. Bartholomew, Claude le Jeune (c. 1528 to 1600) and Loys Bourgeois (b. c. 1510). Goudimel and le Jeune made many settings of the psalms, varying in style from simple homophony, in which the element of chordal treatment is strongly marked, to quite elaborate polyphony. Bourgeois was for many years editor of the Genevan Psalter, and his settings are almost entirely chordal in style, with one note to a syllable.

Martin Luther was himself a practical musician, and laid great stress on congregational singing in his reformed services, though he was not averse to the employment of professional choirs. His great contribution to music was the introduction of the *Chorale* or German hymn into the services, the far-reaching results of which will be seen in later chapters. He was the first religious leader to remark that he did not see why the Devil should have all the best tunes, and promptly clinched his argument by appropriating a number of well-known secular melodies and making 'sacred parodies' of their words. Thus, the words of Heinrich Isaac's melody:

Ex. 18

O Innsbruck I must leave thee, were parodied into *O world I now must leave thee*. Other chorale tunes were adapted from traditional plainsong put into 'measured music', and yet others were original compositions, one of the most famous, *Ein Feste Burg* ('A Sure Stronghold') being reputedly by Luther himself, who also wrote the words. His first Protestant hymnbook appeared in 1524.

In England the musical effects of the Reformation were far-reaching, and yet not so drastic as in Geneva. Whereas Calvin severed any connection with the old Catholic ritual, the reformed English Church retained services based at least to some extent on the traditional 'Offices', together with some of the musical sections. The Chapel Royal, of which records exist as early as 1135, and the great cathedrals, had built up a fine musical tradition which continued unbroken despite the changed aspects of religious belief. Polyphonic music for the Mass was replaced by 'Services' which consisted of settings of the *Venite, Te Deum, Benedictus*,

Kyrie, Creed, Magnificat and *Nunc Dimittis*. Two most notable settings are Tallis' *Dorian* service and Byrd's 'Short' service. In both of these, as in such works as Tye's *Acts of the Apostles*, a simpler, more harmonic style of treatment appears. Byrd's work is almost entirely one note to a syllable, and the tendency to key as opposed to mode is strongly marked.

Besides such large-scale works, we must note the appearance of the 'Anglican Chant' for use with the vernacular prose psalms, and of psalm-tunes for use with the metrical versions. Anglican chants were mainly simple harmonisations of the old Gregorians, with the tune in the tenor. The earliest complete metrical psalter was that of Sternhold and Hopkins, published in 1562; it was a standard work for over a century.

The great importance of the simplification of style which was insisted on by all the reformers lies in the fact that it forced composers to 'think vertically', *i.e.* in terms of chord-progressions rather than of simultaneous melodic lines. We have seen that as far back as Dunstable there were signs of a feeling towards the triad, and Dufay's use of *faux-bourdon* also shows some tendency to harmonic thinking. This tendency was now rapidly intensified, and in the next century the idea of contrapuntal texture based on the decoration of a preconceived chord-basis gradually takes the place of a texture in which the vertical combinations, *i.e.* the chords, arise from the interplay of melodic lines.

Despite the general simplicity demanded by the reformers, contrapuntal music was not banished from the English rite. Byrd's 'Great' service is as polyphonic in texture as any of his Latin works, and the anthem, which may be called the English substitute for the motet, was often written in the traditional complex manner. The finest anthems of the period are those of Gibbons. Of his forty examples, some fifteen are polyphonic, possibly the best known, and certainly one of the finest, being *Hosanna to the Son of David*. Gibbons was not averse to experiment, and was one of the first (though Byrd anticipated him) to write 'verse' anthems, in which solo passages and independent instrumental accompaniment are introduced. This form, new in Gibbons' time, was chiefly popular around the end of the 17th century in the hands of such Restoration composers as Purcell and Blow.

RECORDS

H.M S. Vol. 4, HLP 8/9

CHAPTER SEVEN

THE RISE OF
INSTRUMENTAL MUSIC

OUR study so far has been concerned exclusively with the development of vocal music. It was not until late in the 15th century that composers began to give any serious attention to that for instruments alone. The undeveloped state of the instruments themselves and the fact that composers were so largely concerned with the provision of music for the Church naturally brought about concentration on the vocal rather than on the instrumental side. Little seems to have been written purely for instrumental performance, and there was little or no differentiation of style.

From the earliest times there was a wealth of dance tunes for the *vielle* or *fiedel*, but their composers are unknown. In any case, the 'serious' composer had other things to do than to write such pieces. Of medieval instrumental music written for use in church a number of short organ preludes survive, rambling and formless affairs which show clearly the undeveloped state of the instrument and the composers' lack of grasp of a suitable style. The earliest extant keyboard music is in the *Robertsbridge Codex* of about 1325, an organ *estampie*. It is to some extent stylised, being in dance rhythm but not suitable for actual dancing.

Instruments, as we have seen, were often combined with or substituted for voices, and by the 16th century many had reached a high state of development. Brief consideration of the most important now follows.

The organ had progressed far beyond its condition in the days of the *pulsator organorum*, having one or more manageable keyboards and a considerable variety of stops. It was most advanced in Germany, where an adequate pedal department was considered essential. As early as the first quarter of the 16th century, in an organ built by Arnold Schlick in Heidelberg, four of the sixteen stops were on the pedal, and as we move on towards the 17th century we find this department tending to increase more and more, both in size and variety. In England, Italy and France the organ was less developed and remained so until much later; pedals were either lacking or but poorly provided with registers.

Of domestic instruments the chief were the lute, the viols, recorders, and the various keyboard instruments.

The lute was of great antiquity. Its body was shaped rather like a pear cut in half from top to bottom. The strings were plucked by the fingers and the tone was restrained and gentle. Like many other instruments of the time, and since, lutes were made in families of five or more different sizes, the most popular being the theorbo or tenor lute. Its notation was called 'tablature' and was designed to show the positions of the fingers on the fingerboard, not the actual sounds to be played.* The ordinary staff notation was not used. Of its nature the lute was incapable of true polyphony, though by the end of the 16th century such composers as Molinaro were achieving some remarkable effects of 'faking'.

In Spain the place of the lute was taken by the vihuela, an ancestor of the guitar. The number of strings and their tuning, the notation and the manner of playing the two instruments were similar, as was also the style of writing for them.

The viol was a development of the medieval *vielle*, one

* 'A true tablature rather directed the player *what to do* than told him what music to play' (Scholes, *Oxford Companion*). Tablatures for various instruments survived into the 18th century. Even in Bach's time an organ tablature was still in use by the more conservative composers in Germany, and the theorist F. E. Niedt, in his *Musikalische Handleitung* of 1700, castigates severely and amusingly those who still clung to such an antiquated system. The only present-day survivals of the tablature system are in connection with such instruments as the mandoline and the ukulele.

form of which was held in front of the body, not under the chin. This was gradually transformed into the *viola da gamba* or 'leg viol', and from it came a large family, all held either resting on the knees or between them. As compared with their relations the violin family, viols have a flat back, sloping shoulders, six strings instead of four, and 'C'-shaped sound holes. The tone was sombre, lacking the brightness and incisiveness of the violins. A 'chest of viols' was an actual chest in which a small set of various sizes was kept for domestic use.

Family groups included the recorders, a type of end-blown flute (as opposed to the side-blown or 'transverse' flute of the modern orchestra), with a round and gentle tone. At the beginning of the 16th century four sizes were in use, but by the 18th there were no fewer than nine,

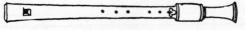

Recorder

ranging from the *sopranino*, roughly equivalent to a piccolo, to the great bass, an impracticable sort of instrument with a penchant for leaping up an octave on the slightest provocation—or on no provocation at all.

Of the four domestic keyboard instruments three, the virginals, the spinet and the harpsichord, were related in their method of tone production, the strings being plucked and the tone consequently tending to be 'twangy'. The tone of the harpsichord was louder and richer than that of its companions, and even before 1600 instruments were being built with mechanism enabling differing qualities of tone to be produced.* Later, two-manual harpsichords were developed, each keyboard controlling its own set of strings (see frontispiece).

In the clavichord, a more essentially domestic instrument

* The reader is referred to Donington's *The Instruments of Music* (Methuen) for details.

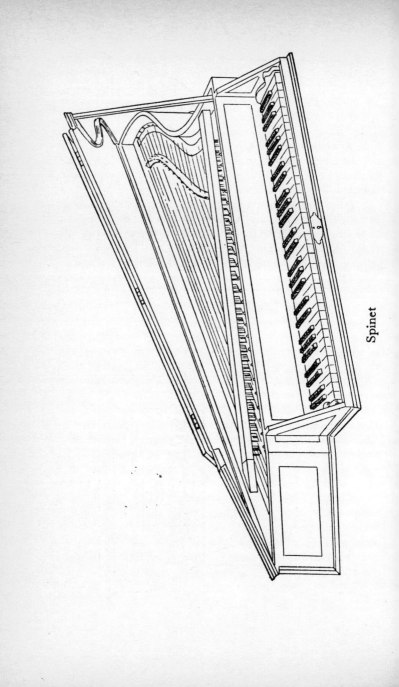

Spinet

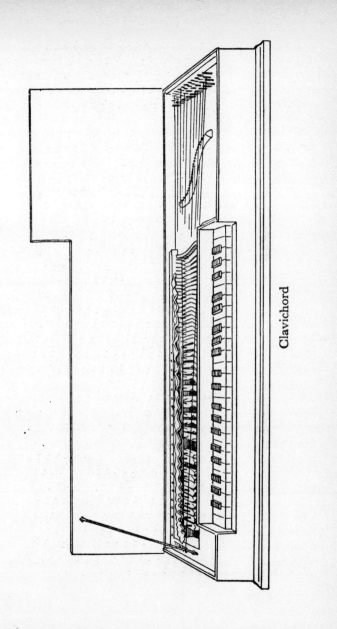

Clavichord

than the harpsichord, the strings were struck by a metal tangent fixed to the rear end of the key. There was no intervening mechanism as in the case of the plucked-string instruments, and the tone could be varied, within somewhat narrow limits, according to the degree of force applied to the key.

Other instruments, for church or open-air rather than for domestic use, were the sackbuts (trombones) and the shawms and pommers. These last were the ancestors of

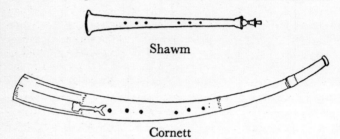

Shawm

Cornett

the oboe and bassoon, including the 'great bass pommer' or 'bombard', a ten-foot giant which needed one man to blow it and another to support it at the front.* There were also cornetts, trumpet-like affairs of wood, or occasionally of ivory, with a cup-shaped mouthpiece.

When composers first began to take a serious interest in writing instrumental music they were faced with the problem of what kind of pieces to write. Broadly speaking, this was solved in three directions, (a) dances, (b) adaptations of the current vocal polyphonic style and (c) variations on a theme. A fourth but less important solution was the writing of descriptive music.

In much of the early music no particular instruments were specified, and it would seem that it was intended to be played on whatever might be available. Large quantities of dances appeared, some for specified instruments,

* A practice which survives perhaps only in one part of the world, with the monstrous temple trumpets of Tibet.

some not. Of the latter, important collections were printed in 1529 and 1530 by the Parisian publisher Pierre Attaignant, comprising pavanes, galliards, basse danses and branles. They do not possess any great musical distinction, but are noteworthy in that, at a time when other kinds of music were predominantly contrapuntal, they are entirely homophonic, as music for the dance must naturally be, once it ceases to be purely melodic. We have seen how from the time of Dunstable there was an increasing feeling for chords and chord-progression, and the composition of dances played an important part in the development of this. The harmony of the Attaignant dances is of the simplest character, some, indeed, employing little but tonic and dominant. Use of the major scale is common.

Attaignant's sets of dances were not arranged according to any plan. The *First Dance Book* of 1530, for example, lumps together 'nine basses danses, two branles, twenty-five pavanes with fifteen galliards in music for four parts'. But even at this early stage the grouping of dances into sets, generally contrasting pairs, was quite common, the second of a pair often being a variation on the first. The pairing of a slow dance and a quick one was most common, the most popular group being the pavane and galliard. The pavane was a stately affair, more of a procession than a dance in the usual sense,* while the galliard was quick, gay, and in triple time as opposed to the duple of its companion. Galliards were frequently written as variations of their associated pavanes. This pairing of dances is historically of great importance, since it is the genesis of the 17th- and 18th-century form, the *Suite*.

The internal organisation of individual dances is notable in view of its bearing on the development of later instrumental forms. From the earliest days dance tunes had been sectional in construction, conformably to the pattern of the dances themselves. In some cases the contrast between

* Compare the Polish *Polonaise*. Such processional dances were common all over Europe.

sections is very strong as, for example, in a Hornpipe by
Hugh Aston, found in a MS. of about 1500. This has five
sections so strongly contrasted that but for the fact that all
but the last end with a half-close, it might as well be five
separate pieces. It is also a good example of the harmonic
simplicity already mentioned; solidly based on the major
scale, the chord-scheme is almost entirely tonic and dominant, with a very occasional supertonic or subdominant.
Attaignant's dances are all clearly sectionalised, though in
varying ways and without any strong contrasts of style.
Towards the end of the 16th century the stylised treatment
of dances led to some conventionalisation of structure,
generally into two or three main periods. In the case of
the latter the music falls into three clearly defined *different*
sections, though there are occasional instances of a true
ternary (ABA) design. There is even one in Attaignant's
collection of 1530. More important is the frequent use of
the two-period, binary plan, of which a well-known example
is Byrd's *Earl of Salisbury's Pavane.* This is as rigidly binary
as anything suggested by any textbook on Form. First
sentence of eight bars leading to a half-close, balanced by
another sentence of similar length ending with a full-close.
It happens also to be a particularly beautiful piece of music.
The importance of the binary design is that as the Suite
developed (see Chapter 9) practically all its movements
were written in this form, and further that from it ultimately grew the sonata form which is the structural basis
of much of the work of the composers of the 'classical'
period.

Examples of the polyphonic style transferred to instruments appear as early as Obrecht, who died in 1505. Such
pieces were usually known as *canzonas.* This term originally signified a certain variety of lyric verse, and was later
adopted for the musical setting of such poetry in a somewhat madrigalian style. From this it came to be used for
instrumental pieces in the same style. In early canzonas
the use of a tenor *cantus firmus* was common, as in the case

of Obrecht's *A maiden sat*, based on a Dutch folksong, but this was by no means obligatory. Isaac also produced interesting works of this kind.

Of rather similar construction was the *ricercar* or *ricercare*, though this term has had a number of different implications. Literally it implies research, a seeking-out, and in this sense might imply a kind of prelude in which, as the historian Dr. Burney says, 'the composer seems to search or look out for the strains and touches of harmony, which he is to use in the regular piece to be played afterwards'. In the 16th century it was often used with this implication in Italian lute music, the ricercare being a short prelude to a transcription of a song. The contrapuntal ricercare was a deliberate imitation of the polyphonic motet, employing all such devices as canon, augmentation, etc., as the composer chose. Willaert's ricercares are of considerable importance, written for three melodic instruments such as viols or recorders. The Italian Girolamo Cavazzoni (b. *c.* 1515) may also be mentioned, being the first writer of ricercares for the organ. He is notable, too, for the freedom of his part-writing, in which the number of voices is apt to vary frequently within a single composition.

The term *Fantasia* (in England 'Fancy') might also imply a piece in canzona style, but equally it might mean something of a rambling nature, simply 'following the dictates of the composer's fancy'.

We have seen that in pairs of dances the second was not infrequently a variation on the first. The practice of writing variations on a theme was developed quickly and with considerable skill by many composers. Within rather restricted limits, great ingenuity was shown in embellishing the tune, and in applying new figures of accompaniment to it. The theme might be made up by the composer, or might equally well be some popular song. Variations were written largely for the keyboard instruments and for the lute.

Turning now to the composers and the instruments for which they wrote, we may note first two important schools, of vihuelists in Spain and of lutenists in Italy. The Spanish school flourished in the first half of the 16th century, notable composers being Luis de Milan, Luis de Narvaez and Anriquez de Valderrano. Narvaez was a particularly good writer of variations, and showed great ingenuity in producing a pseudo-contrapuntal texture on an instrument which

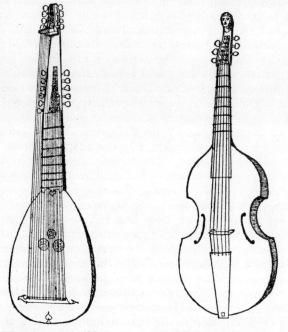

Theorbo or Archlute   Viola da Gamba

is fundamentally non-contrapuntal. This ingenuity is also characteristic of some of the Italians, whose school flourished more towards the end of the century. Some of the finest and cleverest work is that of Simone Molinaro, who in 1599 was *maestro di capella* at the cathedral of Genoa. His compositions show genuine melodic inventiveness, and evidence that he was no mean performer. His *Intavolatura di Liuto*, published in the year of his appointment to Genoa, contains examples of such dances as the *Saltarello* and the *Passamezzo* (in as many as ten separate sections, each ending in the tonic), as well as a number of galliards in three or four sections. Molinaro was almost fantastically clever at 'faking' a contrapuntal texture in his fantasias, not only in his original compositions, but also in his arrangements of canzonas by other composers, *e.g.* Clemens non Papa. Like many of his contemporaries, he often gave fanciful titles to his dances, sometimes, as with Byrd's *Earl of Salisbury* pavane, in a dedicatory fashion, but sometimes for no apparent reason beyond caprice. This is also the case with the lutenist Santino Garsi, who entitles one of his galliards 'The lie in the throat'.

In France the lutenist school, beginning in the latter part of the 16th century, reached its climax considerably later, in the person of Denis Gaultier (d. 1672). He, too, followed the fashion of using 'fancy' titles, *e.g.* 'The virtuous coquette'.

Of English lutenists Dowland and Campian were the most renowned, but the former's fame rests chiefly on his ayres, while the latter appears to have written nothing for lute alone. England, however, produced the greatest virginal music of the century, from the pens of Byrd, Gibbons and Dr. John Bull (1563 to 1628). Bull lived much abroad, his fame on the continent being great, and from 1613 to his death was organist at Antwerp Cathedral. He was a virtuoso of keyboard instruments, with the same visionary insight into the possibilities of technique and sonority as was later to distinguish Domenico Scarlatti and Franz Liszt.

Commenting on the English virginal music of this period, Dr. E. H. Fellowes says: 'No other European country has anything that can remotely be compared with it. More than 600 pieces are in existence, and nearly a quarter of these are by Byrd.' Especially notable, as being the first known engraved book of keyboard music, is the collection called *Parthenia*, of 1611. It contains works of only Byrd,

Gibbons and Bull, and consists largely of pavanes and galliards. Other collections of the time are *My Ladye Nevell's
Booke* and the *Fitzwilliam Virginal Book* (so called because
it was the property of the Viscount Fitzwilliam who presented it to Cambridge University in 1816), together with
the original books of Benjamin Cosyn and Will Forster
(1624). These last are in manuscript. Besides dances,
including allemandes, corantos and jigs, there are numerous
fantasies, preludes, and sets of variations.

In Spain the outstanding writer for keyboard instruments
was the blind Antonio de Cabézon (1510 to 1566), who played
a leading part in the development of variation writing.

For the viols the chief types of composition were the canzona, the ricercare and the fantasie or fancy. Here again
the English composers are outstanding, in particular Byrd
and Gibbons. Both showed great mastery in applying the
contemporary vocal style to instruments, and both produced works which are not only technically ingenious but
also of considerable musical value.

The organ music of the period is of great variety. Canzonas abound, Cavazzoni being notable in this direction,
and a large amount of music exists written for liturgical
purposes. The practice of writing preludial movements
continued. These, although often far from being highly
organised, gradually became less utterly rambling than
those of earlier times, and began to exploit the possibilities
of short-value notes in the form of extended scalic runs.
There are numerous pieces based on plainsong hymns, the
cantus firmus being more or less decorated, with harmonisation which might be quite simple or moderately contrapuntal. These 'organ hymns' appear very early in the 16th
century, there being extant examples by Arnold Schlick,
who died about 1517, and the Englishman John Redford
(1485 to 1545). They are noteworthy as anticipations of
the Chorale Prelude which took such a strong hold of
German composers once the Lutheran reformation was
firmly established.

Also for liturgical purposes are many sets of 'verses for the tones'. These were used in connection with the singing of the psalms, which inevitably became monotonous with the unvarying repetition of the same melodic formula for each verse. The practice grew up of replacing the plainchant of the even-numbered verses by polyphonic settings for the choir or by organ 'versets', based on the 'tone' to which the psalm was being chanted. In the latter case clergy, choir and congregation meanwhile repeated the words of the missing verse silently. Sets of such versets were published in 1531 by Attaignant, and Cabézon among others wrote numerous examples. A rather similar practice obtained at times even in the performance of a plainsong Mass. Certain portions of each movement were replaced by an organ piece of a more or less contrapuntal character, based on the omitted plainsong. The name of Cavazzoni may again be noted in this connection.

Such works as the above had, however, relatively little effect on the ultimate development of organ music as such. More important are the many *toccatas* which appear from about the middle of the century onwards. The term *toccata* comes from the verb *toccare*, to touch. Nowadays it tends to imply a piece designed primarily to exhibit the performer's dexterity and virtuosity, as, for example, Schumann's *Toccata* for piano, and the movements for organ by such composers as Guilmant and Widor, which are often of greater value as extended finger exercises than as music; but the original significance of toccata was not unlike that of *sonata*, *i.e.* something played as opposed to something sung. There was, however, always a proportion of brilliant scalic passage work intended, to quote Grove, 'to exhibit the touch and execution of the performer'. Toccatas for the organ date from about 1550, though the earliest known use of the title is for a lute piece of 1536 by Castelione. Both the Gabrielis wrote in this form, but possibly the greatest of the early writers of toccatas was Claudio Merulo (1533 to 1604), who served at St. Mark's, Venice, as organist from 1557 to 1584. He was renowned as a masterly performer. His toccatas are interesting in their alternation of sections in brilliant virtuoso style with others in the ricercare manner. He was one of the first to realise the effectiveness of contrast between quick movement and steady, solid passages which exploited the inexorable sustaining power of the organ. He may be considered as one of the most important founders of the Italian organ school which flourished in the next century.

Essays in programme or illustrative music range from the reasonably effective to the almost ludicrous, and are important chiefly in that they were the ultimate origin of a type of composition which eventually led to such works as the symphonic poems of Liszt, Richard Strauss and other 19th- and 20th-century composers. Among the more effective pieces is John Mundy's (d. 1630) virginal fantasia depicting, in the words of Sir Hubert Parry, various states of the atmosphere—*A cleare day*, *Lightning*, etc. Martin Peerson (*c.* 1580 to 1650) also wrote some charming little tone pictures, such as *The fall of the leaf*, in which a quietly autumnal feeling is created. In Chapter 6 mention was made of Jannequin's vocal battle piece, and such pieces appeared also for virginals, *e.g.* that by Byrd, in which an attempt is made to illustrate the various stages of the battle, albeit in a rather elementary manner. Battle pieces were even written for that least bellicose of instruments, the lute. The Italian Santino Garsi, who flourished round the turn of the century, produced one of almost incredible naïvety, consisting mainly of passages suggesting trumpets and drums, all with carefully detailed instructions as to their meaning.

RECORDS

Composer	Title	Catalogue No.
	HMS Vol. 4 (Mono only)	HLP 9
Gesualdo	*Gagliarda del principe*	72810
	(also includes works by Frescobaldi, Gabrielli, etc.)	

CHAPTER EIGHT

VOCAL MUSIC IN
THE SEVENTEENTH CENTURY

IN the preceding chapters it has been shown how the leadership in European music passed from one country to another. From the France of Pérotin and Machaut it passed to England (Dunstable), then to the Burgundians (Dufay) and from them to the Netherlanders. They, in their turn, taught the Italians and the Spaniards. We have seen, too, how the Elizabethans adopted the madrigal and developed it, in their own way, to a height hardly reached elsewhere. Each race produced its own supreme genius of polyphony; the Italians Palestrina, the Flemings Lassus, the Spaniards Victoria and the English Byrd. In the early 17th century the lead passed to the Italians, and it is their new developments which we have now to consider. But before doing so it is necessary to sketch briefly the changes of outlook which brought about these developments, and the new technical methods involved.

Shortly before 1600 a band of men, described by one writer* as 'a noisy group of *litterati*', came together in Florence and launched an attack on the current polyphonic style of composition. They are known as the *Camerata*, and were led by Counts Bardi and Corsi. Other important members were Giulio Caccini, a singer, Jacopo Peri, Vincenzo Galilei and Ottavio Rinuccini, a poet. The basis of their attack was that the contrapuntal style obscured the poetry, which admittedly it did, since for much of the time each of the voices would be singing different words. Counterpoint was therefore anathema and music, hitherto the predominant factor, must be treated rather as the hand-maid of poetry. Some members of the group, however,

* Dr. Manuel Bukofzer, *Music in the Baroque Era.*

were amateurs, so that at the back of their attack may possibly have been a realisation that the technique of vocal polyphony needed lengthy professional training, which they did not possess. Galilei's attitude is rather curious, since as a professional musician he had already proved himself a capable contrapuntist.

An avowed aim of the *Camerata* was the revival of what they considered to be the ancient Greek method of declamation, in the form of a musical intensification of the text. Their attitude to the musical expression of the words was different from that of the polyphonic composers. The use of *musica reservata* by Lassus has been mentioned, and no group of composers showed greater ability in this direction than did the Elizabethans. But *musica reservata* included, among other things, the musical illustration of individual words, not merely the expression of their general mood. The word 'run', for example, would be expressed by a quick-moving scalic passage, and so on. The *Camerata* decried such methods, insisting that the music should agree with the mood of the words as a whole. Moods were classified into a series of 'affections', *i.e.* emotions, and the 'affection' of the music must correspond to that of the words. There were even stereotyped musical figures to represent the various verbal affections.

As so often happens with new movements of any kind, there was a good deal of pamphleteering and letter-writing, the exponents of the new theories expressing themselves in no measured terms. Bardi, in his *Discourse on Ancient Music and Good Singing* (*c.* 1580), contrasts counterpoint and the 'art of good singing' much to the detriment of the former. Caccini, writing in 1602, refers to the 'old way of composition' which causes 'a laceration of the poetry'. Agostino Agazzari, in 1607, castigates composers who wish 'to stand solely on the observance of canonic treatment and imitation of the notes, not on the passion and expression of the words'. Examples could be multiplied almost indefinitely.

It must not be thought that the new outlook brought

about a complete and immediate break with the old ideals. Whereas in the great days of polyphony there was one over-all prevailing style of composition, whether sacred or secular, two styles now came to be recognised. The old style—*stilo antico*—persisted in a good deal of music for the church, though increasingly influenced by the new or 'modern' style—*stilo moderno*. The two styles were also known as *prima* and *seconda prattica*,* first and second practices, and training in the former was still considered indispensable to the professional composer. Many musicians wrote equally well in either style. Monteverdi, one of the greatest figures of the time, wrote a number of sets of madrigals, some employing *stilo antico* and some *stilo moderno*. When attacked for his advanced use of dissonance in the latter he simply retorted that it was justified, since he was not composing in the old style. Giovanni Gabrieli, too, exhibits mastery of both styles, his earlier works being clearly in *stilo antico*, and his later ones in *stilo moderno*.

In the course of the century further distinctions of style, though in a different connection, and apart from any question of *antico* or *moderno*, came to be recognised, *viz.* church music, chamber music and theatre music. These distinctions obviously operated according to the purpose for which the music was written, and offer another contrast with the outlook of the preceding generation. In the 16th century there was, broadly speaking, little difference in the style of, for example, a motet and a polyphonic madrigal;† such a work as Gibbons' *What is our life* could be set to sacred words with no violation of propriety, while there is little if any difference between the style of a Palestrina motet and that of one of his early madrigals. The 17th-century composer tended to adopt one style in writing for the opera, another for the church, and so on, though there was at times a good deal of overlapping.

* The inventor of these terms appears to have been Monteverdi.

† Though naturally such forms as the ballett and the ayre were automatically non-ecclesiastical in style.

The technical results of the new ideas were manifold, and can only be dealt with in the barest outline. The appropriate style of declamation was, as we have seen, deemed to be of prime importance. The *Camerata* strove to achieve a type of simple melody, with the simplest possible accompaniment, which could follow the exact inflexions of the declaiming voice, and so enhance and intensify the meaning of the words. It was *musica parlante*, speaking music, for which the term *recitative* is usually employed, also called *stile rappresentativo* or 'representative style'. According to Bardi's son, Pietro, Galilei was 'the first to let us hear singing in the *stile rappresentativo*'. A most important early example of this was a collection of vocal pieces published in 1602 under the title of *Le Nuove Musiche* —'The New Music'. Although experimental, a good deal of emotional intensity and dramatic force is at times achieved, as in Caccini's well-known *Amarilli*.

In all these compositions a notable feature is the rhythmic freedom of the voice part, which is made to approximate to some extent to speech-rhythm. Equally notable is the increasingly free use of dissonance, brief mention of which was made in Chapter 3. Unprepared discords become more and more common, and great stress is laid on the use by the voice of the more 'affective' intervals, *e.g.* the diminished 4th and chromatic progressions.

The accompanimental methods of monody* are of great importance, since (*a*) they show an almost sudden swerve to the use of chords as such, far more than might have been anticipated, despite the tendencies already noted in Chapter 6, and (*b*) they firmly established a practice, already in use to some extent, known as *basso continuo* or 'thorough bass', which persisted for about the next 150 years. Lute accompaniments to ayres often tried to preserve a kind of faked contrapuntal texture; but the *Camerata* eschewed counterpoint, and thus the only possible harmonic

* This term is frequently used for music of the kind under discussion, distinguishing it from polyphony.

support to the voice was chordal. Accompaniments to monody might well be played on a lute, but all that the player had was a figured bass line from which he was expected to 'realise', that is to build up, his chordal progressions. Until about the middle of the 18th century all vocal compositions and the majority of instrumental ones included in the score a part for *continuo*. The bass line itself would be played by some low-pitched instrument such as a 'cello, while it became the regular practice for the 'realisation' to be played on harpsichord or organ. Thus, whatever the texture of the upper parts, there was always a harmonic background. To what extent this would be purely chordal or, alternatively, contrapuntal, would depend on the style of the movement concerned and on the ability of the player.

One further point must be mentioned. We have seen that largely owing to the use of *musica ficta* the individual characteristics of the modes gradually became obscured; the 17th century saw the final disintegration of the modal system and its supplanting by the major- and minor-scale system. In the early years there is often considerable vagueness of tonality, composers seeming to hover between the modes and the later system; some, indeed, employ either at will. Even in the second half of the century we find that Purcell, for example, uses the major scale pure and simple in some of his more 'modern' pieces; but in some movements in his anthems, and in his string fantasias, he deliberately adopts a more archaic, backward-looking idiom. By the end of the 17th century, however, the modes were dead, and the bases of composition were the major and minor scales, though there were, for reasons which will appear later, certain inevitable restrictions. The complete and unrestricted establishment of the new scale-system was the work of Bach.

We turn now to the types of composition which first saw light in the 17th century, which was an extraordinarily fertile period. Although much of the rest of this chapter will be devoted to music in Italy, it must be remembered that the new ideas which have been outlined above spread rapidly all over Europe. Each country tended to stress one or more particular aspects of composition, these aspects being affected by, among other things, social and religious conditions. Not that the music of any one country was isolated from that of its neighbours; there was, as there always has been, continual 'cross-fertilisation', often due to the travels of the composers themselves and the natural desire of the younger men to seek the help or instruction of the most eminent musicians of any country.

The principles of *Nuove Musiche* found complete expression in opera. Before the end of the 16th century there had been written 'madrigal-operas', entertainments in which a drama was enacted, interspersed with the singing of madrigals. In other words, a kind of play with incidental music. (Compare Adam de la Hale's *Robin et Marion*.) More purely musical was such a work as *Amfiparnasso* of Orazio Vecchi (*c.* 1551 to 1605), called by the composer *Commedia Armonica*, which consisted of a whole series of unaccompanied five-part madrigals. But such works, whatever their purely musical virtues, had little if any value as dramatic representations, and it was exactly this matter of the application of music to dramatic ends which was exercising the minds of the *Camerata*. The first true opera, that is drama set to music, was *Dafne* by Peri, produced in 1597 but now lost. Like most of its successors for nearly two hundred years, its plot was based on an ancient Greek story—an obvious result of the Bardi group's preoccupation with Greek tragedy. In 1600 came *Eurydice*, partly by Peri and partly by Caccini, followed in the same year by Caccini's own setting of the same libretto, which was by Rinuccini. The style of these works is entirely monodic, with a somewhat haphazard collection of accompanying instruments. It may be imagined that the effect would be hardly exciting to 20th-century ears, but there was soon to appear a genius of great inventiveness and dramatic power, Claudio

Monteverdi (1567 to 1643), *maestro di capella** to the Duke of Mantua. His first opera, *Orfeo*, produced in 1607, shows great power of dramatic expression, and requires a large and heterogeneous collection of instruments for an orchestra. In later works he tended to be less orchestrally adventurous, and there are clear signs of the beginnings of the use of the string orchestra as the main instrumental support. Monteverdi soon began to turn away from the use of uninterrupted recitative. The use of a chorus in dramatically appropriate places was accepted, and we now find the aria, *i.e.* a properly organised melody commenting on the action, beginning to appear as a break in the monotony. A most expressive example is the famous 'Lament of Ariadne' from *Arianna*, produced in 1608. Monteverdi is notable as an innovator in orchestral technique, and is credited with the invention of the string *tremolando*.

The earliest operas were performed privately, but in 1637 the first public opera house was opened, the *Teatro di San Cassiano* in Venice. Here was produced, in 1640, Monteverdi's *L'Adone* and also *Le Nozze di Peleo e di Teti* by his pupil Cavalli† (1602 to 1676). Cavalli, possibly more than his master, and certainly in opposition to the original ideas of the *Camerata*, cultivated easy-flowing and rhythmic melody, as did also his contemporary, Marc' Antonio Cesti (1623 to 1669). The public found this much to their taste, and quite quickly recitative, the original sole constituent of opera, fell into the background. It was now used simply to carry on the action of the plot, while melodious arias, which often became vehicles for vocal display, came to be regarded as the most important movements. So much so that a composer commissioned to write an opera would begin by setting the recitatives, but would not tackle the

---

* This term, together with the corresponding German *kapellmeister*, has not necessarily any ecclesiastical significance. The *capella* or *kapelle* of a house or institution was the body of musicians attached to it, and the *maestro* or *meister* was the musical director.

† His full name was Pier-Francesco Caletti-Bruni, but the nickname Cavalli is generally used.

arias until he had heard, and assessed the capabilities of, the singers engaged to take part.

Before the end of the century Venice had no fewer than eleven opera houses, employing a group of composers including Legrenzi, Sartorio, Ziani and Strozzi. Other cities were not backward in taking to opera, but hardly to the same extent; Rome, for example, had but three houses.

After the middle of the century the greatest name in opera is Alessandro Scarlatti (1658 or 1659 to 1721), the founder of the Neapolitan school. A superb melodist, it is to him that we owe the standardisation of the aria into ternary form (statement, digression, restatement). He employed two varieties of recitative, the *recitativo secco*, simple and quick-moving, with figured bass accompaniment on the harpsichord, and *recitativo accompagnato* (or *stromentato*), 'accompanied recitative', which was used for the more emotionally intense passages. His use of the stereotyped ternary ('*da capo*') aria was only part of the conventionalisation of opera which persisted for many years until an attempt to break it down was made by Gluck in the 18th century. Of Scarlatti's fellow Neapolitans, Alessandro Stradella (1645 to 1682) is perhaps the most noteworthy.

Scarlatti is notable for the popularisation, if not the invention, of a stereotyped form of operatic overture. The overture originated as a kind of preliminary flourish, a summons to attention, but in Scarlatti's hands it became a three-movement affair—quick, slow, quick—under the title of *Sinfonia avanti l'opera*. Although on a small scale, its historical importance is considerable, since it was the germ of the classical symphony.

In France the earliest operas were closely associated with the Court ballet, and for a long period ballet was considered an essential in opera.* Early attempts to introduce

* Writing as late as 1834, Hector Berlioz remarks, 'at the Opéra, an excuse for a ballet would be found, even in a representation of the Last Judgment'!

Italian opera were unsuccessful, despite the powerful influence of Cardinal Mazarin during the reign of Louis XIV. In 1646 came the private production of what is usually described as the first real French opera, the Abbé Mailly's *Akebar, Roi de Mogol*, and in 1659 began the association of the musician Robert Cambert with the librettist Pierre Perrin. Their most successful work was *Pomone* (1671), the first French opera to be publicly performed in Paris. But their success was not to last. In 1646 one Giovanni Batista Lulli* (1632 to 1687) had come to Paris as page-boy to Mlle. de Montpensier, niece of Louis XIV. His musical ability soon became apparent, and in 1653 he was appointed the King's composer of dance music, rapidly achieving almost a monopoly of the writing of court ballets, in which the King himself often took part. In 1672 Lulli secured for himself the patent hitherto held by Perrin to establish an 'Academy of Music', and thereafter produced some twenty operas in conjunction with the librettist Quinault. The first of these, *Les Fêtes de l'Amour et de Bacchus*, is described as the first 'legitimate' French opera. As with the contemporary Italian works, the subjects of Lulli's operas are chiefly drawn from classical mythology, and all begin with a prologue glorifying *Le Roi Soleil*. The inclusion of ballet was invariable, and much greater use was made of the chorus than in Italian opera. Lulli did not use the Italian *recitativo secco*, preferring instead excellently managed declamation in the form of accompanied recitative. His arias, modelled on those of Cavalli, avoid the Italian conventionality of structure, and are often of considerable emotional power. The well-known *Bois Épais* is an excellent example of Lulli at his best.

To Lulli is ascribed the invention of the 'French' overture. Its plan was (*a*) a slow introduction, generally with much dotted-note rhythm, (*b*) a quick fugal movement, followed by (*c*) one or more dances, or a repetition of the opening movement. Unlike the Italian overture, Lulli's

* Also known by the French form of his name, Jean Baptiste Lully.

form, although still in use by Handel nearly a hundred years later, had no further development.

In Germany opera began with the setting of a German translation of Rinuccini's *Dafne* by Heinrich Schütz (1585 to 1672), in 1627. The music is lost. After this, Italian works were imported, sung in the original tongue. German opera proper dates from 1678, when Johann Theile's *Adam und Eva* was given in Hamburg. In that city Reinhard Keiser (1674 to 1739), the real father of German opera, reigned supreme from the end of the 17th century up to about 1739. His work is entirely German in style, exhibiting characteristic Teutonic earnestness.

In England opera only just managed to exist at all. There seems to be no record of any truly operatic performance until Sir William Davenant's *The Siege of Rhodes* in 1657.* To what extent this was a real opera is perhaps a little conjectural, though it is usually referred to as 'the first English opera'. The music is lost, and the only clue to its character is the composer's statement that the dialogue was in recitative. It was followed by the same writer's *The Cruelty of the Spaniards in Peru*.

Throughout the 17th century, with one outstanding exception, the nearest English equivalent to opera was the *Masque*, a form of entertainment which was also cultivated in France and Italy. The French Court Ballet was of similar type. The Masque, whose origins are of considerable antiquity, combined music, poetry, dancing, pageantry and lavish scenic and mechanical effects, which latter were also a great feature of the French opera. Possibly the two most famous masques were Matthew Locke's setting of Shirley's *Cupid and Death*, and Henry Lawes' setting of Milton's *Comus*. The form survived into the 18th century, Arne's *Alfred* appearing as late as 1740.

The one great English opera of the period is *Dido and*

---

* The fact that this was during the Commonwealth period is in itself a refutation of the widely-held theory that the Puritans deprecated music of any kind. See Scholes' *Oxford Companion*, art. 'Puritans and Music', on this.

Aeneas by Henry Purcell (1659 to 1695). The dialogue is in recitative and some dances are included. The most notable movement is Dido's 'Lament', one of the most poignantly moving pieces of music ever written. Rather oddly, perhaps, *Dido* was composed for performance by the pupils at an academy for young ladies, and we may be permitted to wonder whether the student who took the part of Dido could possibly have realised the full emotional scope of her lament.

Parallel with the development of opera ran that of oratorio. The ultimate origins of this form go back to the 13th century, in the *laudi*, simple devotional songs in the vernacular. Many were written by Franciscan monks. Later they were often cast in dialogue form, and by the 14th century were being dramatised into religious plays with music, performed by companies called *laudesi*. From the dramatised *laudi* evolved, early in the 16th century, the *sacre rappresentazioni* (sacred representations) of which lavish performances were given in Florence and the surrounding country. They were practically operas on sacred subjects, including *laudi*, secular songs, instrumental interludes and dancing.

In 1556 St. Philip Neri, founder of the Order of Oratorians, instituted in Rome popular services which incorporated elements from plays on sacred subjects as well as the singing of *laudi spirituali*. The services continued after his death in 1595, but their character rapidly changed with the introduction into them of the *sacre rappresentazioni*. In 1600 such a work by Emilio di Cavalieri (*c.* 1550 to 1602) was performed in the Oratorio della Vallicella, called *La Rappresentazione di Anima e di Corpo*—the Representation of Soul and Body. This is often called the first oratorio, but it is actually a *sacra rappresentazione*, including a final dance. Oratorio in the accepted sense was yet to come.

Concurrent with the sacred representation was the *Dialogo* (Dialogue), which prefigured oratorio to a greater extent. It consisted of dialogues in simple recitative between two persons, interspersed with choral movements. These latter were often of a 'reflective' character, anticipating the reflective arias which, as in opera, became such an important part of oratorio proper. Notable among composers of *Dialoghi* is Giovanni Anerio (*c.* 1567 to *c.* 1620), who showed a fondness for such cumbersome titles as *Teatro Armonico Spirituale di Madrigali a cinque, sei, sette e otto voci* (1619), which may be translated literally as 'The Spiritual Harmonic Theatre of Madrigals for 5, 6, 7 and 8 voices'. We note the use of the term 'madrigal' and the inclusion under that title of movements in recitative. The choral movements are often of a contrapuntal character, showing the persistence of the *stilo antico*.

In the years after 1600, in the hands of such men as Domenico Mazzocchi and Giovanni Carissimi (*c.* 1604 to 1674), the incipient oratorio, like opera, gradually became transformed, and on rather similar lines. The aria made its way in, and a *Historicus* or Narrator was introduced to make clear the progress of the story.* Stage representation ceased, and the form became essentially what it is to-day, the musical presentation of some sacred story, including recitatives, solos, duets, etc., and choral movements, all with instrumental accompaniment. The stories were taken largely from the Old Testament. Carissimi, for example, uses those of Jephtha, Abraham and Isaac, Job, and the Judgment of Solomon.

In the latter part of the century the most notable composer is Alessandro Scarlatti, equally great in opera and oratorio. As in his operas he used the *da capo* plan of aria, and this rapidly became normal practice everywhere. We may note his *Sacrifice of Abraham* and *Martyrdom of St. Theodosia*, and mention may also be made of his contemporaries Giovanni Colonna (*c.* 1645 to 1682) and Antonio Caldara (1670 to 1735).

---

* The Narrator or Evangelist was of the greatest importance in settings of the Passion. Lack of space forbids any consideration of this form, and the reader is referred to the article in Grove.

In the 17th century oratorio was almost exclusively of Italian cultivation, but the work of the German Heinrich Schütz must not be overlooked. His most important works of the oratorio type are his three settings of the Passion, according to St. Luke, St. John and St. Matthew, and his *Story of the Resurrection*. The Passions are unaccompanied, the solo parts—Evangelist, Christ, Peter, etc.—being in a free recitative which has some affinity with plainsong. The utterances of the 'crowd' are in four-part harmony and lean to the *stilo antico*. The *Story of the Resurrection* employs an accompaniment of strings and organ. Schütz's style is austere, but the works are remarkably telling in their restrained 'affectiveness'.

The madrigal did not long survive the coming of the 'new music'. Works under the old title were still written, but the traditional polyphonic style gave way before the new influences. In the madrigals of Luzzasco Luzzaschi, written before 1600, and in those of Monteverdi, we find instruments used not as mere optional substitutes for voices in the sense of 'apt for viols or voices', but obligatory, and also passages for accompanied solo voice. The most surprising of the late Italian madrigalists was Carlo Gesualdo, Prince of Venosa (1560 to 1614), whose harmonic experiments, much in advance of those of most of his contemporaries, well justify the epithet used above. He was a 'modernist' in the colloquial sense of the word. Frequently he achieves great emotional expressiveness, and as a rule his startling chord-progressions and modulations 'come off'. This cannot be said, however, of the procedures of some of his lesser imitators, such as Benedetti and Belli, some of whose efforts sound like experimentalism gone mad. The work of Gesualdo actually led nowhere, but it is interesting as the final outcome of a style initiated by Willaert and da Rore, and is well worth some study.

As a medium of domestic music-making the madrigal gave place to the cantata, and large numbers of works of this period which were published as the former might

equally well be called the latter. In its most elementary
form the cantata was a short story told in recitative, with
a simple accompaniment, under the title of *Cantata da
Camera* or *Chamber Cantata*. As in opera and oratorio, the
aria soon made its way into the form, alternating with the
recitative. The accompaniment tended to become more
elaborate, and two voices in dialogue were often employed.
Carissimi wrote a number of such works, as did also Scarlatti.
Carissimi was the first to write cantatas on sacred themes
—the *Cantata da Chiesa* or *Church Cantata*, which was a kind
of miniature oratorio for one or two solo voices with accompaniment. In some of these cantatas the tendency towards
the typical 18th-century style of Handel is very clearly seen.
Especially notable is the introduction of florid *coloratura*
passages which obviously prefigure the kind of writing
which Handel used in such movements as *Rejoice Greatly*
in *Messiah*.

In England the secular cantata was very popular as a
substitute for the madrigal, monologues and dialogues
appearing in quantity. To quote Sir Hubert Parry in the
Oxford History of Music: 'The cardinal idea of the form is
the semi-histrionic presentation of some imagined situation
under domestic conditions, in which, without scenic acces-
sories of any kind, characters whose histories and circumstances are well-known to the audience, or personified
abstractions, carry on poetic discourse in musical terms.'
Such compositions were produced by Henry Lawes and
his brother William, Laniere and Coleman. Sacred cantatas, too, were popular, those of Pelham Humfrey, for
example, containing many fine movements.

The cantata, like the madrigal of earlier times, was for
domestic performance. Public concerts in the present-day
sense did not originate until late in the 17th century, the
first being founded in London in 1672 by John Banister,
followed in 1678 by those of Thomas Britton. On the continent possibly the first, as opposed to the more or less
private meetings of the various *Collegia Musica*, were the

Concerts Spirituels founded in Paris in 1725 by Philidor. It must be remembered that the system of patronage to which reference has been made involved the employment of large numbers of musicians in the various courts, etc., and that performances by the *kapelle* were always more or less private affairs. Opera, of course, became public once opera houses were established, but opera is not a concert in the accepted sense.

In the paragraph above dealing with the madrigal mention was made of the independent use of instruments as distinct from their introduction as substitutes for, or doublings of, the voices. This independent use was known as *concertato*. The derivation of this term is generally taken to be from the verb *concertare*, to compete. The chief implication of the *concertato* style was that of contrasting groups of performers, in particular of voices and instruments. Although the word *concerto* (with the same derivation) is commonly associated with instrumental music, its earliest use was in connection with vocal works. Andrea and Giovanni Gabrieli produced in 1587 *Centi Concerti* for 6, 7, 8, 10 and 16 voices, the first work in which *concerti* is used as a title. Of importance in this connection are the *Concerti Ecclesiastici* of Lodovico Viadana (*c.* 1564 to 1627), published in 1602, and a work with the same title by the lutenist Molinaro. Viadana's concertos are for from one to four voices, with a figured bass accompaniment for organ. It was the independent part for the instrument which justified the title.

The most important name in the early development of the *concertato* style is Giovanni Gabrieli, whose association with St. Mark's, Venice, has already been noted. He was the first to make any clear differentiation between vocal and instrumental styles in such works, and besides this he made great use of the possibilities of contrast between solo voices and chorus, and between opposing choirs. He also introduced occasional purely instrumental interludes or *sinfonias*. In his later works his 'modernity' is strongly evident in every direction, not only in his use of the *concertato* style, but in his illustrative treatment of the text, use of 'affective' intervals in the voice parts, treatment of dissonance, etc. For such compositions as his motet *In Ecclesiis* (for solo, quartet, chorus, brass and viola), the only appropriate epithet is monumental. The effect of such a work in the vastness of St. Mark's must have been overwhelming.

The *concertato* style passed to Germany through Schütz, the 'Father of German Music'. In 1609 he went to Venice to study with Gabrieli, then at the height of his powers, and in 1619 published his first really important work, the *Psalms of David*, in which the manner of his teacher is evident, together with an increased differentiation between vocal and instrumental styles. In 1625 came the *Cantiones Sacrae*, to Latin texts, in which he goes almost to extremes in his use of dissonance for pictorial purposes. In 1629 Schütz paid a second visit to Italy, this time coming under the influence of Monteverdi, and thereafter produced the three parts of the *Symphoniae Sacrae* and the *Kleine geistliche Konzerte* (Little Sacred Concertos). In these works the various movements range from small-scale monodies with *basso continuo* accompaniment up to monumental compositions such as the famous '*Saul, Saul*', which are on the same scale as Gabrieli's *In Ecclesiis*. In all Schütz's sacred works there is a notable intensity and sincerity of expression, deriving from the firm faith of the devout Lutheran. Whatever the technical method or style, all is intended as a means to one end—the glory of God.

Schütz was by far the greatest German musician of his time, but two of his contemporaries are well worthy of note, Johann Hermann Schein (1586 to 1630) and Samuel Scheidt (1587 to 1654). Schein's *Cymbalum Sionum* (1615) shows the Venetian influence, as does also Scheidt's *Concertus Sacri* (1622), but both are relatively conservative in their harmonic outlook, lacking any signs of the intense use of dissonance such as Schütz displayed in his *Cantiones Sacrae*.

The development of the musical side of the Lutheran

service, at least among the 'orthodox' school as opposed to the Pietists, offered suitable opportunity for the performance of such choral works as have been mentioned above. The hymn which at first followed the recitation of the Latin Creed became replaced by a 'motet', which signified a piece performed by the choir, and which might also go by the title of dialogue, *concertato* or *symphonia sacra*. These movements were selected so that their subject had a close connection with the Gospel of the day and, as is pointed out by the great authority Albert Schweitzer, served as sermons in music preparing the way, as it were, for the spoken sermon which followed later in the service. Ultimately the motet became known as cantata, but this term did not come into use in this particular connection until about 1700, being first employed by one Pastor Neumeister of Hamburg in a series of text for such works. The motet was normally based on a biblical text; the cantata was based on a 'composed' one, sometimes a poetic paraphrase of a passage of scripture, and in any case designed to edify and 'point a moral'.

The normal cantata was arranged in the form of recitatives, arias, duets, etc., and chorus movements, with orchestral accompaniment. Frequently a chorale was included, sometimes for congregational performance, sometimes not. Among the important composers of cantatas are Franz Tunder (1614 to 1667), Dietrich Buxtehude (1637 to 1707) and Wilhelm Zachau (1663 to 1712). From 1641 Tunder, a pupil of Frescobaldi (see Chapter 9), was organist at the Marienkirche in Lübeck, where he established a famous series of sacred recitals known as *Abendmusiken*. He was succeeded by Buxtehude, who raised the musical fame of the church to even greater heights. Zachau was Handel's teacher. The work of all these foreshadows that of Bach, on whom they had considerable influence.

In England the *concertato* style is in evidence in the many verse anthems of the 17th century. The term itself was not used, but in the opposition of a solo group and the full chorus, and the use of independent accompaniment, the principles of the style are present. Throughout the century the verse anthem developed, though with an inevitable break during the Commonwealth period. The Puritans had no objection to music as such, but, in common with others of the more strictly reformed sects, would allow but little, and that of the simplest kind, in their church services. This attitude was adopted, for example, by the German Calvinists, and mention was made in Chapter 1 of its effect on Bach's output while he was at Cöthen. The return of Charles II in 1660 brought about the establishment of the 'Restoration anthem', in which the resources of solo, solo ensemble, chorus and instrumental accompaniment are fully exploited. Simultaneously appears the 'Restoration style', characterised often by a distinctly secular feeling which at times seems to go beyond the limits of propriety. During his exile in France, Charles had heard much of the bright music in favour at the Court of Louis XIV, and it was this style that he required from the composers of his Chapel Royal. 'The prime object of the court music in England was to provide sensuous entertainment and to serve as sonorous ornament.'* The serious style of the early anthems, deriving from the Latin motet, went out of fashion; the royal taste demanded easily comprehensible tunes, and rhythms which induced the tapping of the royal foot. A number of common idioms developed, including that of a jigging dotted-note rhythm for such words as *Alleluia*, though this was hardly specifically English, since Carissimi uses it in at least one of his cantatas, in the same verbal connection.

The most important composers were William Child (1606 to 1697), John Blow (1648/9 to 1708), Pelham Humfrey (1647 to 1674) and Henry Purcell. Purcell is in every way the greatest, and in his work English music of the Restoration period reaches its climax. Apart from his verse anthems, he wrote a few 'full' anthems for from five to

* Bukofzer, *Music in the Baroque Era.*

eight voices, in which he looks back to the polyphony of the Elizabethans, but without recapturing the true tradition. The style is inevitably strongly affected by the new ideas which had developed during the century—declamation, 'affectiveness', and the increasing feeling for counterpoint arising from harmony, as opposed to the old pure polyphony. These anthems show, however, his great mastery of contrapuntal writing, and in the creation of rich and sombre sonorities he is unsurpassed.

Purcell's verse anthems often show the style at its finest. Many are conceived on an extended scale, having accompaniment for string orchestra, with an introductory 'French' overture and instrumental interludes between the verses. His 'Welcome' and 'Birthday' songs, written to celebrate such occasions as the return of the King to London, or a royal birthday, are planned similarly to the anthems, but while containing some fine movements are marred by the fatuous adulatoriness of the texts. Of greater literary value are the odes for St. Cecilia's Day, that of 1692, *Hail bright Cecilia*, containing some of Purcell's finest choral writing.

To sum up, it will be seen that during the 17th century music underwent a great revolution. The polyphonic style and the modal system on which it was based both died out. The flexible rhythmic principles which had their ultimate origin in *musica mensurata* gave way to the relatively rigid system imposed by what is sometimes called 'the tyranny of the barline'. New ideas on the handling of dissonance came to the fore, together with a new attitude to the treatment of words, and the use of voices in general. And over all looms the shadow of instrumental music, gradually ousting the old conceptions of vocal polyphony. It is a century of transition, amazingly fertile in new ideas, and producing much music that is of far more than merely historical interest. Yet it can now be seen as a time of preparation, in which were laid the foundations of the towering edifices erected by Handel and Bach.

RECORDS

| | HMS Vol. 4 (Mono only) | HLP 10 |
| | and Vol. 5 (Mono only) | HLP 11/12 |

Composer	*Title*	*Catalogue No.*
Caccini	Amarilli	SLPX 1289
	(also includes works by Carissimi, Monteverdi, etc.)	
Purcell	Church Music	ZRG 5444
	Ode to St. Cecilia (1692)	2533 042

CHAPTER NINE

INSTRUMENTAL MUSIC
IN THE SEVENTEENTH CENTURY

WE have seen in Chapter 8 how fertile the 17th century was in the development of new vocal forms; it was equally so on the instrumental side. It saw the expansion of dance-pairs into the suite, the rise of the sonata, the concerto, the chorale prelude and other forms of organ music, and the transformation of the ricercare into the fugue. Besides all this, there was the achievement of a truly instrumental style of writing, as opposed to the often tentative efforts of the preceding century, and the rise of important schools of violinists and organists. These were the most important developments, paving the way for the supreme works of genius of Bach and Handel in the first half of the 18th century, and it will be necessary to trace the course of each one separately. Before doing so, however, we must deal further with the viols and their music.

In the 17th century the use of the viols gradually died out, and they were supplanted by the violin and its larger brethren, the viola and violoncello. This was due largely to a change of taste, corresponding in a way to the change which now preferred the solo voice, interpreting the 'affection' of the words, to the old polyphonic complexity of the madrigalists. 'The highest value was set upon those instruments that were best equipped for producing singing tone, and thus for competing with the human voice in tenderness, mellowness and emotional expressiveness. . . . The violin became the queen of all the instruments, outstripping her elder sister, the sombre and heavy viol.'* The home of violin-making was Italy, the principal workshops

* Geiringer, *Musical Instruments*.

being first at Brescia, and later at Cremona, where the Amati family produced instruments with unsurpassed beauty of tone. The greatest of the Amatis was Nicolo, of the third generation. Even greater, perhaps, was the work of his pupil Antonio Stradivari (1644 to 1737), whose violins remain supreme examples of artistic craftsmanship. Almost equally great was Giuseppe Guarneri (1687 to 1742).

The viols did not surrender their supremacy without a struggle, and in England especially their use persisted almost to the end of the century. Thereafter only the bass *viola da gamba* survived in use to some extent—Bach uses it for the accompaniment to one of the arias in his *St. Matthew Passion* of 1729—but with the death of the virtuoso Carl Friedrich Abel in 1787 the viol died too. Among those who opposed the violin may be mentioned Thomas Mace (*c.* 1620 to 1710), a lay clerk of Trinity College, Cambridge, who, in his *Musick's Monument* of 1676, inveighs bitterly against the violins and their music, and looks back regretfully to the good old days of polyphonic viol music.

In England, Fancies for viols were written until late in the century, important composers being Alfonso Ferrabosco, William Lawes, John Cooper (who, presumably for reasons of prestige, Italianised his name to Giovanni Coperario), John Jenkins, and above all Purcell. The quality of their work is apt to be variable, and often shows the intermediate hovering between the modal system and the major and minor scales. Purcell's Fancies at times reach great heights of emotional intensity and are by far the finest of all; they were also the last to be written. The weakness of the Fancy as a form lay in its tendency to be split up into a number of often unrelated sections, a natural consequence of its derivation from the motet or madrigal. But whereas in the vocal forms the words gave logic to the musical plan, the Fancy had no such solid guiding principle. The composer would work a point of imitation for as long, or as briefly, as he chose; and despite the beauty of many individual passages, the impression sometimes remains that there was no particular reason why any given section should last as long as it does, or, alternatively, why it should not have been expanded to twice its length. True, the idea of the form was that the composer could 'follow the dictates of his fancy', but this did not necessarily lead to structural logic and stability.

Another aspect of viol playing which survived in England until the end of the century was the improvisation of variations or 'divisions' on a ground bass. This art is dealt with in Christopher Sympson's *Division Violist* of 1659.

To turn now to the development of instrumental forms in the 17th century. We have noted that the suite originated in the pairing of such dances as the pavane and galliard. Quite early in the century the dancing of these went out of fashion, their place being taken by another slow-quick pair, the *Allemande** and the *Courante* or *Coranto*. At this time there was a fairly well-established and definite sequence of formal ballroom dances, the ball regularly beginning with a slow dance followed by a quick one. After the *Courante* composers of suites most often added a slow *Sarabande*, followed perhaps by other dances such as the *Gavotte*, *Minuet*, *Bourrée*, *Jig* (or *Gigue*). The whole might be introduced by a *Prelude*. Apart from the invariable allemande and courante, there was no set order or scheme in the suite, and it may be well to mention that the basic group of allemande, courante, sarabande and gigue, which is sometimes insisted on by writers of textbooks on Form, applied mainly in Germany, in the latter part of the 17th century and the beginning of the 18th. English, French and Italian composers treated the suite simply as a series of contrasting movements, mainly, but not entirely, based on dances, and bound together chiefly by unity of tonality, all being in the same tonic key.

---

* It is sometimes stated that the Allemande was not a dance. This is incorrect. It was a stately court dance from Switzerland and Germany, originating in the 16th century.

The dance movements were stylised, and their form rapidly became conventionalised into a straightforward binary. The old three-section plan, so common in the 16th century, was discarded, though faint traces of it linger even into the 18th century, in some of Bach's dances.

It was in the 17th century that the great French school of *clavecinists* (=harpsichordists) arose. The founder was Jacques Champion de Chambonnières (*c.* 1597 to 1672), harpsichordist to Louis XIV. His most important successors were Jean François Dandrieu (1684 to 1740) and various members of the Couperin family, of whom the greatest was François (1668 to 1733), known as *Couperin le Grand*. The works of this school show a keen insight into the character of the instrument and its possibilities. Couperin in particular produced a multitude of delightful and ingenious pieces which he grouped into *Ordres* (=suites), often giving them fanciful titles suggesting their moods. The Frenchmen tended to write very lengthy suites, including not only dances, with or without 'fancy' titles, but also a number of programmatic pieces, often in rondo form, having no connection with any dance. Couperin's first *Ordre* (1713) contains no fewer than eighteen movements, of which only eight are dances. He achieved a delicacy and economy of means which have for long been characteristic of the best of French music.

In England the outstanding figure is once again Purcell, whose harpsichord 'Lessons' exhibit his natural tunefulness and his strong grasp of a true keyboard style. His suites generally begin with a prelude, and like Couperin he retains the orthodox allemande and courante; but after that, anything may happen.

In Germany the first important name in connection with the suite is that of Johann Jacob Froberger (1616 to 1667), whose style was to some extent modelled on that of the French school. He was followed by Johann Adam Reinken (1623 to 1722), Buxtehude, Georg Muffat (*c.* 1645 to 1704) and others, all of whom were more or less influenced by the French style. With Buxtehude we find strict adherence to the 'textbook' order of allemande, courante, sarabande and gigue, which remained the standard in Germany until the suite died out in the middle of the 18th century.

In Italy the suite went by the name of *sonata da camera** or chamber sonata, as distinct from the *sonata da chiesa* or church sonata, to be dealt with later. The earliest chamber sonatas, *e.g.* those of Tarquinio Merula,† published in 1637, were not restricted to dances, but were merely suitable for secular rather than for sacred (church) use. Twenty years later, however, the distinction between church and chamber sonatas had become more strongly marked, in that the latter were conceived primarily as dance suites. By the time of Arcangelo Corelli (1653 to 1713) the regular basis of allemande and courante, introduced by a preludial movement and followed by one or more other dances, was fully established. Corelli was one of the founders of the great school of violin playing in Bologna, and in this respect are associated with him the names of Giovanni Battista Vitali (1644 to 1692) and G. B. Bassani (1657 to 1716). The chamber sonatas of these men were written generally for two violins and viola da gamba (or 'cello), with a part for *continuo* to be realised on the harpsichord. Such sonatas were designated *a tre*, *i.e.* for three instruments, the *continuo* being, as it were, taken for granted. The 'trio sonata', whether chamber or church, was part of the staple fare of this period.

The church sonata, like its brother of the chamber, had at first no fixed form; it was simply of a character serious

* The literal meaning of *sonata*, from the verb *sonare*, to sound, is something played, as opposed to *cantata*, something sung. In this sense it may cover a large range of instrumental music, and was so used in the 17th century. The student may be warned to disabuse his mind of any idea that *sonata* necessarily means a work with that title in the style of, say, Mozart or Beethoven. *Sonata*, the past participle, was originally associated with the noun *canzona*, a *canzona sonata* (or *canzona da sonare*) being a 'played canzona'.

† Not to be confused with the organist Merulo.

enough for use during a sacred service, and derived from the 16th-century *canzona sonata*. Such a work is the well-known *Sonata pian' e forte* of Giovanni Gabrieli, a monumental piece for two brass choirs (except that the highest part in the second choir is for violin). In this, contrasts of soft and loud are deliberately used for the first time. Sonatas *a tre* appear quite early in the 17th century, for example in the works of Giovanni Battista Fontana (d. 1630), as do also 'solo' sonatas for a single violin and *continuo*. They are of no fixed plan, but consist of a series of short sections in contrasting styles and speeds. Merula produced similar works under the title of *canzone*, as did many others, *e.g.* Massimiliano Neri. Until about the middle of the century the terms 'sonata' and 'canzona' are practically interchangeable, but the latter title gradually dropped out of use. The plan and order of the movements, however, remained variable, though it gradually became customary for one of them to be fugal in style.

In some of the sonatas of Vitali, *e.g.* those of his op. 2 of 1667, we find fairly strongly suggested the basis of what was later to become the normal plan until well into the 18th century. A slow introductory section, *grave*, precedes a quick movement in fugal style. This is followed by a melodious *largo*, and the work concludes with another quick movement, sometimes in the style of a gigue. This was established as the standard plan by Corelli, though he does not always adhere strictly to it. By his time (his op. 1 and op. 3, consisting of church sonatas, were published respectively in 1681 and 1689) the distinction between church and chamber styles was tending to break down. His slow third movements are often of the sarabande type, and his last ones gigues. This crossing of the two styles ultimately obliterated the original distinction. The preludes, too, of Corelli's chamber sonatas could equally well serve as movements for church sonatas.

The Italian style of sonata reached England in time for Purcell to show that in it his genius was not less than that of his continental contemporaries. His two sets of *Sonatas of III Parts* are fully equal to other similar publications, and he admits in his preface to the first set (1683) that he has 'faithfully endeavour'd a just imitation of the most fam'd Italian Masters'.

In Germany the one really great name in the line of sonatists is that of Heinrich Biber (1644 to 1704), whose works have been described as 'the first German violin music of any artistic worth at all' (Grove). Like Purcell, he shows Italian influence, but exhibits also considerable individuality and grave sincerity. His compositions prove that he was no mean virtuoso.

The instrumental concerto was based on the same fundamental principles as the vocal one, *i.e.* the playing off against each other of two contrasted groups. This is seen in essence in Gabrieli's *Sonata pian' e forte*, and still more in one of his canzonas, where a small body of instruments contrasts with a larger one. Similar methods are found in the canzonas of other Venetians of the time, *e.g.* Neri and Francesco Usper. Rather later we find sonatas for trumpet accompanied by string orchestra by such writers as Stradella and Vitali, in which the idea of contrast is still more strongly marked.

The essential principles of the style, as they are found in the greatest examples of the form, those of Handel and Bach, were first fully worked out by Corelli and Torelli (d. 1708), both members of the Bolognese school, who produced what is known as the *Concerto Grosso*. The contrast lay between the *concertino* or solo group, in Corelli's case consisting of a string trio (two violins and 'cello), and the *ripieni* or '*tutti*' strings. Like his sonatas, Corelli's concertos fall into two types, church and chamber, the former being for use before, during or after High Mass. Formally there is little sign of any conventional layout; everything depends on the contrasting of the two groups of performers. Torelli established what was to remain the normal three-movement plan—quick, slow, quick. He exhibits, more than Corelli, the

'concerto style'—the vigorous, pounding metrical pulsation
in the *allegros*, and the general feeling of 'busyness'.*

In some of the later *concerti grossi* of Corelli there is a
tendency for the first violin to take the lead over the other
members of the *concertino*. This led to the writing of 'solo'
concertos, for a single violin with accompaniment by the
string orchestra. As far as is known, the first such works
were by Torelli, though they were not published until a
year after his death. In them the solo part begins to demand a certain amount of virtuosity, but the emphasis
remains primarily on contrast between solo and *tutti*. (The
'display' concerto, designed to allow the soloist to show off
his technical ability, was a product of the late 18th and
the 19th centuries. In the period with which we are dealing the technical ability demanded of the soloist was generally little greater than that required of the orchestra. The
same applies to the *concertino* in a *concerto grosso*.)   Other
composers of solo concertos were Tomasso Albinoni (? 1674
to 1745) and Giuseppe Jacchini, who wrote the first 'cello
concerto.

Further progress was made by Antonio Vivaldi (*c.* 1676
to 1741) of Venice, who also made considerable advances
in violin technique. In his *concerti grossi* he varied the composition of the *concertino*, sometimes using a group of wind
instruments. More than Torelli he exploits what has been
called the 'relentless mechanical beat of the concerto
style',† and in the strength and character of his themes
he often anticipates Bach, who, indeed, learned much
from the study of his works. Among Vivaldi's Venetian
contemporaries who emulated his style are Francesco
Gasparini (1668 to 1727), Benedetto Marcello (1686 to

* Lack of space forbids any consideration of the structural principles
of the movements. The form used for the *allegros* is generally known as
Ritornello form, and the reader is referred to R. O. Morris's *The Structure
of Music* for a simple explanation of it. The Introduction to Vol. 3 of
Tovey's *Essays in Musical Analysis* contains a most illuminating discussion
of the form.

† Bukofzer, *Music in the Baroque Era.*

1739) and Giuseppe Valentini (b. *c.* 1680). In the next generation comes Francesco Geminiani (1674 to 1762). He was a pupil of Corelli and Scarlatti and was rather conservative in his outlook. He used a string quartet for *concertino*, adding the viola to the usual trio. Much of his life was spent in England (he died in Dublin), and he was the author of the first 'method' for the violin, entitled *The Art of Playing the Violin*. Rather younger than Geminiani was Pietro Locatelli (1693 to 1764). His solo concertos demand technical ability of a truly virtuoso standard, and in them we see the coming of a new conception of the form. No longer is it primarily a matter of contrast, with the soloist as it were the first among equals; the orchestra now begins to recede into the background, as mere subordinate accompaniment.

It may be noted that at this time no concertos were written for harpsichord. This instrument was used for the *continuo*, as a background. It is not until Bach's *5th Brandenburg Concerto* that we find the harpsichord used as a solo instrument, which duty it shares with a flute and a violin. (There are also seven concertos by Bach for solo harpsichord and orchestra, but at least five of these are transcriptions of works originally for violin and orchestra. They are later in date than the *5th Brandenburg*.) The earliest sonatas will be considered in the next chapter.

In music for the organ, a vastly important branch, there arose two great schools; the southern, based on Italy, and the northern, based on the Netherlands and Germany. Of the former, we have already noted the Venetian Merulo as one of the founders. After him the emphasis shifts to Rome, where Girolamo Frescobaldi (1583 to 1643), organist of St. Peter's, was renowned as one of the most brilliant performers of his day. His toccatas show a great advance on those of the Gabrielis and Merulo in their careful planning of contrasted sections and their truly dramatic effect. They also exhibit much greater coherence in the more brilliant passages, the vaguely rambling scales of the earlier

composers being organised into shapely and logically designed figuration. In passing, it may be mentioned that
Frescobaldi seems to have had an adequate appreciation
of the technical difficulty of some of his compositions. At
the end of one toccata he writes, '*non senza fatiga si giunge
al fine*', which may be freely translated as, 'you won't get
through this without feeling tired'.

Of equal importance to Frescobaldi's toccatas are his
organ ricercares. At the beginning of the century the ricercare, derived from the vocal motet, occurred commonly in
two guises. In one the same principle was used as in the
fantasia, *i.e.* it consisted of a series of fugal sections, each
based on a new theme. In the other, the *ricercare sopra un
soggetto* ('on a subject'), only one basic theme was used for
fugal treatment. This type had two possibilities. There
might be a series of fugal expositions on various modifications of the theme, or alternatively the theme itself might
be kept more or less unchanged, but used in a series of
expositions with a new countersubject for each. The ricercare 'on a subject' was established by Frescobaldi, and
developed gradually into the fugue as we know it in the
hands of Bach. Like the fancy, the ricercare had the
structural weakness of being so highly sectionalised, though
in the examples 'on a subject' this is not so noticeable as
in the other type, since at least one basic theme ran through
the whole piece. But even so, it was inevitably chopped
up in effect, and composers gradually realised that it was
more effective and satisfactory to work out the possibilities
of a single unvaried theme to the limit, rather than to piece
together a series of more or less brief snippets. Possibly
the most distinguished pupil of Frescobaldi was Froberger,
a Catholic Saxon, whose work shows increased facility in
the methods of organisation initiated by his teacher, and
possibly an even greater appreciation of the characteristics
of the organ. With him may be associated another Saxon,
Johann Kasper Kerll (1627 to 1693), who may also have
studied with Frescobaldi.

The purely Italian school soon declined in importance, the initiative passing to southern Germany. Besides the two Saxons just mentioned, we may note Georg Muffat, the last of the German Catholic organists of any real importance. His most notable work is the *Apparatus Musico-Organisticus* of 1690, which contains, among other things, twelve toccatas. Structurally they are variable, but the principle of brilliant *bravura* sections contrasting with steady-moving passages designed to exploit the sustaining power of the organ, as well as the inclusion of sections in fugal style, still holds good. The toccata had not begun to degenerate into a mere show-piece. In Muffat's work, still more than in that of his predecessors, there is an increased power of organisation of runs into coherent patterns; the feeling for design becomes continually stronger.

In the north-west of Europe a school of organists flourished whose work was based on the requirements of the reformed faith. The father of this school was Jan Pieterszoon Sweelinck (1562 to 1621) of Amsterdam. The organs of the Netherlands and northern Germany had already a well-developed pedal department, unlike those of Italy, and Sweelinck provides some of the earliest examples of independent pedal parts. He is most notable for his development of the ricercare into the fully worked-out fugue, at a time when the Italians were still content with the *ricercare sopra un soggetto*.

Through his pupils Sweelinck's influence spread throughout northern Germany, among the most important being Samuel Scheidt and Heinrich Scheidemann (1596 to 1663). Their contemporary Herman Schein (1586 to 1630) was of the same school, though not a pupil of its founder. In the next generation appears Reinken, who followed Scheidemann at St. Catherine's Church, Hamburg, and whose fame was so great that the young Bach walked long distances to hear and play to him. With these men must be mentioned two of Bach's uncles—Johann Christoph (1642 to 1703) and Johann Michael (1648 to 1694), and Johann Pachelbel of

Nuremburg (1653 to 1706), who serves as a link between the southern and northern schools. He was a pupil of Kerll, and so came to some extent under the influence of Frescobaldi. A little earlier, and perhaps the greatest of all organists before Bach, was Buxtehude, born in 1637. A Swede, he was for long the chief musician in Lübeck, and Bach was willing to walk 200 miles to sit at his feet. These are only an important few of a great galaxy of Lutheran organists on whose work was founded Bach's colossal superstructure.

The most important types of composition evolved by the north Germans for use in the reformed services were those based on the chorale. Luther's introduction of the chorale into the church service was eagerly welcomed, and we cannot do better than to quote Sir Hubert Parry, in the *Oxford History of Music*, on the subject: 'The influence which the German chorales exerted upon the German Protestant organists was of the utmost importance, and the seriousness and deep feeling, which were engendered in their attempts to set them and adorn them, were answerable for a great deal of the nobility in their organ music. . . . The chorales . . . were a kind of religious folk-songs. They came spontaneously from the hearts of the people, and had their roots in the deepest sentiments of the race. . . . Upon these tunes the organist-composers of the 17th century expended all the best of their artistic powers. The tunes became symbols, which were enshrined in all the richest devices of expressive ornament and contrapuntal skill, woven fugal artifice, and melodic sweetness, which the devotion of the composers could achieve.'

Although the term 'chorale prelude' is used loosely to describe all kinds of pieces based thematically on chorales, there were actually four different types. The chorale prelude proper, used in the service to introduce the congregational singing of the hymn (much as the present-day organist 'gives out' the first line or two) was generally fairly terse, the melody, decorated or otherwise, being usually in the top part. In many cases, each line of the tune was preceded by a more or less free fugal exposition based on it. This procedure was used by the early writers as far back as Scheidt, and many fine examples were written by Pachelbel. Although perhaps the commonest method of treatment, it was but one among many. Kipling's rhyme—

> 'There are nine-and-sixty ways
> Of constructing tribal lays,
> And every single one of them is right'

might well apply to chorale preludes.

Other types of chorale composition were (a) the chorale fugue, in which the first line of the tune served as the subject of an extended fugue*—also found in Pachelbel's work; (b) the chorale partita, or variations on a chorale—Pachelbel, Böhm and Buxtehude are important here; and (c) the chorale fantasia, which might be of considerable length, designed to show off both the instrument and the ability of the performer.

Besides works based on chorales, toccatas were popular, those of Reinken and Buxtehude being the most notable. Both men had first-rate instruments at their disposal, and both possessed consummate technique which they were not unwilling to display. The prelude and fugue, too, gradually took shape, but as yet lacked the intense concentration of thought and economy of material which characterises the greatest of those by Bach. By the time of Buxtehude, and especially noticeable in his work, a purely instrumental style of writing for the organ had been evolved, free from the influence of the old vocal style and exploiting the effective possibilities of the instrument to the highest degree.

Summing up, we may say that during the 17th-century instrumental music underwent as great a revolution as did that for voices. In all branches the influence of the old

* Bach's so-called 'Giant Fugue' is an example.

vocal polyphony was shaken off; chord-progression, instead of arising chiefly from the interweaving of separate melodic lines, became an essential foundation over which the interplay of contrapuntal parts could be carried out. Purely instrumental forms and a purely instrumental style of writing were evolved. The supersession of the modal system by the major and minor scales involved new methods of tuning, to allow for the possibility of modulation, *i.e.* movement from one key to another. As long as music remained basically modal, 'just temperament', tuning in accordance with the natural laws of Acoustics, was adequate; but this was not by any means satisfactory in dealing with a 'key system', and a modification called 'mean tone' temperament was first worked out. For a few keys around C major this was good enough, but beyond two or three sharps or flats, and especially in minor keys, the effect became more and more unpleasant, extreme keys such as B and F sharp being excruciatingly out of tune. The ultimate solution was found in 'equal temperament' in which every one of the semitones of the chromatic octave is slightly out of tune by strict acoustic theory, but so slightly as to be imperceptible to all but the keenest of ears. By the use of equal temperament all keys and all modulations became equally available. The first suggestion of this method of tuning appears in a work of the Spaniard Ramos de Pareja, in 1482, and it is also dealt with by the Italian theorist Zarlino (1517 to 1590). John Bull must have understood the system, since his Fantasia on *Ut, re, mi, fa, sol, la* ranges through every major key. In the course of the 17th century more and more works appear in which equal temperament is, at least by implication, taken for granted. Buxtehude, for example, writes a toccata based on E major which, although it does not modulate widely, would nevertheless be unbearable on anything but a 'tempered' instrument. And a number of works appeared containing pieces in most of the twenty-four possible keys. A suite by Andreas Werckmeister (1645 to 1706) uses seventeen of them, while Johann

Ferdinand Fischer (d. *c.* 1738) in his *Ariadne Musica* adds two more. The eventual outcome was, of course, Bach's *Forty-eight*, of which the full title was *The Well-Tempered Clavier**—two preludes and fugues in each of the twenty-four major and minor keys.

RECORDS

Composer	Title	Catalogue No.
Albinoni	Sonatas a 5 in A and G minor (Op. 2 Nos. 3 and 6)	
Corelli	Concerto Grosso Op. 6 No. 9	HQS 1232
Vivaldi	Concerto in D	
	Concerto in G minor,	
	Sonata in E flat (*Al Santo Sepolcro*)	
	Sonatas for Recorder and Continuo, Op. 13 (*Il Pastor Fido*)	TV 34228S
	4 Concerti for Violin and Strings (*The Seasons*)	ZRG 654
Sweelinck	Echo Fantasia, etc.	198445
	(also includes works by Clemens and Willaert)	
Buxtehude	Miscellaneous Organ Works	72532
Purcell	Various Consort Pieces	SAWT 9535
	Musick's Handmaid (excerpts)	3C310
	Suite in G minor, etc.	
	(also includes works by Bull, Byrd. Farnaby and Gibbons)	
Couperin	Ordres No. 6 and 22	HQS 1085
	8 Preludes from *L'art de toucher le clavecin*	
Frescobaldi	2 Toccatas	SAWT 9463
	Fantasia	
	(also includes works by Bach and Boehm	
	See also HMS Vol. 4, HLP 10 (Mono only)	
	Concerti Grossi	2530 070

* Clavier literally means keyboard, and is used in this period to cover both harpsichord and clavichord.

CHAPTER TEN

THE AGE OF BACH AND HANDEL

THE first half of the eighteenth century is over-shadowed by the colossal genius of Bach and Handel. There are, however, certain lesser but by no means negligible composers who may first be briefly considered. Of these the most striking and important is Domenico Scarlatti (1685 to 1757), son of Alessandro.

Although he wrote a number of operas, cantatas and other vocal works, Scarlatti is chiefly famous for his harp-sichord sonatas. He was the great virtuoso of his time, with outstanding technique and an almost fantastic insight into the possibilities of his instrument. In these respects he is comparable to Liszt, taking the art of playing and writing for the harpsichord to the ultimate limit. Despite the advances made in keyboard technique since his day, many of his works remain quite difficult enough for any but the above-average player, the more so since their texture is always so economical. Arrangements of some of his pieces by such 19th-century virtuosi as von Bülow are in a way easier than the originals, since in the latter there is no room for error of any kind. In this, Scarlatti is comparable to Mozart. Any pianist knows that such a piece as Mozart's *Rondo in A minor*, so deceptively simple, is far more testing than, say, a Liszt Rhapsody, where the occasional handful of wrong notes (though hardly to be recommended) may be lost in the welter of sound.

Scarlatti wrote over 500 sonatas, many under the title of *Exercises for Harpsichord*. The majority are short one-movement affairs in binary form, though there are a number which subdivide into a series of movements. See, for example, the sonata in G minor (Longo 36),* in four

* The standard edition is that of Longo, published by Ricordi.

contrasted sections, all based on the same tonic key. In his use of binary form Scarlatti shows some notable features, the most important being his frequent employment of 'corresponding cadence figures'. The last section of the first part, generally in the dominant or relative major key, and ranging from a few bars to something quite extensive, is reproduced in the tonic at the end of the second part. This is to some extent a foreshadowing of the 'second subject group' which is a normal feature of the sonata form of the next generation. But Scarlatti is far from being rigid or stereotyped in his handling of form. It may be fundamentally binary, but the organisation of the internal details is infinitely variable and, it may be said, is a fascinating study. Equally important is his frequent use of contrasting moods within a single movement. In the greater part of instrumental music of all kinds up to about the middle of the 18th century we find the principle of 'one movement, one mood'; changes in the emotional temperature take place only within narrow limits. An opening mood of vigour and cheerfulness is maintained throughout, as is, similarly, a sad mood or a reflective one, and so on. Any concerto of the period furnishes an adequate example of this consistency. But with Scarlatti we often find quite strong, almost capricious changes. For example, in Longo No. 12, D major, in both halves of the binary form there is a sudden change, after a bar's rest, from a bright and happy major-key start to a really mournful, minor-key continuation. Here again Scarlatti in a way looks forward to the practice of later generations, in whose sonata form movements a vigorous, rhythmic first subject may be opposed by a melodious and strongly contrasted second group.

The first clavier sonatas, as distinct from suites, were written by Johann Kuhnau (1660 to 1722), who was Bach's immediate predecessor as Cantor at St. Thomas's, Leipzig. These sonatas are in three or more movements, and include *Six Biblical Sonatas*, remarkable instances of programme music. We have seen that in the 16th century a certain amount of illustrative music was written, and the principle was carried on in, for example, the suites of the French lutenists and clavecinists. But apart from 'battle' pieces, the 'story' programme was rare. Kuhnau, however, took Old Testament stories and illustrated them step by step, in separate movements, with elucidatory comments above the music. At times he indulges in rather naïve attempts at realism, as, for example, in *The Combat between David and Goliath*, where the flight of the stone from David's sling is expressed (perhaps not altogether so naïvely) thus:

Ex. 19

followed, as the commenting text informs us, by the fall of Goliath:

Ex. 20

Contemporary with Kuhnau was the Belgian J. B. Loeillet, who is less widely known than he deserves to be. In his sonatas for flute or oboe he often achieves really remarkable emotional intensity, and occasionally produces a movement quite worthy of Bach.

Rather younger was Joachim Quantz (1697 to 1773),

a brilliant flautist and a sound musician. In his treatise on flute playing he has much of value to say about interpretation and musical aesthetics. He refers to Bach as 'a man worthy of admiration', but this is in connection with his organ playing. From 1741 to his death, Quantz was flautist and composer to Frederick the Great, and in this position had the possibly uncomfortable privilege of teaching that monarch to play the flute. His output of works for his instrument—concertos, trios, solos, etc.—was immense, and, like Vivaldi's interminable list of *concerti grossi*, shows how composers of the time, the 'Age of Patronage', were forced by the conditions of their appointments to go on turning out work after work to satisfy the demands of their employers. The amazing thing is not so much that they were able to do this, as that the quality is often so high. Quantz, for example, though by no means a composer of the first rank, nevertheless rarely falls below a high level of competence. The difficulties under which the 'tied' composer might labour are made clear in the *Letters of an Attentive Traveller* by J. F. Reichardt, who was for a time kapellmeister to Frederick the Great. Writing in 1774, he contrasts the operas of Hasse and Graun. He points out that Hasse, serving a sympathetic master at the Dresden court, 'worked freely and, unhampered by the taste or will of any person, wrote as he felt and as he wished. . . . Graun, on the other hand, less generally known, worked only according to the taste of his king [Frederick]; what failed to please him was struck out, even though it were the best piece in the opera.'

In Germany alone there were over three hundred states, ranging from important and extensive ones like that of Prussia, to others which were quite insignificant. But wherever (and however) the money could be found, the Arts, especially Music, were cultivated, after the fashion set by Louis XIV. The rulers of such states vied with each other in the size of their *kapelle*, the magnificence of their opera houses, and in their efforts to obtain the services of the most famous musicians of the time. This system had its advantages, in that the musician might be assured of a reasonably safe livelihood, and with the right kind of employer might be able, like Hasse, to 'write as he felt and as he wished'. But a ruler like Frederick might, from the point of view of musical progress, be a distinct handicap.

Johann Sebastian Bach and George Frederick Handel were born in the same year as Scarlatti, 1685; Bach at Eisenach in Thuringia, on March 21st (Old Style); Handel at Halle in Saxony, on February 23rd. It would be a ridiculous overstatement to suggest that there any resemblance ceases, but there are sufficient fundamental differences between the two men and their work to warrant a series of comparisons.

Bach came of a long line of professional musicians;* Handel's family tree seems to have provided him with no musical ancestors. Bach was trained to be a professional musician as a matter of course; Handel had to overcome paternal opposition. He was intended for the Law, and although his father died in 1696, it was not until 1703, when he had finished his course of study at the university of Halle, that he was free to follow his own inclinations. Handel was widely travelled; Bach remained all his life within one narrow area in central Germany, his longest journey being to Lübeck in 1705, to hear Buxtehude. Bach married twice and was the father of twenty children; Handel remained a bachelor all his life. Handel was a master of opera; Bach never touched that form.† Bach was a devout Lutheran (his library at his death consisted largely of theological works); Handel's faith, while doubtless equally sincere, was of a less strictly doctrinal character. Handel was

* Space forbids the tracing of Bach's ancestry. The founder of the line was one Hans Bach, who was living in 1561; Johann Sebastian was his great-great-great grandson. Some sixty of the family have been identified by name, fifty-three of them being musicians.

† His attitude to opera is attested by his remark to his eldest son: 'Well, Friedemann, shall we go over to Dresden to hear the pretty tunes?' See C. S. Terry, Bach, a Biography.

for much of his life a freelance; Bach was always in the service of either the Church or some princely court. Such a list of contrasts could be extended almost indefinitely, and perhaps the most important of all is that Handel always tended to bear in mind the taste of his public, though he never merely pandered to it, whereas Bach wrote simply to satisfy his own conscience. We can generally feel that Handel, to put it colloquially, had an eye on the man in the back row of the gallery. Bach was but little concerned with the effect of his music on his audience, an attitude which at times drew the censure of his employers. Unfortunately for posterity, the two men never met, though on two occasions Bach endeavoured to get in personal touch with his great contemporary. In one respect at least their characters were similar—neither seems to have suffered fools gladly. Both seem to have had a certain streak of obstinacy, which in Bach's case sometimes degenerated into what can only be called 'cussedness'. When reproached by the Consistorium of Arnstadt for having prolonged four weeks' leave of absence to four months, his reply was to the effect of, 'Well, you've got a deputy'—and that seems to have been all he had to say.

Handel's musical life dates from 1693, when he began to study with Zachau. Zachau was a thoroughly sound musician, and it is worth noting that a number of turns of phrase which are generally labelled as 'typically Handelian' are to be found in the work of the older man. In 1703 Handel went to Hamburg, being employed at the opera house under Keiser. Here, in 1705, was produced his first opera, *Almira*. Four years later he was in Italy, where he learned all there was to be known about the Italian style of writing, and where was produced, among other works, the opera *Agrippina* (1709). In 1710 he became Kapellmeister to the Elector of Hanover, who was later to become George I of England. His only other comparable appointment was in the same capacity to the Duke of Chandos, from 1717 to 1720, for whose private chapel he wrote the twelve *Chandos* anthems. In them he showed that he had nothing to learn of the art of choral writing for the English rite. Handel's first visit to London, in 1710, was brief, but his second, in 1712, was the beginning of permanent residence in this country.

From 1712 until his death in 1759 Handel's life as a composer falls into two periods. Up to 1740 he was mainly concerned with the writing of opera, and thereafter with oratorio. Until 1728 he was a director, with Buononcini and Ariosto, of the 'Royal Academy of Music', an operatic venture begun in 1719 with the support of the king. Court intrigue—the king was at loggerheads with the Prince of Wales—and rivalries within the company itself caused the final bankruptcy and collapse of the Academy, and in the next few years Handel produced operas either in conjunction with the impresario Heidegger, or on his own.

In his earliest operas, *Almira* and *Rodrigo*, Handel shows the influence of Keiser. *Agrippina* leans to the methods of the Venetian school of Legrenzi and Caldara, with which he came in contact in the early part of his stay in Italy. Later works, *e.g.* his first London opera, *Rinaldo* (1711), show the influence of his Neapolitan friend Alessandro Scarlatti, and this influence persists, with much of its conventionality, until *Orlando* of 1732.* From this time he began to show less regard for convention, but public taste was changing, and the purely Italian style was no longer so favoured as formerly. This was partly due to the production in 1728 of *The Beggar's Opera*. This was a 'ballad opera', and like all of its kind was in the vernacular, with spoken dialogue. The subjects of ballad operas were not mythological or historical, as were those of the Italian type, but were taken from everyday life. There were no long *da capo* arias, designed chiefly for the singers to display their ability. Instead, many of the tunes were well-known contemporary songs. Ballad opera was a live, quick-moving and

* It may be noted that although Handel's operas were of the Italian variety, he quite often opens with a 'French' overture.

easily understood kind of work, which made an immediate appeal to a public which had grown tired of the grandiose artificiality of the Italian style. Handel struggled against the current, but by 1740, when he wrote his operatic swan-song, *Deidamia*, he realised that his day as a composer of operas was ended.

As early as 1708 Handel had written two Italian oratorios, *The Resurrection* and *The Triumph of Time and Truth*, in which the influence of the Roman Carissimi is evident. Others had appeared at intervals before the final group of master works of his later years, *e.g.* the first and second versions of *Esther* (1720 and 1732), *Deborah* and *Athalia* (1733). Besides these, mention must be made of a setting of the Passion text of Brockes, in 1716, which is unfortunately too little known. Of the few oratorios which are now performed with any frequency, the first was *Israel in Egypt* of 1738, which year also saw the composition of *Saul*. Both were first performed in 1739. In 1741 followed the best known of all oratorios, *Messiah*, and the last to be written was *Jephtha* of 1751, though an English version of *The Triumph of Time and Truth*, much expanded, appeared in 1757, two years before the composer's death. In all these works Handel shows his mastery of all kinds of vocal writing. From the simplicity and fervour of *I know that my Redeemer liveth* to the brilliant coloratura of *Rejoice Greatly*, every variety of aria is to be found, while in *Israel in Egypt* the chorus for the first time becomes the protagonist. Of its thirty-nine numbers, no fewer than twenty-eight are choral.

Although Handel was as capable a contrapuntist as any composer of his time, on the whole he lacks the intense concentration of Bach. A comparison is sometimes drawn between their respective settings of the words 'Glory to God in the highest', and may well suffice here. Handel, in his version in *Messiah*, gives us an initial hammer-blow with 'Glory to God', followed by a sudden hush at 'and peace on earth', an effect calculated to make an immediate appeal to the non-musician. Bach, in the *Christmas Oratorio*, gives us page after page of magnificent rolling counterpoint which appeals more to the trained musician.   Such movements as 'Glory to God', or the 'Alleluia' chorus stand at one end of Handel's scale; at the other lies the setting of the first two words of *Messiah*—'Comfort ye'—one of the greatest strokes of genius in the whole of music.

Apart from his operas and oratorios, there are various suites for harpsichord, which show that Handel was by no means hidebound in his attitude to that form.   No. 2, for example, contains no dances at all.   The *concerti grossi* follow the tradition of Vivaldi, as do also the various sonatas.

Bach's father died when the boy was but ten years old, and he received his musical education at first from his elder brother Johann Christoph, a pupil of Pachelbel, at Ohrdruf. In 1700 he was admitted to the Michaelisschüle at Lüneburg, where he remained for three years, coming under the influence of Böhm, who was himself a pupil of Reinken. It was during this period that Bach for the first time walked the thirty miles to Hamburg to hear that great old man, bringing back impressions which for long showed in his compositions.   At this time, too, he trudged sixty miles to Celle, where he encountered music in the French style, and again returned with impressions that remained.   After a short period in the service of Duke Johann Ernst, younger brother of the reigning Duke of Weimar, Bach obtained his first independent appointment, as organist at the New Church at Arnstadt, far south of Lüneburg, but only a few miles from his birthplace.   While there, thanks to his willingness to undertake long walks, he came under the influence of Buxtehude.   In 1707 he moved to become organist of St. Blasius's Church in Mulhaüsen.   The remainder of his life has been briefly outlined in Chapter 1.

Handel may be said to have summed up the Italian style of writing which had evolved during the 17th century. Bach, studying and copying the music of both Italy and France, adopted what he thought best from both and incorporated it into the essential German style to which he had been brought up, and which he raised to the highest perfection. It was for Handel to develop Italian opera and oratorio to a point not hitherto attained. In all other branches of music, for orchestra, harpsichord and organ, in cantatas and Passions, Bach was supreme. Hardly acknowledged in his lifetime as anything more than a composer of competent kapellmeister status, and forgotten after his death, the publication of Forkel's monograph in 1802, and the work done by Mendelssohn (who arranged, in 1829, a centenary performance of the *St. Matthew Passion*) and others, led to a revival of interest in his works which has lasted to the present day and shows no signs of diminishing.

The early organ works, of the Weimar period (1708 to 1717), show much of the influence of the northern school, Reinken and Buxtehude. Such are, for example, the well-known *Toccata and Fugue* in D minor, and the great *Prelude and Fugue* in D major. Their brilliant style and somewhat loose construction are in the Buxtehude tradition, and they reveal, incidentally, the young organist with a fine technique which he was not unwilling to display. With increasing age and experience we find greater concentration and tautness of texture, as, for example, in the great *Passacaglia* in C minor. This tendency reaches its climax in the works of the Leipzig period, such as the 'Great' B minor prelude and fugue and that in C major. The subject-matter becomes increasingly terse and the treatment of it more and more intensified. Throughout his life, except during his time at Cöthen (1717 to 1723), Bach wrote Chorale Preludes, employing every possible method of treatment, and adding always the intangible something which was the fruit of his own genius. From his Weimar days comes the *Little Organ Book*, unfortunately never completed, a model of succinctness, a string of musical pearls.

Cöthen saw the composition of the *Brandenburg Concertos* (so called from their dedication to the ruler of that state), in which the models of Corelli and Vivaldi are raised to the highest power. In them Bach varies the composition of the *concertino* to a far greater degree than had any of his predecessors, and shows that even greater rhythmic drive was possible than had been achieved by Vivaldi. We may note also the four *Overtures* (suites) for orchestra, the violin concertos and sonatas, as well as many other purely instrumental works. It was at Cöthen that the first book of *The Well-Tempered Clavier* was completed (the second book dates from 1744, at Leipzig). This has been aptly described by C. S. Terry as 'his conclusive contribution to the controversy raging round the tuning of the clavichord'. After the *Forty-eight* there was nothing more to be said on the matter.

To the Leipzig period, from 1723, belong most of the cantatas (though some date from his appointment as *konzertmeister* at Weimar in 1714), the latest and greatest of the organ works, including the six 'Schübler' chorale preludes and those in the *Clavierübung*, the *St. John* and *St. Matthew Passions* and the *Mass in B Minor*. This last, the first of the great 'concert' masses, was written (and partly compiled by adaptations from cantatas) to enable Bach to obtain the post of court composer to the Elector of Saxony, which coveted title he hoped might improve his standing with the authorities in Leipzig. His rather prickly temper often involved him in difficulties with them.

The great event in Bach's later life was his visit to Frederick the Great at Potsdam, in 1747. This was arranged by his son Carl Philipp Emanuel, at that time in the king's service, and resulted in the composition of the *Musical Offering*, a series of pieces based on a subject given by Frederick. The great six-part ricercare in it is a masterpiece among masterpieces. In his dedication Bach refers to the king's 'truly royal subject', and proceeds to treat it in a truly royal manner.

Towards the end of his life Bach began work on what he intended to be a complete exposition of everything fugal, the *Art of Fugue*, but died before finishing it. Technically it is stupendous; musically it stands almost alone.

With Bach, as with most of the great composers, we see maturity in age bringing an increase of intensity and economy in his compositions. Technical ability, so great as to be almost superhuman, is used simply to serve expressive ends; structure becomes more and more tightly knit. The occasional straggliness of the early works gives way to the concentration of the later ones. The difference is noticeable even in works which are separated by only a few years. Compare, for example, the treatment of the words 'wept bitterly' in Peter's denial in the *St. John Passion* of 1723 with that in the *St. Matthew* of 1729. The former is moving, but the latter, only half as long, is almost unbearable in its despair.

With the death of Bach in 1750 and Handel in 1759 an era comes to an end. Between them they summed up all the tendencies of music since 1600, but by their later years tastes were changing. The complexities of the contrapuntal style were no longer acceptable, and such music became known as 'learned', in a rather derogatory sense. The development of the new style will be the subject of our next chapter.

RECORDS

Composer	Title	Catalogue No.
Scarlatti	Sonatas for Harpsichord	VICS 1532
	Sonatas for Harpsichord }	SAWT 9422
Handel	Suite 8 }	
	(also includes works by Rameau and Boehm)	
	Concerti Grossi	ST 1043
	Organ Concerti Nos. 1, 5, 7, 8	ASD 2352
	Water Music	6500 047
	Giulio Cesare (complete)	SER 5561/3
	Giulio Cesare (excerpts)	SDD 213
	Messiah (complete)	SLS 774

Composer	Title	Catalogue No.
Bach	*Mass in B minor* (complete)	2710 001
	Mass in B minor (excerpts)	136 300
	St. Matthew Passion (complete)	2712 001
	St. Matthew Passion (excerpts)	136 233
	Motets Nos. 1, 3, 5	HQS 1114
	Cantata No. 147 and Motets 2, 4, 6	HQS 1254
	Various Chorale Preludes	HQS 1166
	Concerti for Violin in A minor and E } Concerto for 2 violins in D minor	2870 126
	Brandenburg Concerti	SET 410/11
	Toccata and Fugue in D minor } Prelude Fugue in D } Fantasia and Fugue in G minor } Trio Sonata 2	138907
	48 Preludes and Fugues Bk. 1	HQS 1042/3
	Bk. 2	HQS 1065/6

CHAPTER ELEVEN

THE RISE OF CLASSICISM

IN the second quarter of the 18th century, while Bach and Handel were producing their greatest works, there arose changes of taste which involved corresponding changes in the style of music. We have seen how, at the beginning of the 17th century, there was a swing away from polyphony (at least in certain cases) to homophony. From about 1730 onwards there was a rather similar swing away from the contrapuntal style* to music in which the stress was on the vertical aspect rather than on the horizontal. Besides this, a lighter, less generally serious style evolved, usually known as the *style galant*, which aimed chiefly at grace and elegance. Broadly speaking, such music was of a kind to be heard rather than carefully listened to; it required but little of the mental concentration which was needed for the appreciation of, say, a Bach concerto.

Anticipations of the new style are numerous, as in the clavecin pieces of Couperin and his successor Jean Philippe Rameau (1683 to 1764), while Domenico Scarlatti's sonatas show a complete lack of interest in anything truly contrapuntal.† The cantatas of Georg Philipp Telemann (1681 to 1767) and Christoph Graupner (1683 to 1760) show leanings to the *style galant*, as does the work of some of the successors of Vivaldi, *e.g.* Pietro Locatelli (1693 to 1764) and

---

* It must be pointed out that this chapter will not deal with opera, which is, of course, essentially non-contrapuntal.

† Dr. Bukofzer, in *Music in the Baroque Era*, suggests that in Scarlatti's work 'the nearing classic style manifests itself openly'.

Francesco Veracini (c. 1683 to 1750). It is noticeable that the traditional trio sonata now falls into disuse, its place being taken by the solo sonata. The initial slow movement of the sonata drops out, and the *allegro* movement takes first place, losing its fugal character and becoming homophonic. Thus, the normal plan becomes that of the Italian overture—quick, slow, quick.

It is at this time that the foundations of the clavier sonata,* which reached its climax in the pianoforte sonatas of Beethoven, were laid, the most important composer being Bach's third son, Carl Philipp Emanuel (1714 to 1788). He worked on the three movement plan. His first movements are basically binary. Using the 'corresponding cadence figures' mentioned in connection with Scarlatti, which were also much employed by his father in suite movements, he gradually increased their contrast with the opening material, thus pointing the way to the true second subject group of the later, fully-developed form. In his slow movements, he shows a considerable advance on the practice of the older composers, using a wide range of keys and styles, and even indulging in experiments in recitative. Possibly more than any of his predecessors except Scarlatti, he achieved a true keyboard style. His important book *The True Manner of Keyboard Performance* remains a mine of information on the musical practice of his time. Despite his professed admiration for the works of his father, he seems to have held a poor opinion of 'learned music', and to

* The ousting of the harpsichord by the piano took place in the second half of the century. The piano was invented about 1709 by Cristofori in Florence, being distinguished from the older instrument by the fact that its strings were struck by hammers, not plucked. This gave the player control by the fingers over gradations of tone; hence the name originally used by the inventor, *gravicembalo* (=harpsichord) *col piano e forte*. The new invention was exploited in Germany by Silbermann, who found Bach critical of his early efforts; the Cantor preferred his clavichord. Later, more developed examples, which Bach was able to try when he visited Potsdam, he found more satisfactory. By the end of the century the harpsichord was obsolescent, though as late as 1802 some of Beethoven's sonatas were published as 'for harpsichord or pianoforte'.

have considered lack of contrapuntal ability no great matter.

The symphony began to develop contemporaneously with the sonata. Works under the title of symphony, apart from the *sinfonia avanti l'opera*, had been written well back in the 17th century. There exists one of 1629 for two violins and bass by Bartolomeo Mont'-Albano, and another of 1650 for two violins, viola and bass viol by Gregorio Allegri. But these are really canzonas under another name. The term 'symphony' was also sometimes used for introductory movements (apart from opera), as in the case of that to Bach's C minor Partita (=suite) for clavier. As an independent form, deriving from the Italian overture, the symphony really dates from around 1740, and its rise was at least partly due to the establishment of public concerts. The demand for symphonies became very great, and composers found it desirable to write them apart from any operatic connection. Such symphonies were, and still are, sonatas for orchestra, their structural development following that of the solo sonata for clavier or violin. The normal plan was of three movements, as in the Italian overture. To this was often added a minuet between the last two movements, a carry-over from the *divertimento* type of work, which might run to a large number of movements, including various dances.

The early orchestras were small, and their composition was variable. There was always a basis of strings—1st and 2nd violins, violas, 'cellos and basses (whose parts were normally identical), with harpsichord *continuo*. Above these might be a pair of flutes or oboes, and two horns. Later it became customary to employ a pair of both flutes and oboes, plus one or two bassoons, two trumpets and two kettledrums, the last two being omitted in the quiet slow movements. Clarinets do not appear until the end of the century.* Orchestration in the modern sense of the term

---

* The clarinet was invented by Johann Denner of Nuremburg in 1694, and at first was naturally of a very crude nature. Handel wrote an overture for two clarinets and *corno da caccia*.

now begins to develop,* with some considerable differences in the use of the instruments as compared with the preceding generation. In Bach and Handel we find, rather naturally in view of their fundamentally contrapuntal texture, that little distinction is made in the style of writing for the various instruments. A passage first stated on the violins, and entirely suited to them, may later appear transferred literally to flutes or oboes. Where these composers show their appreciation of tone colour is in their choice of instruments for particular movements.† This is especially noticeable in the accompaniments to vocal pieces. For example, when Bach accompanies the aria *For love of us my Saviour suffered* in the *St. Matthew Passion* by a flute and two *oboi da caccia*,‡ we can only feel that the colour is entirely 'right'. Similarly with the solo violin which is added to the quartet in the aria *Have mercy, Lord, on me*. Quite as much as the voice does it express Peter's utter despair. Examples could be multiplied indefinitely.

17th- and early 18th-century orchestration was naturally largely conditioned by the doctrine of 'affections'. As long as the principle of 'one movement, one mood' held good, anything approaching the kaleidoscopic changes of colour which became normal in later ages was obviously out of the question. One of the most important changes which came over music in the second half of the 18th century was the tendency to strong contrasts of emotional temperature within a single movement. In this, as has been pointed out, Scarlatti was a pioneer.

* Space has forbidden any consideration of Bach's use of the orchestra in the preceding chapter. The student should realise that although he lived before the rise of orchestration in the present-day sense of the term, Bach's handling of the orchestra was, in its own way, as masterly as that of any later composer. But the whole method and approach were different, being bound up with the generally contrapuntal style of writing.

† For a simple example of the early 18th-century style of orchestration the reader may refer to one of the oboe concertos of Handel. Less simple, but possibly more instructive, are the first and third movements of Bach's 2nd Brandenburg Concerto.

‡ The 'hunting oboe', predecessor of the cor anglais.

In Bach and Handel we find that the wood wind and the violas are expected to work as hard as the violins. But in the new *galant* style the wind are largely relegated to holding notes, their parts often being almost devoid of melodic interest. The violas cling tightly to the 'cellos and spend much of their time doubling the parts of their larger brothers. The standard of viola playing was generally low, for which reason composers of the *galant* period rarely gave the viola a truly independent or important part. We must assume that Bach and Handel took not inconsiderable risks in their writing for this instrument.

As to the changed use of wood wind, we must realise that the new style of writing was based, roughly speaking, on a melody (in the broadest sense of the term) and a bass, with non-contrapuntal inner parts. The upper strings did most of the melodic work; the wind, plus the *continuo*, provided a background. But this must not be taken too literally; as the new style developed so did the use and individualisation of the instruments. Mozart made perhaps more progress in this direction than anybody; even Haydn, after all he had done to develop the new style, said late in life that it was a pity he had to die just as he was learning how to use the wood wind.

The list of early symphonists is lengthy. Among the more important are Giovanni Battista Sammartini (*c.* 1700 to 1775), Baldassare Galuppi (1706 to 1785), on whose (imaginary) toccata Browning wrote his poem, Georg Christoph Wagenseil (1715 to 1777), Karl Friedrich Abel (1725 to 1787), who, with Bach's youngest son Johann Christian (1735 to 1782) was active for many years in London, and Karl Ditters von Dittersdorf (1739 to 1799). All these were concerned with the gradual evolution of the symphony as we know it. Specially important are Johann Stamitz (1717 to 1757) and his son Karl (1746 to 1801). Johann was in charge of the orchestra at the electoral court of Mannheim, where his renderings reached a height of expressiveness hitherto almost unknown. He was one of the first to make full use, in orchestral performance, of a gradual increase or decrease of tone as opposed to the 'terrace' dynamics, *i.e.* 'block' contrasts of degrees of tone, of the preceding period, and the 'Mannheim *crescendo*' was famous throughout musical Europe.* Mozart was greatly influenced by the performances he heard at Mannheim.

The two greatest figures of the second half of the 18th century are Joseph Haydn and Wolfgang Amadeus Mozart. Haydn, the son of a wheelwright, was born at Rohrau in Austria on March 31st, 1732. Like Handel, he seems to have had no notable musical ancestry, but from a very early age gave signs of talent. At the age of eight he was admitted as a chorister at St. Stephen's Cathedral in Vienna, where he remained until 1748. The pretext for his dismissal, his voice having broken, was a practical joke which he had perpetrated on one of his fellows. He was now thrown on his own resources, and until 1756 was miserably poor. He managed, however, to obtain and study the important theoretical works of the time and so gradually built up his technique as a composer. In 1759 he obtained an appointment with Count Morzin, with a small but secure salary of about £20 a year plus board and lodging, and proceeded to marry the daughter of a wigmaker who was a perpetual cross to him until she died in 1800. It is extraordinary that Haydn, saddled with a vixen of a wife who, as he himself said, 'cared not a straw whether he was an artist or a shoemaker', could write so much music of a happy and carefree nature. As a composer he must have been able to shut himself up in a mental world of his own. From 1761 to 1790 he was in the service of the enormously wealthy Esterhazys. The second of these, Prince Nicholas 'the Magnificent', who succeeded to the title in 1762, was one of the greatest benefactors of music in the whole of

* *Crescendo* and *diminuendo* were not, as is sometimes implied, Stamitz's invention. They had been in use in opera since the time of Caccini, and Geminiani employed them in instrumental music. Italian musicians in the early part of the 18th century used swelling and diminishing of tone in all kinds of music.

the Age of Patronage.   Although Haydn had to wear a
livery like any other servant, his relations with his employer
were easy, his salary generous, and he was given every
encouragement, like Hasse at Dresden, to 'write as he felt
and as he wished'.   After 1790 he was free of any appointment, with a comfortable pension.   Then followed his two
visits to London under the aegis of the impresario Salomon.
He died in Vienna on May 31st, 1809, famous all over
Europe, honoured by all.

In Haydn we see the work of the early sonatists and
symphonists developed to a point from which Beethoven
was able to take his departure.   The clavier sonatas are
built on the foundations laid by Emanuel Bach, to whose
work Haydn admitted he owed much.   From Bach's more
or less tentative development of binary form he gradually
evolved the settled outline of the full sonata form.   It remained for Beethoven to develop real differentiation in the
character of thematic material within a movement.   Haydn
was often content to allow a second subject to grow from
the first, the only real difference being that of key.   Mozart
on the whole went farther, but hardly the whole distance.
Haydn is notable for his adventurousness in key plan, far
beyond anything that Emanuel Bach ever attempted.   In
the E flat sonata, op. 82, for example, the slow movement
is in the very distant key of E major.

The early symphonies (Haydn wrote altogether over a
hundred) are mostly in the *galant* style, the orchestra small
and its treatment relatively undeveloped.   This was natural
enough, since in his early days the symphony was not considered a very important branch of art.   Performances must
have been often rough and ready.   As Sir Hubert Parry
says in the article *Symphony* in Grove, 'with regard to deep
meaning, refinement, poetical intention, or originality, they
(the audiences) appear to have cared very little.   They
wanted to be healthily pleased and entertained, not stirred
with deep emotion; and the purposes of composers in those
days were consequently not exalted to any high pitch, but

were limited to a simple and unpretentious supply. . . .
Haydn was influenced by these considerations till the last.'
In the latest symphonies, however, the two 'Salomon' sets,
composed for his visits to London, the mature hand of the
great master is evident; the former master of the *galant* style
has now become the great classic. While there is not the
emotional depth of, say, Mozart's great G minor, the craftsmanship is superb and the orchestration impeccable; and
the wealth of delightful ideas shows that increasing age
brought no diminution of inventiveness and spontaneity.

Haydn is sometimes called the Father of the Symphony;
equally he was the Father of the String Quartet. In his
young days there was but little distinction between symphony and quartet. The latter derived mainly from the
sonata for strings and *continuo*, *via* such works as the *quadri*
of Sammartini and his fellow-countryman Giuseppe Tartini
(1692 to 1770), an outstanding violinist of the generation
after Vivaldi. These men occasionally dispensed with the
continuo, leaving the strings to stand on their own feet.
Besides such works were a multitude of divertimenti,
cassations and serenades, consisting of an indefinite number
of movements, and designed primarily for open-air performance. For this reason they lacked a *continuo* part. Haydn's
earliest quartets are of the divertimento type, but those of
op. 3 (the opus number is that of a publisher, not the composer), dating from the middle 1760's, are more truly
quartets in the accepted sense. They are in four movements, the third being a minuet. The inclusion of this
movement, as in the symphony, was a relic of the divertimento, which often contained two or more. With op. 9
and op. 17 (1769 and 1771 respectively) we find the true
quartet style firmly established. The part-writing is of
greater interest, and the viola, in particular, is now expected to pull his weight with greater independence. The
six quartets of op. 33 (1781), written 'in an entirely new
and special manner', are a landmark in their mastery of
thematic development. We have by now moved a long

way from the slightly developed binary form of Emanuel Bach. The later quartets show increasing mastery in all directions, including mastery of counterpoint.*

It is impossible to deal, even in the barest outline, with much of Haydn's other work, but reference must be made to his two great choral works, *The Creation* and *The Seasons*. The former was the outcome of his experiences in London, where he had attended various performances of Handel's oratorios, and had been overwhelmed by their power. *The Creation* was written in 1797 and, allowing for the inevitable differences in idiom, is the true successor of the oratorios of Handel. *The Seasons*, written in 1800, was on the whole less successful. Haydn was in poor health and did not find the libretto really attractive. He remarked that whereas the characters in *The Creation* were angels, in *The Seasons* they were merely peasants.

Haydn, apart from his natural ability, achieved his mastery by struggle and hard work over a period of years. Mozart, if not 'born fully armed', may be considered possibly the most naturally gifted musician who has ever lived. He was born in Salzburg on January 27th, 1756, his father, Leopold, being a violinist (later vice-kapellmeister) in the private orchestra of the Prince Archbishop of that city. From his earliest years the young Mozart's great talent was evident, and he received careful instruction from his father, who was a musician of considerable attainments. (His *Method for the Violin* was for long a standard work and is still to be studied with profit.) At the age of six, Wolfgang and his sister Marianne, also musically gifted, were dragged round Europe and to England as infant prodigies. Unlike Haydn, Mozart travelled widely throughout his life—Mannheim, Paris, Rome, Milan, etc.—though his father would have much preferred him to remain in a settled post.

* Despite public distaste for 'learned' music, composers' training was still largely based on contrapuntal practice, and both Haydn and Mozart were brilliant contrapuntists. The writer has even heard the opinion expressed, by a musician of great erudition and experience, that Mozart was a greater contrapuntist than Bach.

Leopold was of a careful disposition, always with an eye to a steady income and the favour of his employer. His son, possibly the most tidy and economical composer who ever lived, showed increasing fecklessness as he grew older, and when away from home was perpetually chased by cautionary letters and admonitions from his father. In 1782 he married Constanze Weber, having previously had an affaire with her elder sister Aloysia, thereby adding to his difficulties with Leopold. As time went on he became deeply in debt (his begging letters to his friend and fellow Freemason Michael Puchberg, always with promises of speedy repayment, make pitiable reading), and, dying on December 5th, 1791, was buried in a pauper's grave outside Vienna.

Mozart's early works are naturally enough in the *style galant*, but are distinguished from those of his contemporaries by their superior craftsmanship and elegance. He was at first strongly influenced by the style of Christian Bach, whom he met as a child in London, and again, at the age of twenty-two, in Paris. In 1781 he first met Haydn, an encounter which turned out to be mutually profitable. Although Haydn was the elder by some twenty-four years, each learned from the other. From Haydn Mozart learned much of the possibilities of form and expression; while from Mozart Haydn learned 'a rounder phrase, a richer harmonisation, and a fuller command of the orchestra' (Grove).

It is from this time that the clever young exponent of the *style galant* develops into the great classic, in whose later works, as in those of his elder contemporary, the elements of structural balance, proportion and pure beauty are unsurpassed. Not that the emotional side is eliminated; there is much more than mere well-balanced 'patterning'. One has only to think of the great G minor symphony to realise this. But, with comparatively rare exceptions, the emotion is strictly controlled; its free expression, so strongly characteristic of the Romantics of the 19th century, is not the prime object. Occasionally it wells up irresistibly, as in the slow movement of the A major piano concerto (K. 488) or that of the *Sinfonia Concertante* for violin, viola and orchestra; but it is never allowed to override perfect balance and symmetry of form.

In his symphonies and chamber music Mozart followed much the same line of development as Haydn. Both, as they progressed, achieved greater mastery of form, greater technical mastery of the medium, and greater depth of meaning. Mozart, as the shorter-lived, progressed more rapidly and possibly farther. Even more than is the case with Haydn, his craftsmanship is pure delight. Everything is vital to the total effect, and there is never a note too many. Above all composers, Mozart understood the art of concealing art, and of obtaining the maximum effectiveness by the simplest of means. Pages of examples could be quoted, did space permit. For a single, superb instance, the reader may turn to the second movement of the G minor string quintet, noting how the cadence figure of the minuet, put from minor into major key (a mechanical procedure if ever there was one), becomes the opening of the trio. The incredible effect of this transformation can only be realised fully, of course, in the context of complete performance. It is comparable only with such strokes of genius as the first entry of the fugue subject in Beethoven's sonata op. 110, or Bach's ultimate affirmation of faith in 'Truly, this was the Son of God' in the *St. Matthew Passion*.

No sketch of Mozart's work can omit reference to his concertos. Brilliant both as a clavierist and a violinist, he wrote equally well for both instruments, but whereas the last complete concerto for violin was written in 1777, the last for piano was in the year of his death. It is in the concertos for piano that we find, as in the later symphonies and chamber music, the quintessential Mozart. In them he exhibits the complete range of his style, from the *galanterie* of the first, written at the age of seventeen, to the sheer

beauty of the famous A major of 1786 and the tragedy of
the great C minor of the same year.

On the purely technical side, the concertos show the
rise and development of the 'display' element. This
had begun to creep into works for the violin as early
as Torelli, and the tendency was intensified as time
passed, in the works of such composers as Veracini and
Tartini. With the gradual decline in importance of
the *continuo* during the century, the harpsichord and
the piano came into their own as individuals in concerted music. Haydn wrote a small number of piano
concertos, but the first of real importance are those of
Mozart. All are in three movements, lacking the minuet.
In the first movements there are traces of the old concerto
form of the preceding period, especially in the orchestral
introduction which serves as an 'opening ritornello'.* The
second movement is most frequently an *andante*† and the
finale often a rondo, sometimes of distinctly complex internal
construction. The display element is strictly controlled,
and of limpid clarity; the day of handfuls of notes, splashed
liberally all over the keyboard, was as yet far distant. In
his passage-work, as in everything else, Mozart means every
note to say something to the point.

At this stage we may pause to note the gradual speeding-
up of the *tempo* of musical change. (We do not use the
word 'progress' here, as it is apt to lead to misunderstanding.) It took about 300 years for music to evolve from the
beginnings of the old organum up to measurable music.
Then another 150 before *Ars Nova* appeared. Another 300
to the climax of the polyphonic style, and about 150 to
the masterpieces of Bach and Handel. But now we find

---

* There is a good deal of misunderstanding regarding the form of
these movements, and the frequent statement that they are in 'sonata
form with a double exposition' is not strictly correct. See Tovey,
Essays in Musical Analysis, introduction to Vol. 3, and Hutchings,
Companion to Mozart's Pianoforte Concertos, for a full discussion.

† Which term, it may be pointed out, means 'going', *i.e.* moving, *not*
'slow'.

a new style reaching a climax in three-quarters of a century, and we shall see later how further changes, both in outlook and technical method, followed in comparatively rapid succession. It took over 600 years for the modal system to be played out, but the major and minor scale system, at least according to some contemporary musicians, is already, after less than 300, reaching the end of its tether. But this, of course, is purely a matter of personal opinion.

RECORDS

Composer	Title	Catalogue No
Haydn	String Quartets in F and D minor	SXL 6093
	Symphonies No. 45 (*Farewell*) and 104 (*London*)	135 034
	Symphonies 94 (*Surprise*) and 101 (*Clock*)	138 782
	Keyboard Sonatas 20, 44, 46	61112
	The Creation	2707 044
Mozart	Sinfonia Concertante	ASD 2462
	Sinfonia Concertante (wind)	
	Sinfonia Concertante (Violin and Viola)	73030
	Symphonies Nos. 35 (*Haffner*) and 39	61023
	Symphonies Nos. 40 and 41 (*Jupiter*)	SAX 2486
	Piano Concerti in A and D (K. 488 and K. 451)	138 870
	Clarinet Concerto and Flute and Harp Concerto	SAL 3535
	Clarinet Quintet and Clarinet Trio	6500 073
	String Quartets 14 and 18	138 909
	Serenade No. 10 for 13 wind instruments	SXL 6049

CHAPTER TWELVE

DEVELOPMENTS IN OPERA

WE must now retrace our steps to follow the course pursued by opera from the point at which we left it in Chapter 8.

In Italy, by the early years of the 18th century, opera was bogged down in a mass of conventions, especially in the Neapolitan school of Scarlatti and his successors. Subjects for libretti were restricted almost, if not entirely, to classical mythology or ancient history; there was a set number of characters, the number and order of whose arias were strictly regulated; ensemble numbers, except for an occasional duet, were almost unheard-of. The action of the story was carried along by recitative with the barest of accompaniment, the arias, expressing the characters' reactions to the situations in which they found themselves, being really outside the action and serving largely as *media* for the singers to exhibit their vocal talents. The heroine, for example, finding herself about to be cast into the deepest dungeon, or led away to the torture chamber, holds up the action while she expresses at length, and in ternary form, her feelings on her predicament, her captors awaiting the end of her outburst with exemplary patience. No wonder Dr. Johnson defined opera, in his dictionary, as 'an exotic and irrational entertainment'! The irrationality was in no way diminished by the employment of male sopranos for heroic parts. True, many of the arias, as separate pieces, had considerable musical value, but an opera as a whole was, as Prof. Dent puts it,* 'just a concert in costume'. The orchestra was small, mostly strings with harpsichord *continuo*, and the overture was often of negligible value. In any case, few if any of the audience

* *Opera* (Pelican Books).

bothered to listen to it. It had rarely any recognisable connection with the opera itself, and served to cover up the shuffling of feet and the conversation of the audience who were awaiting the appearance of their pet singers.

In France the Lullian tradition was carried on by Rameau. The subjects of the French operas were similar to those of the Italian, but in the musical setting there was more insistence on declamation as opposed to pure singing; mere vocal pyrotechnics, as in the *aria di bravura* of Italy, were discountenanced. Besides this, choral movements were a regular constituent, as was ballet. The orchestra, too, was used with greater ingenuity than was common in Italy. Instead of merely providing a subordinate accompaniment, it was sometimes used, at least by Rameau, for descriptive purposes, a possibility entirely overlooked by the Italians.

From very early times it had been customary to provide light relief between the acts of a tragedy, by *Intermezzi*. In the period before 1600, for example, madrigals would be sung, and with the development of opera a similar practice obtained. Gradually the *Intermezzi* achieved character and coherence of their own. By the beginning of the 18th century they had become little two-act affairs, which were interlocked with the three acts of the opera proper, with which they had no connection either in plot or music.* In due course the *Intermezzi* became separated from the opera, achieving independence as an individual form. This independence was largely the work of Giovanni Battista Pergolesi (1710 to 1736), whose *La Serva Padrona* is the most famous of all such works. Separated from the *opera seria*, the 'serious opera', the *Intermezzo* became known as *opera buffa*—comic

---

* The writer was interested to find a similar procedure occurring in India as recently as 1943. A travelling company of entertainers whom he saw alternated the acts of an historical drama with low comedy turns. The idea seems to have been similar to that of the *Intermezzi* as explained by Rousseau in his *Dictionary of Music* (1767), 'to cheer and repose the spirit of the spectator, saddened by thoughts of the tragic and strained by its attention to matters of gravity'. Though, judging by the applause, the comedy turns did little to 'repose' the spirits of the sepoys who formed the bulk of the audience!

opera. It was bound by no conventions and so achieved real vitality.

In 1752 an Italian troupe, *Les Bouffons*, arrived in Paris to perform their *Intermezzi*, and almost immediately arose the *Guerre des Bouffons* between those who supported the Italians and those, more conservative, who preferred the traditional French style deriving from Lully. Throughout much of the 17th and 18th centuries Paris was an operatic battleground—the Parisians took their opera very seriously —the grounds of contention being mainly whether the purely musical side, as in Italian opera, or the dramatic side, as in the French, was to be considered the more important. Pamphleteering was rife. The pro-French writers complained that all the Italians thought of was singing; the Italian faction retorted to the effect that the French had no good singers anyway. Argument went back and forth on the importance or otherwise of stage machinery, dancing, use of chorus, etc., often conducted in a remarkably virulent manner. Among the more prominent pamphleteers were the Abbé François Raguenet (b. 1660) and Le Cerf de La Viéville. In England, Joseph Addison (1672 to 1719) had many witty things to say of the traditional Italian style, while in Italy itself Benedetto Marcello satirised the native opera and the vanity of the singers.

With the arrival of *Les Bouffons* warfare flared up violently, two of the most important supporters of *opera buffa* being F. W. von Grimm (1723 to 1807) and Jean Jacques Rousseau (1712 to 1778). The latter, in his *Letter on French Music*, generally lauds the Italians and their performances as compared with the French, concluding 'that there is neither measure nor melody in French music, because the language is not capable of them; that French singing is continual squalling; . . . that its harmony is crude and devoid of expression', and so on. Finally, 'that the French have no music and cannot have any; or that if they ever have, it will be so much the worse for them'. A somewhat startling condemnation of the national art from one who only three years earlier had written strongly supporting French opera against Italian. Rousseau himself wrote an *Intermezzo*, in French, in the Italian style, called *Le Devin du Village*. Pergolesi's *La Serva Padrona*, poorly received in Paris at its first presentation in 1746, eventually made its way into favour, and had ultimately considerable influence on French opera.

After Pergolesi, the great name in Italian *opera buffa* is Domenico Cimarosa (1749 to 1801), famous especially for *The Secret Marriage*. It is from this time that the tradition of the French *opéra-comique*, stemming from *opera buffa*, was built up by such composers as François Philidor (1726 to 1795), famous also as a chess player, Pierre Monsigny (1729 to 1817) and André Grétry (1741 to 1813). *Opéra comique* had spoken dialogue and, like *opera buffa*, was far removed from the formality and heaviness of the Lully-Rameau style. Its last great representative was Daniel Auber (1786 to 1871), who possessed a remarkable *flair* for writing works which appealed to the least musically educated audience. Like many of his contemporaries and predecessors, his facility in composition was amazing, his operas numbering forty-six, including the 'grand' opera *Masaniello*. In this work he showed considerable originality, and a rather unexpected ability to handle the grand manner.

The *Guerre des Bouffons* having died down, Paris was almost immediately plunged into another operatic struggle, that of the Gluckists *versus* the Piccinnists. Christoph Willibald Gluck (1714 to 1787) began by writing successfully in the conventional Italian manner. A visit to Paris in 1746 enabled him to hear works by Rameau, which gave him cause to reflect on the possible weaknesses of the Italian style. He was not the only one to feel that it had reached a ridiculous pitch of irrationality; the Italian Francesco Algarotti, in his *Saggio sopra l'opera in musica* (1755), was highly critical. He demanded, among other things, that the recitative should be given greater importance, and that brilliant passages in the arias should be introduced only when really appropriate. He admits that occasional movements by such composers as Jommelli (1714 to 1774) and Hasse (1699 to 1783) are worthy of praise, but the general tone of his complaint is that the true aims of the founders of opera, a hundred and fifty years earlier, had been completely forgotten. As a 'concert in costume' it might be effective enough; as a dramatic unity it did not exist.

The results of Gluck's reflections appeared first in his *Orfeo* of 1762. The most popular librettist of the time, whose works were set by all the most famous musicians, was Metastasio. His libretti were designed exactly to suit the conventions of *opera seria*. Gluck had set some of his libretti, but for his new ideas he needed a writer of sympathy and originality, whom he found in Raniero da Calzabigi. *Orfeo* was, however, only a halfway house, and it was not until 1767, in the Preface to *Alceste*, that Gluck first fully expounded his ideas on what opera should and should not be. In the dedication of this work he begins by saying: 'When I undertook to write the music for *Alceste*, I resolved to divest it entirely of all those abuses . . . which have so long disfigured Italian opera.' His aims, he explains, are 'to restrict music to its true office of serving poetry by means of expression and by following the situations of the story, without interrupting the action or stifling it with a useless superfluity of ornaments'. In other words, to return to the methods and aims of the *Camerata*. He deplores the undramatic formality of the *da capo* aria and insists that the action of the plot must not be held up 'unreasonably or wantonly'. Further, 'the overture ought to apprise the spectators of the nature of the action that is to be represented and to form, so to speak, its argument'. In this he anticipates Wagner, who, a century later, insisted that an opera begins not with the rise of the curtain, but with the first note of the overture.* We may mention that

---

* Gluck was not, however, the originator of this idea. In essence it is found in many overtures to Venetian operas of the mid-17th century, even to thematic material being taken from that in the main scenes of the opera.

Gluck in his 'reformed' operas used the orchestra to accompany the recitatives, instead of the traditional harpsichord.

Such theories, and their application in practice, did not please the opera public of Vienna, which city had by this time become the chief centre of Italian opera. In 1772 Gluck wrote, to a French libretto, *Iphigénie en Aulide*, produced in Paris in 1774. Largely due to the support of Marie Antoinette, his former singing pupil, it was a success, and was followed by the presentation of *Orphée et Eurydice* (adapted from *Orfeo*) and *Alceste*. The war of the Gluckists and the Piccinnists broke out in 1777. Piccinni was the protégé of the Italian faction, and his *Roland* was to be produced four months after Gluck's *Armide*. The contest was waged with great violence, and eventually the two composers were invited to set the same libretto, *Iphigénie en Tauride*. Gluck's version, produced in 1779, was a great success; Piccinni's, two years later, was a comparative failure. Even so, the argument was carried on after Gluck had returned to Vienna.

Except for Etienne Méhul (1763 to 1817) the French composers remained unaffected directly by Gluck's reforms; Méhul's greatest work was the sacred opera *Joseph*. The Italian conventions, however, gradually broke down, and although in Italian opera the accent remained primarily on the singing, the complete unreality and formality of *opera seria* eventually passed away.

In Germany a type of opera known as the *singspiel* grew up during the 18th century. Originally it was related to the English ballad opera—spoken dialogue in the vernacular with interpolated songs—but by degrees evolved into something more approaching true opera, without recitative. Singspiels were often based on everyday stories, the mythological-historical subjects of *opera seria* being excluded. Nor were there any conventions in the form. The initial impulse seems to have come from the performance of a German version of the ballad opera *The Devil to Pay* by

Charles Coffey, which had a great success in Leipzig in 1764, and led to the composition of a number of similar pieces by Johann Adam Hiller (1728 to 1804) in conjunction with the poet C. F. Weisse. Hiller is often called the father of the *singspiel*. Dittersdorf's *Doctor and Apothecary* is one of the most famous of all such works.

Of Mozart's operas, *The Magic Flute* (which the composer referred to as 'my German opera'), is described on the title-page as a *singspiel*, while *The Flight from the Seraglio* and the less-known *Theatre Director* are of the same class, though much more developed in every way than the works of Hiller or Dittersdorf. Mozart wrote two *opere serie*, *Idomeneo* and *La Clemenza di Tito*. Of the others, apart from those already mentioned, *Figaro* and *Così fan tutte* are *opere buffe*, while *Don Giovanni* is described as a *Dramma Giocoso*, a 'humorous drama'. But neither *Figaro* nor *Don Giovanni* is comedy pure and simple. The former is in essence a social satire, its libretto being arranged, by Lorenzo da Ponte, from a comedy by Beaumarchais which at the time was banned by the authorities. *Don Giovanni*, based on a story of considerable antiquity, may almost be considered as a 'cautionary tale'. Neither has the often trivial plot, nor the trivial music, of the general run of *opere buffe*. They lie, as it were, between serious and comic opera, and are the ancestors of such works as Strauss's *Der Rosenkavalier*. This the composer describes as a 'comedy with music', but again there is much more under the surface than mere comedy.

There is no particular virtue in trying to decide which of Mozart's operas is the greatest. As with so many of his works, he simply does everything better than any of his contemporaries, always with the greatest simplicity and ease. It is doubtful, for example, whether it would be possible to achieve greater beauty with a most elementary harmonic progression and an almost static voice part than Mozart does in the opening of the aria *Dove sono* in *Figaro*. Especially notable, too, is his power of characterisation.

With only the minimum of resources, he defines each of his characters with the greatest clarity.

As with Gluck, the overture is an integral part of the work; that of *Don Giovanni* leads without break into the first scene. (Gluck does the same in *Iphigénie en Tauride*.) In the overtures to both *Don Giovanni* and *The Magic Flute* there are brief references to music which will be heard later in the opera. This is an important anticipation of the practice of later composers; Weber, for example, used material from the body of the opera for much of his overtures, while some of Wagner's introductory movements, *e.g. Mastersingers* and *Parsifal*, are entirely based on themes to be heard later.

By the end of the 18th century the old French tradition of opera, dating back to Lulli, had disintegrated, but 'grand opera' continued, however reformed. Plots became less stereotyped as literary romanticism began to have its effect. Stories were based on Oriental romance, on fairy tales, on the chivalry of the Middle Ages, and so on. Musically there was gradually greater freedom, and a tendency to carry on the action continuously, rather than to confine the movement of the plot to recitative or spoken dialogue. Concerted numbers became longer and more important, while spectacular and melodramatic elements came more to the fore. In all these directions Luigi Cherubini (1760 to 1842) excelled, and we may note his *Lodoiska* and *Les Deux Journées*. Cherubini, Italian born, was for many years director of the Paris Conservatory of Music, and was a learned writer of technical treatises.

From the beginning of the 19th century Parisian grand opera became more and more of a spectacle, in accordance with prevailing taste. The style is well exemplified in Spontini's *La Vestale* (1807), Halévy's *La Juive*, and reaches its height in the operas of Giacomo Meyerbeer (1791 to 1864), *e.g. Robert the Devil*, *The Huguenots* and *L'Africaine*. All such works demanded a large cast and orchestra, spectacular scenic effects, and were full of brilliant solos, large-scale concerted numbers, and melodramatic incident. Although many of his contemporaries had hard things to say of Meyerbeer, and whatever the underlying vulgarity of much of his music, he certainly understood public taste, in Berlin as well as in Paris. Wagner referred to him as 'a Jew banker who composes music',* but did not disdain to learn and use some of his effective tricks of orchestration.

In Italian opera the solo voice still remained the predominant factor, but, as in France, the old insistence on the mythological-historical plot faded away. The old conventions died out, and 'romantic' subjects came into the picture. Concerted numbers, especially the 'concerted finale', also began to appear. The greatest Italian of the early 19th century was Gioachino Rossini (1792 to 1868), a master of melody, of the voice and of the orchestra. His most famous works are *The Barber of Seville* (1816) (of which the plot is actually the first part of Beaumarchais's story of Figaro, Mozart's work being the second part) and *William Tell* (1829). This latter was his thirty-sixth opera, and after it he wrote no more. In the remaining thirty-nine years of his life he seems to have been more interested in gastronomy than in composition.

Of other Italians, Gaetano Donizetti (1797 to 1848) and Vincenzo Bellini (1801 to 1835) were chiefly concerned with carrying on the tradition of opera as a vehicle for vocal (solo) melody and technique. Both were accomplished melodists, but neither showed any great ingenuity in either harmony or use of the orchestra.

We see, then, that from about the middle of the 18th century as great changes came about in opera as in other forms of writing. In Italy, despite the continued insistence on the exploitation of pure singing, convention and formality gave way to greater freedom of design, and to a wider range of subject-matter. In France opera branched out in a number of different directions. The establishment of

* Meyerbeer came of a German-Jewish business family. His real name was Jacob Liebmann Beer.

opéra comique helped in breaking down the old rigidity, and although good declamation remained of the utmost importance, a more easily appreciated and melodious style of vocal writing evolved, together with the spectacular element. Of German opera we shall speak later.

RECORDS

Composer	Title	Catalogue No.
Gluck	*Orpheus and Euridice* (complete)	SET 443/4
	Orpheus and Euridice (excerpts)	SET 495
Mozart	*Marriage of Figaro* (complete)	SLS 955
	Marriage of Figaro (excerpts)	136 283
	Don Giovani (complete)	SET 421/5
	Don Giovani (excerpts)	SET 496
	The Magic Flute (complete)	2709 017
	The Magic Flute (excerpts)	136 440
	The Seraglio (in English, complete)	SLS 932
Rossini	*The Barber of Seville* (complete)	SET 285/7
	The Barber of Seville (excerpts)	SXL 6271
Donizetti	*Lucia di Lammermoor* (complete)	SLS 797
	Lucia di Lammermoor (excerpts)	SXL 2315
Meyerbeer	*Les Huguenots* (complete)	SET 460/3
	Les Huguenots (excerpts)	SET 513
Cherubini	*Medée* (complete)	SET 376/8
	Medée (excerpts)	SET 476
	Arias by Bellini, Meyerbeer and Charpentier	ASD 2513

CHAPTER THIRTEEN

BEETHOVEN

IN the latter part of the 18th century the 'Age of Patronage' was drawing to a close. The day of the 'tame musician' was nearing its end, and the professional composer, instead of being the paid servant of some wealthy amateur, more or less bound to provide music to suit his employer's taste, became a freelance. The change was, of course, gradual, and the old system survived, dwindling, well into the 19th century. The last of the really great kapellmeisters was Haydn; Mozart, by the time he was twenty-six, had been ignominiously discharged by his employer, Hieronymous Colloredo, Archbishop of Salzburg, and thenceforward had to make his own way independently, as a consequence finding life none too easy. Many composers still had their patrons, on whom they relied for encouragement and possibly some kind of periodical financial assistance; but it was no longer taken for granted that the musician would seek an assured livelihood in some salaried court or church post. Even when such a post was held, as in the case of Liszt's appointment as director of music at the court of Saxe-Weimar, the composer expected, and was granted, freedom to write what he wished and as he wished.

After Mozart the first of the great freelances was Ludwig van Beethoven, born in Bonn on December 16th, 1770, died in Vienna on March 26th, 1827. His father, a tenor singer at the court of the Elector of Cologne, gave him his first musical instruction, and he also received training from Christian Neefe, who, from 1783, was director of music to the Elector. In this year, while still only twelve years old, Beethoven became the 'orchestral harpsichordist'—

unpaid—and thus early obtained experience of a responsible position. In 1787 he visited Vienna, where he had a few lessons from Mozart, and in 1792 he settled there permanently. Lessons in counterpoint with Haydn were not a success and soon ceased, but he persevered with the theorist Albrechtsberger until 1795. Albrechtsberger, a distinctly conservative contrapuntist, seems not to have been greatly impressed. At the age of about thirty Beethoven began to go deaf, ultimately becoming completely so.

Although a freelance, Beethoven nevertheless accepted the patronage, in the new sense, of many of the nobility in Vienna. For some years he lived in the house of Prince Karl Lichnowsky, who made him a yearly allowance. The dedications of many of his works show that he was in close touch with many wealthy and titled people.

In the work of Beethoven three periods are usually distinguished, though there is some overlapping. In the first period we see the influence of Mozart and Haydn, the obvious models for a young composer of the time, but rarely without something which is essentially Beethoven and nobody else. It may be a turn of phrase, an abrupt and forceful manner of expression (as in the first subject of the piano sonata, op. 2, No. 1), a modification of the conventional form (as in the last movement of the same work), or any one of a dozen things. Beethoven the individualist is always there. Notable, too, is the great intensity of emotional power which at times comes to the surface, as in the brooding of the slow movement of op. 2, No. 2, and still more in that of the D major sonata, op. 10, No. 3. Composers of the preceding period rarely 'let themselves go' emotionally, and when they did, as is evident from some of Mozart's letters, it was with a certain amount of trepidation as to the reactions of their audience. Beethoven, like Bach, was but little concerned with what his auditors wanted; they had to take what he gave them.

The first period takes us to about the year 1802, in which the second of the nine symphonies was written. But the

move into the second period was already under way, as is
evident in the piano sonatas of opp. 26 and 27, which include
the so-called 'Moonlight' sonata—a publisher's title, not the
composer's—of 1801, and those of op. 31 of 1802. In these
it is obvious that the real Beethoven, independent, forceful,
and entirely sure of himself, has emerged. The fury of the
first movement of the D minor sonata, op. 31, No. 2, is
something which had never before been expressed in music,
while perhaps only Bach had plumbed such depths as are
found in its slow movement.

In this second period are found a great body of works of
all kinds—the third to the eighth symphonies, the piano
sonatas up to op. 90, the string quartets up to op. 95, the
piano concertos in G major and E flat major, the violin
concerto, the overture to *Coriolanus*, the *Kreutzer* sonata
for violin and piano, the *Rassoumovsky* quartets, op. 59, and
the one opera *Fidelio*, to mention some of the chief. In
many of them we are impressed by the enormous scale on
which the composer works, as compared with his predecessors. For example, the miniature score of the whole of
Mozart's *Jupiter* symphony runs to eighty-four pages; the
first movement alone of Beethoven's *Eroica* takes eighty-
one. This is not to suggest that greater length necessarily
implies greater value; Mozart was capable of packing into
a single page more meaning than many other composers
could achieve in a dozen. But Beethoven, like Mozart,
holds our attention from the first note to the last.

The compositions of the first and second periods show
a number of important technical advances, though it is to
be noted that in many of them Beethoven was to some
extent anticipated by Haydn and Mozart. In works of
the sonata type he tends to employ a wider range of keys,
though Haydn, as we have seen, was far from being hidebound. It was, for example, distinctly unexpected of Beethoven to put the slow movement of his C minor piano
concerto in the key of E major. In sonata form first movements there are instances of unusual keys for the second

subject group as, for example, in the *Waldstein* sonata, C major, where it is in E major. The structure of the second group becomes more consistently complex (though here he was anticipated by Mozart), and its character also. If the reader will refer to the second group of Mozart's sonata in F, K. 332, and compare with it that of, say, Beethoven's *Appassionata* or *Waldstein* sonatas, this will be readily apparent.

In development sections there is a tendency to greater length; every possible deduction is made, as it were, from the material selected for discussion. The range of modulation, too, is apt to be wider than had formerly been customary, though again Mozart pointed the way. The development of the first movement of the *Eroica* symphony, for example, at one point finds itself in the extremely remote key of E minor. But in Mozart's G minor symphony the development begins in F sharp minor, equally remote from the tonic, and reached by a really startling harmonic short cut. Even in quite early works, *e.g.* the last movement of the sonata op. 2, No. 2, Beethoven realised the potentialities of the coda. Mozart, yet again, had set the ball rolling, as in the last movement of his *Jupiter* symphony, where the coda is a comprehensive summing-up. Not that Beethoven invariably wrote long codas; it depended on whether he felt one to be appropriate. The first movement of the *Eroica* offers an example which is almost a second development, and shows the composer's genius for holding our attention while arguing a point, as it were, down to the last detail.

There is a tendency, too, towards greater continuity within extended movements, the various sections moving into each other almost imperceptibly. Often in the works of earlier composers we feel that the bridge passage is more or less mechanical padding, a link that has got to be there, and that the second group is ushered in, as it were, with a flourish of trumpets. With Beethoven the bridge tends to become an integral part of the material, and the second group, however contrasted, to flow out of it.

The *scherzo* in sonata or symphony is often assumed to be Beethoven's invention, but he was anticipated to some extent by Haydn, some of whose minuets, as in the quartets of op. 33, approach the style. Beethoven, while in most cases retaining the 3/4 time-signature, definitely changed the character of the movement. As early as op. 2, No. 2, we find a *scherzo* in which there is but little trace of its ancestry. In the 5th symphony the literal conception of a *scherzo* as a playful movement becomes metamorphosed, at least in the first and last sections, into something almost macabre. The 5th symphony is a work of great import-ance in the development of symphonic writing, and in it we can trace the distance which Beethoven had travelled. The very opening is a revelation. There is no concession to convention, not even so much as the two introductory chords which, in the *Eroica*, are all that he uses to replace the frequent conventional slow introduction of the earlier symphonists. Beethoven simply hurls his subject-matter—four notes—at his audience, and proceeds to build prac-tically the whole movement on the well-known rhythmic figure, rising to heights of almost shattering intensity. The tension is relaxed in the slow movement, but returns in a different guise in the *scherzo*. This leads without break into the *finale*—another new departure—and the *finale* itself is interrupted by a reference back to the theme of the *scherzo*. This is the first instance of such thematic cross-referencing, and is especially notable in two ways. Firstly, it led to further such developments by later composers, and secondly it shows, mechanically, what is evident purely musically in so many of Beethoven's sonatas, etc., that he viewed the work as a unified whole. Not that he was the first in this. Such works as Mozart's *G minor* or *Jupiter* symphonies, or the *G minor Quintet*, are one and indi-visible. But it cannot be denied that in many of the earlier sonatas and symphonies and quartets, one slow movement or *finale* would suit as well as another.

The 5th symphony shows, too, advances in the use of the orchestra. From his first symphony (1800) Beethoven had used clarinets regularly, and in the *Eroica* he employed three horns instead of the usual two, obviously to allow for the notable horn passage which opens the trio of the *scherzo*. In the 5th there are only two horns, but the last movement brings in piccolo, double bassoon and three trombones, the first time these had been used in such a work. Mozart uses the double bassoon in his *Masonic Funeral Music*, but trombones were usually reserved for use in opera, especially in connection with funeral music and the supernatural. The entry of the statue in the last act of *Don Giovanni* is an example of the latter. Not until the *9th Symphony* does Beethoven employ four horns, and trombones appear again only in the 'storm' movement of the *Pastoral Symphony* and in the second and last movements of the 9th. The use of voices (soloists and chorus) in the last movement of the 9th was another forward-looking innovation, with progeny including such works as Mendelssohn's *Hymn of Praise*, Vaughan Williams's *Sea Symphony* and Holst's *Choral Symphony*.

Beethoven's one opera, *Fidelio*, ranks among the greatest of all, while his *Mass in D* stands on a peak with Bach's *B minor*. Comparison of these two works would be fruitless; their composers' outlook and approach were entirely different, and each work is supreme in its own way.

In the works of the third period, which include the last quartets and the piano sonatas from op. 101 onwards, Beethoven begins to move away from strict adherence to the traditional forms. As with all great composers, his organisation of the internal details had always been conditioned by emotional intention, *i.e.* by the message which he wished to convey, even though the basic outlines were those customarily followed at the time. In these latest works the conventional plans are modified or discarded if the composer feels them inadequate for the expression of his thought. In this, Beethoven points the way to the

'Romantics', to whom form was subservient to emotional expression. But, unlike some of his successors, he was always the great architect; his designs, whether for single movements or for whole works, and however unorthodox by conventional or textbook standards, are always perfect in themselves. The relationship between form and content* is indivisible. The thematic material, too, tends to be of a new character. As opposed to the subject which was so often melodic, or based on figuration, Beethoven used matter which can be best described as germinal—a cell from which a movement *grows*. His frequent adoption of fugue in later works shows this, since fugue,† of all styles of composition, is that in which the principle of continuous growth from a germinal cell, the subject, is basic. The use of variations, too, shows the same principle in operation, the 'cell' being the theme, and the variations exploring its implications.

In his last works Beethoven was preoccupied with *thinking* in musical terms. In the same way as a Bertrand Russell or a de Madariaga expresses his philosophical deductions in an essay, so Beethoven gives us the fruits of his meditations in sound. It is music not for 'entertainment', in however high a sense we interpret the word, but to give expression to thought. For this purpose, fugue and variations, neither of them 'forms' in the conventional sense, offered possibilities beyond those of sonata and other traditional forms. This is not to suggest that Beethoven was the first to 'think in sound'. Bach had done so in the *Art of Fugue* (notwithstanding its pedagogical aim) and in the great *Ricercare* of the *Musical Offering*, to name no other examples. But Beethoven, withdrawn into himself by the total deafness of his later years, did so on a far greater scale than any earlier composer. No better summing up

* 'Content' implies 'meaning', that which the composer wishes to express, emotionally and in every other way, regardless of the form in which he casts his music.

† It is undesirable to think of fugue as a 'form'. As Sir Donald Tovey so often pointed out, it is a 'texture'.

of the works of the last period can be found than that
of Edward Dannreuther: 'He passes beyond the horizon of
a mere singer and poet, and touches upon the domain of
the seer and the prophet; where, in unison with all genuine
mystics and ethical teachers, he delivers a message of religious love and resignation, identification with the suffer-
ings of all living creatures, deprecation of self, negation of
personality, release from the world.'

RECORDS

Composer	Title	Catalogue No.
Beethoven	Piano Sonatas	
	Op. 2/1, Op. 10/1, 2/3	SXL 6097
	Op. 13 (*Pathétique*) Op. 27/2	HQS 1076
	Op. 57 (*Appassionata, Moonlight*)	
	Op. 109, Op. 110	61172
	Violin Sonatas	
	Op. 12/1 and Op. 30/3	SAL 3416
	Op. 23 and Op. 47	SAL 3419
	The 9 Symphonies, 7 Overtures and	
	Incidental Music to *Egmont*	SLS 788
	Piano Trio No. 6 (*Archduke*) and No. 10	ASD 2572
	String Quartets Op. 127 and Op. 135	HQS 1177
	String Quartet Op. 59/1 (Rassoumovsky)	HQS 1159
	An die ferne Geliebte	ASD 2601
	Missa Solemnis	2707 030

CHAPTER FOURTEEN

THE ROMANTICS AND THEIR MUSIC

UNTIL the latter part of the 18th century practically all music was written for a specific purpose or occasion. It might be for the Church, for a court or civic function, for the opera house, for domestic or instructional use, or what not; but fundamentally it was *Gebrauchsmusik*—utility music. Composing was looked upon largely as a 'job of work'; 'art for art's sake' was unheard-of. Even such a masterpiece as the *St. Matthew Passion* was written simply because Bach needed a new setting for use at St. Thomas's Church. Had someone commented to him on its greatness (a most unlikely happening at the time), he would probably have replied, as he did in another connection, that anyone could do as well if he worked hard enough.

It has already been noted that the decline of the patronage system brought about changes in the conditions under which composers worked. Official posts in the Church and the opera house still remained, but the old system of regularly composing to order no longer held good. Simultaneously there came about a change in the composers' attitude to their art. The utilitarian approach died out, and the musician, at least in his own estimation, became an 'artist', whose aim was at all costs to express *himself*, without restrictions or inhibitions. The new conditions and outlook were part and parcel of the general tendency towards greater freedom, of which the French Revolution and similar smaller movements were but the more violent manifestations. Comparable tendencies are observable among the poets. The rather rigid formalism of the 'Age of Reason' gave way to a more humanistic and natural approach. To the cool, classical poise of an Alexander Pope succeeds the vision of a William Blake, the lyricism of a Shelley. In Germany the new movement, Romanticism,* is represented by such poets as Goethe, Schiller and the brothers August and Friedrich Schlegel. The almost rigid versification of the 18th century, what has been called 'the stiff couplets and clenched quatrains'† was replaced by greater flexibility and variety. The poet *sang*, and the musician, conversely, began to consider himself as a poet in musical sound, a tone-poet.

It is at this time that we find, too, the rise of the 'literary' musician, as well as of the musical literary man. In former times almost all books on music, from *Musica Enchiriadis* onwards, had been of an instructional nature. There were, of course, numerous writings on opera, but these were mostly either propaganda or simply controversial. Aesthetics had hardly been touched, rather naturally as long as composing was regarded largely as a 'job to be done'. The new generation of composer-critics addressed themselves not merely to musicians or students, but to the musically educated public, as in the *Dramatic and Musical Notices* of Carl Maria von Weber (1786 to 1826). Weber was the first of the line, and was followed by Hector Berlioz (1803 to 1869), more appreciated in his lifetime as a musical journalist than as a composer. In 1834 Robert Schumann (1810 to 1856) founded the *New Journal for Music* with the avowed object of encouraging the poetic principle in music. Franz Liszt (1811 to 1886) wrote voluminously on a wide range of subjects, while possibly the most verbose and controversial of all was Richard Wagner (1813 to 1883), whose writings were chiefly designed as propaganda for his own works.

Of the musical *littérateurs* whose writings provided both

---

* Despite what was said in Chapter 1, this label is retained for convenience.

† Louis Untermeyer in *The Albatross Book of Living Verse*.

background and encouragement to the romantic movement, the most important were Johann Paul Richter (1763 to 1825), usually known as Jean Paul, and E. T. A. Hoffmann (1776 to 1822). They were the high priests of Romanticism, and both exerted a great influence on Schumann, who was in some ways the most romantic-minded of all romantic musicians.

We now see a change in the social and cultural background of the musician. Formerly the great composer had most frequently come of a family of musicians. There were, of course, notable exceptions—Handel, son of a surgeon, Haydn, son of a wheelwright, and so on. But we may also think of the Gabrielis, the Scarlattis, the Bach family, Mozart and Beethoven. In any case, the musician was generally of humble origin. With the coming of the romantics we find composers from a wider range of social strata. Berlioz and Spohr were sons of physicians; Schumann's father was a bookseller of considerable culture; Mendelssohn came of a wealthy and cultured family of Jewish bankers. The status, too, of the musician rose. Under the patronage system he normally occupied a subordinate position; now he was admitted to terms of something like equality with wealthy and titled people, while Mendelssohn was on relatively easy terms with the British Royal Family.

The basic aims of the Romantics were, very broadly speaking, freedom and self-expression. The musical results of these aims, again in very general terms, were (a) a greater appreciation of sound as such; (b) a relaxation and broadening of the attitude to the importance and function of form; (c) free and unrestricted expression of personal emotion; (d) a tendency to ally music to some literary or other non-musical background. We may note also the cultivation of small-scale works and concentration on the solo song.

With regard to (a), the vital factor is the development of the orchestra. From Weber and Schubert onwards, new possibilities of colour and sonority are continually explored;

composers are not concerned merely with the music as such, in its melodic and harmonic aspects, but with its actual sound-effect, *i.e.* with the sensuous side. Weber's magic horn which opens the overture to *Oberon* (the horn was considered a most romantic instrument), or Schubert's visionary use of the trombones in his great C major symphony, stand at the beginning. Near the end of the period lies the orchestral virtuosity of Wagner, taken still further by Richard Strauss and Edward Elgar. In between stands Berlioz, who could play only the flute and the guitar, but whose orchestral imagination was unrivalled. His *Traité d'Instrumentation* (1844) is still a standard work. The orchestra tended to increase in size. To Beethoven's standard requirements were added two more horns and three trombones. Berlioz, in some of his works, demands huge forces, and Wagner's colossal music-dramas needed an orchestra of comparable size—triple wood wind, as many as eight horns, and so on. But the introduction of new or extra instruments was not merely to achieve a greater volume of sound; both Berlioz and Wagner are sparing in their use of the full orchestra. Composers wanted a wider range of colour. Anyone who has heard the *Ring* will realise that, for example, *only* the bass clarinet could produce the exact psychological effect that Wagner intended in certain cases.

The romantics' attitude to form is expressed in Berlioz's statement that music must not be based on 'rule' but on 'direct reaction to feeling'. Liszt says much the same: 'The artist may pursue the beautiful outside the rules of the school.' The interaction of form and content has always presented composers with a problem. The early symphonists of the *galant* style often solved this problem by almost eliminating any worth-while meaning. Much of their work is little more than well-ordered patterning with notes. Haydn and Mozart had the genius to combine structural stability with vital content, within the accepted limits of classical form. The musical god of the romantic school was Beethoven; to them he was the great emancipator who 'broke the bonds of form'. Beethoven was quite as much of a 'self-expressionist' as any professed romantic; but they seem at times to have overlooked the fact that however far he may have departed from the classical forms of Haydn and Mozart, however much he may have adapted form in order to express his meaning, he was still the great architect. His forms can still stand as examples of structural perfection.

The formal problems of the romantics were intensified by their fondness for illustrative music, since a 'programme', whether an actual story or merely some more or less vaguely poetical background, would not necessarily fit into the confines of a classical form. Berlioz's programme symphonies, the *Fantastic* and *Harold in Italy*, still retain, broadly, the traditional outlines. The former has five movements instead of the usual four and uses a kind of motto theme, the *idée fixe*, which acts as a psychological connecting thread. But there is no attempt at a complete break with tradition; they are symphonies with a programme, but still symphonies. (At least one writer has argued that Berlioz is actually more of a classic than a romantic.) Liszt, however, realised that the idea of programme music could only be carried out logically by breaking with formal tradition and allowing the form to be dictated by the programme in each individual case. Hence his adoption of the title *symphonic poem*, and hence, also, the varied forms of his works in this *genre*. Liszt was also largely responsible for developing the system of thematic metamorphosis, by which means ideas or characters can be shown in different lights or situations. The principle is that a basic theme can be varied in character, and consequently in meaning and significance, by some kind of modification, often, though not necessarily, rhythmic. Examples from *Les Préludes* (of which, by the way, the programme was written after the music, not before it) will make this clear. In the opening 'Moods of Spring and Love' appears this theme:

Ex. 21

changed a little later to:

Ex. 22

In the next section, 'Storms of Life', it is modified to:

Ex. 23

and later to:

Ex. 24

Finally, in 'Strife and Victory', it becomes:

Ex. 25

Although the symphonic poem originated from the symphony, it did not replace it; the two forms have tended to run parallel, each developing on its own lines. The first important symphonist of the romantic era was Franz Schubert (1797 to 1828). His early symphonies are in the Mozart tradition, relatively brief and essentially tuneful. Schubert was, and remains, unexcelled as a melodist, and next to Mozart he was possibly the most naturally gifted of all composers. In his last two symphonies, the great C major and the *Unfinished*, he showed himself capable of thinking in a really extended and dramatic manner, yet without losing anything of his essential tunefulness. He effected a fusion of the dramatic and the lyrical. The C major may seem to some to be diffuse and repetitive— Schumann remarked on the 'heavenly length' of its second movement—but not a bar can be cut without marring the symmetry and balance. Schubert died before the romantic attitude to form was fully defined, but in his *Wanderer Fantasie* for piano, he looked forward to later developments in his use of the 'cyclic' principle. This involves the derivation, by metamorphosis, of some, if not all, of the thematic material of later movements from that stated initially, either in an introduction or in the exposition of the first movement. In the *Wanderer* the opening subject is the basis of the principal material of each of the three succeeding movements. The cyclic idea is a method—mechanical, though its results may be musical enough—of ensuring, or endeavouring to ensure, the homogeneity of a work as a whole;* a homogeneity which the great classics achieved superbly without any such adventitious aid.

Chronologically the next important symphonist is Berlioz, whose methods have already been briefly considered. Then comes Mendelssohn (1809 to 1847).† He has been described as a romantic-classicist—romantic in his attitude to musical sound and in his lyricism, classic in his attitude to form.

* The principle is seen as far back as the 16th century in the 'cyclic' masses, *i.e.* those in which material such as a plainsong tune is used thematically for the various movements. It may even be traced as far back as Machaut—see the remark on p. 58 regarding his use of a basic motive.

† His full name was Jakob Ludwig Felix Mendelssohn-Bartholdy.

To him, Beethoven was not the breaker of the bonds of form; he was rather the perfector of it. Mendelssohn rarely touches great depths; there is, in fact, a not infrequent tendency to shallowness in his work. He lacks the fire of a Berlioz, the earnestness of a Schumann, the histrionic ability (and weakness) of a Liszt. But of all the romantics he was perhaps the finest craftsman and in this may be compared with Mozart. Like his great predecessor, he understood 'economy of means', and while he never indulged in orchestral virtuosity, there was little he did not know about the orchestra and its possibilities, in so far as they were applicable to his own rather limited style. His *Italian* symphony, for example, is full of the deftest touches, which are a delight both to the amateur and to the trained musician. The two flutes wandering about at the top of the score in the slow movement, for instance, and the 'horns of elfland faintly blowing' in the trio of the minuet*—even though two of them are bassoons:

Ex. 26

Schumann's four symphonies, while containing much delightful music, are marred by his lack of ability as an orchestrator. Structurally the most interesting is No. 4 (originally No. 2), which makes some use of the cyclic principle.

This same principle was used by Liszt in his two symphonies, which are really extended symphonic poems with a non-musical background. Their titles are *Symphony on Dante's Divine Comedy* and *A Faust Symphony*. Both make great use of thematic metamorphosis, and both include choral parts. Perhaps the most outstanding example of

* A volume could be written on the romantics' fondness for the horn. From Weber to Strauss, none could resist its allure.

formal experiment on cyclic lines was Liszt's piano sonata
in B minor. It is in one huge movement, retaining the
essential outlines of sonata form. The working out is interrupted by an *intermezzo* which serves as a slow movement,
after which development is resumed in fugal style. Practically all the thematic material is derived from three terse
subjects announced in the introduction.

The 19th century saw the rise of the concert overture.
Apart from their function as introductions to operas or oratorios, numerous overtures had been written to plays, *e.g.*
Beethoven's *Coriolanus,* or for special occasions, *e.g.* his *Con-
secration of the House,* written for the opening of the Joseph-
stadt Theatre in Vienna. With Mendelssohn's *Hebrides*
overture (1830, revised 1832) the title appears with a new
signification—a single movement, at first usually based on
sonata form, not introducing anything—and not even necessarily used to 'open' a concert. Although many such works
have been written as abstract music—Beethoven, for instance, wrote one about 1807, describing it as a 'Characteristic Overture'—most have a more or less programmatic
background; they are a kind of miniature symphonic
poem. The *Hebrides* was inspired by a visit to those islands.
Wagner's *Faust Overture,* originally intended as the first
movement of a symphony, is another great example.

Chamber music did not attract the romantics as it did
their predecessors. Schubert's quartets, etc., develop from
those of Mozart and Beethoven; in many ways he had the
classic outlook. But for most of the romantics the string
quartet and allied forms were too purely abstract; they
were not really suitable *media* for the expression of 'direct
reaction to feeling'. Mendelssohn, classically minded, wrote
some fine works and Schumann also produced a few, of
which the best-known and possibly the finest is the *Piano
Quintet* in E flat. In any case, chamber music was primarily domestic music, or at least was originally conceived
as such, and domestic music-making now began to change
its character. From being mainly a concerted affair, as

it had been since the days of the *sonata a tre,* it became more a matter for a solo performer; the domestic supremacy of the piano now begins, with such composers as Mendelssohn, with his *Songs without Words,* and Schumann, with his numerous small-scale pieces (*Fantasiestücke, Scenes of Childhood, Waldscenen,* etc.), to supply the literature. Such works as Beethoven's *Bagatelles,* terse mood-pictures, had pointed the way, but the intensive cultivation of the short, possibly miniature composition is an outcome of romanticism. In their little tone pictures, the composers could express themselves in a concentrated and intimate manner, in contrast to the expansiveness of their more extended works.

It is a rather odd contradiction that the romantic era, while stressing for the first time the small-scale tone picture, was also the era of the greatest virtuosity. We have noted how the Italian violinists tended gradually to exalt the soloist in their concertos, and mention has been made of the rise of the display concerto in the latter part of the 18th century. The purely technical difficulty of concert works, whether concertos or sonatas, increased continually, as is evident in those of Beethoven, who, in his early years, was famed as a pianist. But with him the difficulties are a matter of necessity; his thoughts could not be expressed otherwise. There is no suggestion of difficulty for difficulty's sake; it is simply a means to a purely musical end. With such composers as Weber, Thalberg, Herz and Hunten, however, we find a strong tendency to brilliance for its own sake—'showing off'. But the virtuosity of these paled before that of the violinist Nicoló Paganini (1782 to 1840), whose technique was such that many believed him to be in league with the Devil, and who took the art of violin-playing to a stage never yet exceeded. What Paganini could do as a violinist, Liszt decided to emulate at the piano, and achieved his aim. In his early life he spent many years as a touring virtuoso, astounding all Europe by his amazing brilliance. In his compositions for piano he discovered and exploited hitherto unheard-of effects and sonorities, and his influence still persists. Liszt, however, was not merely a purveyor of pianistic fireworks, as were Herz, Hunten and Thalberg. Admittedly he was not averse to playing to the gallery; but his interpretations of Beethoven, for example, were revelatory, while Chopin once wrote: 'I should like to steal from him the way to play my own *Etudes*.'

What Liszt achieved in brilliance, Chopin matched in poetry. He was born, near Warsaw, in 1810, and died in Paris in 1849. Chopin was a pianist pure and simple, and his compositions in other *media* are negligible. Schumann's famous remark, 'Hats off, gentlemen, a genius', is evidence enough of the impression made by his work as early as the variations on *La ci darem la mano*, op. 2. (Admittedly Schumann, in his eagerness to encourage young composers, was rather apt to confuse geese and swans, but in this instance he did not err.) Chopin's *Preludes* and many of his *Mazurkas* show him to be unexcelled as a miniaturist, while such works as the *Polonaises* and the *Ballades*, especially perhaps the latter, prove his mastery of the larger scale. There is great originality and a strong poetic impulse in everything he wrote, and while his handling of form is at times distinctly unorthodox, it is fundamentally logical. The *Nocturnes** show that as a melodist he stands in the same class as Schubert, while in the *Etudes* he proved that the study of advanced technique need not involve the dullness of a Czerny.

We come now to some consideration of song writing, an art which comes to the fore for the first time since the days of the Elizabethan lutenists. Not that it had ever been entirely neglected. Both Mozart and Beethoven wrote a certain number of songs, while Johann Rudolf Zumsteeg (1760 to 1802) was a pioneer of the dramatic and narrative ballad. The aim of this form is the description of an event,

* The nocturne, which Chopin raised to the highest pitch of perfection, was given its character, of a melody with arpeggio accompaniment, by the Irishman John Field (1782-1837). It is not the same as the 18th-century *Notturno* meaning literally 'night-music', as used by Mozart in K. 286.

or chain of events. Zumsteeg was followed by the much
greater Carl Loewe (1796 to 1869), whose ballads often
achieve considerable vividness and dramatic power. We
may also note Mendelssohn's teacher, Carl Zelter (1765
to 1832) and Johann Reichardt (1752 to 1814), both of
whom helped to found and develop the German *lied* or
'art song'. Songs of their time are normally strophic, that
is, the same music is used, basically, for each of several
verses, and the voice part is fundamentally a tune. The
instrumental part is a subordinate accompaniment. In
Zumsteeg's ballads, however, the instrumental part is often
of greater importance, not so much a mere accompaniment
as a commentary on the words, and it is in this that we see
the beginnings of the fully developed *lied*, a duet for voice
and piano, in which the instrumental part is as important
as that for the voice.

The first, and in the opinion of many the greatest, exponent of the true *lied* was Schubert. His enormous output of songs, over 600, covers every style, from the simplicity
of the well-known *Heidenröslein* to the intense drama of
Erlkönig. In the former the accompaniment is so slender
that it could almost be dispensed with; in the latter, the
piano part is at least half the making of the song. In
his treatment of the vocal part, Schubert covers an enormous range. *Heidenröslein* might almost be a folk-song;
An die Musik gives us sophisticated melody of extraordinary
beauty; while in *Erlkönig* we have dramatic recitative of
awesome intensity. *Erlkönig* is almost a complete exposition of Romanticism in itself. The storm, the supernatural element, the terrified child, the frenzied galloping
of the horse, and the final tragic climax—'In his arms the child
lay dead'—with the vivid characterisation, are all typical.

Schubert's choice of poems was wide and varied, sometimes perhaps too much so, since his amazing facility—he
once wrote eight songs in a single day—led him at times to
set verses of poor quality. But whatever the value of the
words, the settings themselves always show the maximum

of insight. Schubert was not only born to be a musician;
he was born to be a song writer, and had he written nothing
else, his fame would be assured. Apart from separate songs,
Schubert wrote the song-cycles *Die Schöne Müllerin* ('The
Beautiful Maid of the Mill') and *Die Winterreise* ('Winter
Journey'), the words of both being by the poet Wilhelm
Müller. The idea of a song-cycle is a group of songs with
a continuous underlying theme or story, so that the whole
series constitutes an entity. The idea was not new. The
first known example dates from the early years of the 17th
century. Under the German title of *Liederkreis* (song-*circle*),
Beethoven's *An die ferne Geliebte* ('To the Distant Beloved')
of 1816 antedates Schubert's *Maid of the Mill* by seven years.
Since Schubert's time, numbers of such cycles have been
written, notably Schumann's *Frauenliebe und Leben* ('Woman's
Love and Life') and *Dichterliebe* ('A Poet's Love').

In these, as in all his songs, Schumann proves himself
the true inheritor of the tradition established by Schubert.
Like his predecessor, his treatment of the vocal part is
infinitely varied, as is his inventiveness on the instrumental
side. Schumann wrote no songs until 1840, the year of
his marriage to Clara Wieck. This victory after a long
struggle against the opposition of his prospective father-in-
law unlocked the floodgates of song, and in the one year
he wrote over one hundred. Unlike Schubert, Schumann
rarely if ever set words which lacked some literary distinction.

Of Schumann's contemporaries, Mendelssohn looks back
rather to the strophic style of Zelter and Reichardt, in
which the voice part predominates. Liszt is represented
by a collection of fifty-five songs (1860), many of which,
although hardly comparable in value to those of Schubert
and Schumann, are in the true *lied* tradition. After Liszt
the line passes through Brahms and Hugo Wolf. Brahms
will be considered later. Wolf (1860 to 1903) developed
the 'duet' principle of the *lied* to the limit, and no song-
writer has ever created a juster balance between words and

music. He may best be summed up by a quotation from Grove: 'A song to him was poetry absorbed and recreated in terms of something which was neither melody by itself nor mere declamation, but a fusion of the two.' Hair-splitting arguments as to whether or not he was the greatest of all song-writers are immaterial; we may say that, like Schubert, what he did not know about the writing of songs was not worth the knowing. But, unlike Schubert, he knew little else; songs were his life.

If Mendelssohn was a romantic classicist, Johannes Brahms (1833 to 1897) may be described as a classic romanticist. His early works, *e.g.* the three piano sonatas, the *Scherzo* in E flat minor, etc., are very clearly the production of a whole-hearted romantic outlook. Schumann took him to his heart, and in his article 'New Paths', written in 1853, referred to him as 'one man who would be singled out to make articulate in an ideal way the highest expression of our time, one man who would bring us mastery. . . . Seated at the piano, he at once discovered to us wondrous regions . . . an altogether inspired style of playing which made of the piano an orchestra of lamenting and exultant voices.' This of an unknown youngster of twenty. But Brahms, as he developed, controlled his essential romanticism by a classic regard for form. Not for him were the structural experiments of a Liszt, the discarding of 'rule' advocated by Berlioz. Like Beethoven, he found it possible to express himself to the full, with as much intensity as any belligerent romantic, without disregarding the vital necessity of structural stability and without the continual need for some literary or programmatic impulse. He was, in fact, the true successor of Beethoven, even though he had not quite the same complete mastery of form. Like Beethoven, too, he was a master of variation-writing, his sets on a theme of Handel, on the *St. Anthony Chorale* and on the theme of Paganini ranking with those of the older master and of Bach.

Although Brahms was far from making consistent use of

cyclic methods, there are occasional instances in his work.
In the first piano sonata, op. 1, the first subject of the last
movement is clearly derived from that of the first.

Ex. 27

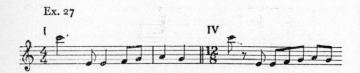

There are occasional instances of thematic cross-referencing,
as in the third symphony where the first subject of the opening movement returns, metamorphosed in significance, to
round off the last. A more subtle case occurs in the second
and fourth movements of the same work. The second
subject of the former:

Ex. 28

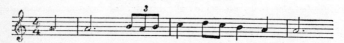

gives rise in the latter to:

Ex. 29

Sir Edward Elgar made the penetrating remark that the
latter is the 'tragic outcome' of the former.

The subtlety that lies in the art of concealing art is often
evident in Brahms. We may instance the G major violin
sonata, in which the three movements are related by the
persistence of a rhythmic motive:

Ex. 30

This kind of thing is far from being obvious, and it is not until the work has been carefully studied that its significance is realised. Similarly, in the second symphony, where the basic motive is melodic:

Ex. 31

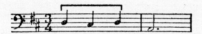

The essential fall and rise of a step occurs in the thematic material of all the movements, being inverted in the third. This kind of 'germinal' procedure was not invented by Brahms, though it clearly opened up a path which has been followed by many later composers. It is seen in Beethoven's *5th Symphony*, where the basic idea of a three-note anacrusis to an accent is quite clear in the first, third and last movements:

Ex. 32

To what extent this was intentional is arguable. Such interrelationships may quite well arise without the composer being aware of them, only to be pointed out after the event by the keen-eyed analyst. Similarly, in the piano sonata, op. 110, where the subject of the fugue:

Ex. 33

may (or may not) be derived from the first subject of the first movement:*

Ex. 34

Brahms approached the symphony with diffidence, his first, in C minor, being produced when he was forty-three years old. He was no orchestral virtuoso, though he had as keen an appreciation of tone-colour as most of his contemporaries. But he rarely insists on sound as such; rather it is the music itself which he forces on our attention. It has sometimes been suggested that Brahms 'could not score', but this is a misstatement. His use of the orchestra, however far removed from that of a Berlioz or a Wagner, is an integral part of his style. A Brahms symphony rescored would cease to be Brahms.

Brahms' classic tendencies are seen in his output of chamber music, which contains some of his finest work. His handling of the instruments is irreproachable, as is his

* It may be well to point out that this game of tracing thematic relationships can be carried to idiotic extremes. If taken far enough it can lead to such fatuity as suggesting that the fugue subject in Brahms' E minor 'cello sonata is derived from the opening of the *St. Matthew Passion*! The reader may care to work this out for himself.

feeling for the appropriate style. Unlike some later composers, he never tries to make a quartet sound like a string orchestra, nor does he 'stunt' with the instruments. As a first-rate pianist himself, it is natural that many of his works for the instrument are of considerable technical difficulty, but here again the classic outlook appears. Even in the two concertos Brahms does not indulge in virtuosity for its own sake; the most difficult or brilliant passages are an integral part of the work, not mere flashy display. The same applies to the far from easy violin concerto. In his later years Brahms produced a number of short but intensely concentrated *Intermezzi* and *Capricci*. They are in varied styles, the *Intermezzi* being in steady *tempo* and the *Capricci* less so. Each is a complete little tone-poem, pin-pointing a mood with singular clarity and distinction, and each is in a perfectly balanced form.

In his songs Brahms relies more on melody than on declamation; while not by any means reducing the piano part to a mere subordinate accompaniment, he tends on the whole to tip the balance in favour of the voice. The strophic plan of treatment is most usual, and in many of the songs there are influences from the German *Volkslied* or folksong. No song-writer surpassed him in emotional intensity or intimacy of expression. His last published compositions were the *Four Serious Songs*, to biblical words, which form a fitting apotheosis to the work of one who, while not perhaps greatly interested in the niceties of ecclesiastical dogma, was one of the most sincere and earnest-minded of all the great musicians.

It remains to deal briefly with choral works of the romantic period. The church music is rarely of any great value. The Masses of Schubert, despite fine moments, lack the true liturgical appropriateness of, say, the Bach cantatas, while many by other composers, *e.g.* Liszt and Schumann, were conceived chiefly as 'concert Masses'. In his oratorios *St. Paul* and *Elijah* Mendelssohn developed the Handel tradition, with some admixture of Bach, in his own idiom;

Liszt's *Christus* and *St. Elizabeth* are effective and highly characteristic of their composer.

Possibly the greatest sacred choral work of the period is Brahms's *German Requiem*, for which the impulse came primarily from the death of his mother in 1865. It is not a requiem Mass, but rather a meditation on death—a forerunner of the *Four Serious Songs*. In it, as in his other choral works—the *Triumph Song*, the *Song of Destiny* and the *Alto Rhapsody*—Brahms proved that his mastery of choral writing was no less than of any other branch of music.

RECORDS

Composer	Title	Catalogue No.
Schubert	Symphonies Nos. 5 and 8	139162
	Symphony No. 9	139043
	Piano Quintet (*The Trout*)	SAL 3621
	Die Schöne Müllerin	ASD 481
	Winterreise	2707 028
	Der Erlkönig (also songs by Wolf and Strauss)	ASD 2404
Mendelssohn	Symphonies Nos. 4 and 5	SAL 3727
	Symphony No. 3 and *Hebrides* Overture	SAX 2342
Berlioz	Overtures, including *Roman Carnival*	SAL 3573
	Symphonie Fantastique	138 964
Schumann	Symphonies Nos. 1 and 4	138 860
	Piano Concerto	SAX 4285
	Dichterliebe, Op. 48 ⎱ *Liederkreis*, Op. 24 ⎰	139 109
	Various Piano Pieces (inc. Abegg vars., etc.)	139 183
	Piano Quintet	72429
Chopin	Piano Concerto No. 1 in E minor	139 383
	Ballades and Études	SXL 6143
	Polonaises	139 420
	Preludes	72943
	Sonata in B minor ⎱ Sonata in B minor ⎰	HQS 1246
Liszt	Hungarian Rhapsodies for Piano (complete.)	TV 34266–8DS
	Hungarian Rhapsodies 1–4 for Orchestra	SXLP 20094
	Les Préludes	139 037
	Piano Concerto in E flat	139 383

Composer	Title	Catalogue No.
Brahms	Piano Concerto in B flat	2530 111
	Violin Concerto and Double Concerto	SLS 786
	Symphony No. 1	ASD 2401
	Symphony No. 2 and Alto Rhapsody	ASD 2746
	Symphony No. 3 and St. Anthony Variations	138 926
	Sympony No. 4	ASD 2560
	Various Piano Pieces including Rhapsodies, Ballades Intermezzi, etc.	SB 6845
	Violin Sonata	ASD 2618
	Four Serious Songs	135 161
	Lieder Recital	ASD 2555
	A German Requiem	SLS 821

CHAPTER FIFTEEN

ROMANTIC OPERA

IN Chapter 12 a brief sketch was given of the way in which the character of opera changed in France and Italy in the period around 1800. In Germany similar changes came about, leading to the style which is usually known as Romantic Opera. As in France, new tendencies appear in the latter part of the 18th century, the first use of the term 'romantic' being in the subtitle of Gotthilf von Baumgarten's setting of a libretto based on that of Grétry's *Zémire et Azor*. It is described as a 'Romantic-Comic Opera'. As well as the lack of conventions which was typical of the *singspiel*, as it was of *opera buffa* and *opéra comique*, we find also the fondness for the fantastic and the Oriental. 'Turkish' opera was a distinct fashion from about 1770 onwards, in Italy, France and Germany,* while Wranitzky's *Oberon, King of the Fairies* may be considered the prototype of the 'fairy-tale opera', of which the best known example is perhaps Humperdinck's *Hansel and Gretel* of 1893.

Weber is usually regarded as the real founder of German romantic opera. His *Der Freischütz*, completed in 1820, raised the *singspiel* to a new level (it has spoken dialogue), while the plot contains all the ingredients which were so dear to the romantics—magic, the supernatural (one of the characters has sold his soul to the Devil), and so on. Especially notable are the vividness of the orchestration and the general effectiveness of both solo and choral writing. *Euryanthe*, which followed in 1823, is based on a medieval plot, and discards the spoken dialogue; it is a full-dress 'grand' opera. *Oberon* (1826) returns to spoken dialogue, and is the direct successor of Wranitzky's work of the same name.

* Mozart's *Seraglio* is an example.

Weber's treatment of the overture shows a notable advance. We have seen how Gluck insisted that the overture should prepare the audience for the opera itself, and how Mozart, in *Don Giovanni*, opens with a reference to the dramatic climax of the whole work. Weber builds his overtures almost entirely from material which is to be used later, thereby stressing still further their integral function.

The romantic style was followed by Heinrich Marschner (1795 to 1861), whose *The Vampire* (1823) and *Templar and Jewess* (1829, based broadly on Scott's *Ivanhoe*) show it at its crudest and most violently melodramatic. His best work is *Hans Heiling* (1833). This is notable for the plan of the prologue, in which spoken dialogue and set 'numbers' are dispensed with. It is 'through-composed', a *continuous* movement for solo and chorus, foreshadowing the continuity on which Wagner insisted in his later works. This style was taken farther by Louis Spohr in his *The Crusaders* (1845) which, to quote the composer's own words, is 'through-composed . . . somewhat as a musical drama'. The use of the term 'musical drama' is significant. Wagner, at that time thirty-two years old, entitled his later works 'music drama' rather than 'opera'.

Schumann's one opera, *Genoveva*, was a complete failure on its production in 1850. Although the value of much of the music was recognised by at least one of the critics, it was hardly theatrical enough for the audiences of the time. It was criticised, too, for its lack of separate 'numbers'. Otto Jahn, the biographer of Mozart, remarked on the great amount of effort it demanded of the listeners, and complained that the possibility of the singers 'being accorded immediate applause is eliminated'. Audiences were as yet far from being trained to sit silent through the hour and a half (or more) which Wagner sometimes demands for a single act, and the singers still preferred the separate recitative and aria, at the end of which they could receive their meed of clapping and *bravos*.

With Richard Wagner (1813 to 1883) we come to the

great reformer of opera, who, in his approach, was the lineal descendant of Gluck. For the greater part of his life he had to struggle against adversity, often, it must be admitted, due to his own impetuosity and lack of consideration for others. In 1849 he had to flee from Germany, chased by a warrant for his arrest as a 'politically dangerous individual', and after a short stay in Paris, settled in Zürich. He was banned from returning to Germany until 1861, when he received permission to re-enter any state except Saxony, where his political activities had originally led to his exile. The ban on Saxony was lifted in 1862. In 1864 he at last achieved an assured position, thanks to the generosity of Ludwig II of Bavaria. At Bayreuth was erected the Festival Theatre, and here he was able to superintend the production of his works on the scale and in the manner which he had always intended but had rarely, if ever, achieved.

Both as a musician and a reformer, Wagner developed slowly. His few early non-operatic works—the piano sonata, op. 1, for example—give no hint of the genius of the *Ring* or the *Mastersingers*, nor do his first two operas, *Die Feen* and *Das Liebesverbot*. The former had to wait until five years after his death for its first performance, while the latter, produced in 1834, was an utter failure. *Rienzi*, his next work, is a grand opera in the manner of Meyerbeer, and as blatant as any work of that composer. In the *Flying Dutchman* (1841), however, we find strong pointers to what was to come. The story is in the best romantic tradition, and is notable also as being a northern legend. A cardinal doctrine of the later Wagner was that plots for operas should be based on folk-lore. Musically the *Dutchman* carries on the tendency to continuity which is seen in such works as *Hans Heiling*. The orchestra begins to occupy a more important position, tending to provide a commentary on the action. The use of the *leit-motif* principle also begins to develop—the principle which is so vital in the thematic construction and the texture of the later works.

The *leit-motif* or 'leading theme' is a passage, generally short, associated with some particular character, scene, idea, etc. It may be primarily melodic, harmonic, rhythmic, or a combination of them. As used by Wagner in his later works, leading themes not only serve in an illustrative capacity, but also give coherence and unity. Their use in the *Flying Dutchman* is undeveloped, but the principle begins to emerge. Of *Tannhäuser* (produced 1845) and *Lohengrin* (completed 1848), both based on Teutonic legends, the latter shows the greater advance in technique. It also shows the musical side of Wagner's nature rapidly developing. While there are still passages which look back to the style of *Rienzi*, though fewer than in *Tannhäuser*, there are others, the prelude to Act 1, for example, in which we can see that whatever Wagner may have thought of himself as poet, dramatist, or what not, he matters most as a musician.

During his exile, Wagner did a great deal of heavy thinking on the problems of opera, expounding his arguments and conclusions in his essays *Art and Revolution* (1849), *The Art Work of the Future* (1850) and *Opera and Drama* (1852). Briefly, and very broadly, his conclusions may be summarised as follows. Opera must go back to the original aims of its founders, and be thought of as musical drama. All the factors concerned—libretto, singing, acting, staging, the orchestra, etc., are of equal importance. The music must no longer be allowed to override the unfolding of the drama; it must be the means of expression of it, not an end in itself. The action must not be held up by the 'set number'; it must unfold continuously. The aria as such must therefore be discarded. The vocal writing must vary between pure recitative and song-like melody, according to the needs of the situation at any given moment. The orchestra, utilising a texture of leading themes, will give a continuous commentary on the action, and must begin, in the overture, by 'exciting our feeling from a general state of tension to a special sensation of premonition'. The plot should be based on national legend, cast into alliterative poetry. We may note that Wagner always wrote his own *libretti*.

In *Rhinegold*, the first of the huge tetralogy of music dramas known as *The Ring of the Nibelungen*,* Wagner carries out his theories with considerable strictness, but in the remaining three, as well as in his other works, *Tristan and Isolda*, *The Mastersingers of Nuremberg*, and *Parsifal*, the musician pure and simple cannot be restrained, so that the music itself tends to become the predominant factor. Not that he ever dropped back to the 'melody opera' of former times. But, as Prof. Gerald Abraham says,† 'Wagner was no rigid doctrinaire'. The poem of *Tristan* is not entirely alliterative, while that of *The Mastersingers* is in normal rhymed verse. The 'set piece' appears, even in *The Valkyrie*; Siegmund's *Spring Song* is an example. Still more outside the strict theory of *Opera and Drama* is the quintet in the last act of *The Mastersingers*, of which Mr. Ernest Newman once remarked that it has no right to be there at all, and yet is the emotional climax of the whole work. The way in which the whole action is held up while five people express their feelings and emotions is almost pure 18th century; but nobody, in the face of such sheer beauty, is likely to cavil on that account. The increasingly important role of the orchestra is evidenced by the fact that sections of the music dramas are sometimes performed as concert pieces, without voices at all. The orchestra, in fact, tells the story in its own idiom; it provides, as it were, an illustrative symphonic poem which runs concurrently with the action on the stage. It must be realised that Wagner, although rightly called a reformer, did not simply sit down and think out in cold blood a new way of writing opera. From the *Dutchman* onwards his ideas gradually crystallised, reaching their full expression in the *Ring* and later works.

* The others, in order, are *The Valkyrie*, *Siegfried*, and *The Twilight of the Gods*.

† In *A Hundred Years of Music*.

Wagner was not only an operatic reformer; he was also a harmonic innovator, or rather developer. In this direction he was to some extent indebted to Liszt, with whom he was for long on terms of intimacy, and whose daughter Cosima he married as his second wife. Liszt's harmonic innovations are at times quite startling, and in some of his latest piano works he anticipates procedures which are customarily associated more with such a composer as Debussy, who was not born until 1862. Wagner was not eager to admit what he had learned from Liszt, though he did so once, in a somewhat secretive manner, in a letter to Hans von Bülow, Cosima's first husband. Broadly speaking, his harmony developed in the direction of intense use of chromaticism, and a loosening of the bonds of key. He did not, like some of his successors, attempt to 'invent' a new system; he simply expanded on the basis of tradition, thereby creating a system which was perfectly adapted to his own expressive ends.

At the other end of the operatic scale from Wagner stands his great contemporary Giuseppe Verdi (1813 to 1901). Verdi was no reformer. He was brought up in the Italian tradition, in which vocal melody was all-important, and raised the style to its highest point. To the Wagnerians his name was anathema, since he stood for all that they despised in opera. His operatic career falls into four periods. The first was a time of apprenticeship, up to 1850, during which he had more or less success with works which are now almost forgotten, such as *Oberto* and *Ernani*. In these the style of Bellini and Donizetti is evident. In the second period are *Rigoletto*, *Il Trovatore* and *La Traviata*. In these he really found himself, taking the style of Donizetti to a climax, but with greater dramatic power and greater earnestness than the older man had ever achieved. To Verdi, despite his adherence to tradition in the importance of the voice and the relative unimportance of the orchestra, opera was far from being a mere 'concert in costume'; it was a serious matter, as it was to the Wagnerians. Mention of opera, or art in general, as 'entertainment' infuriated him. Even in his early operas his characters are alive; they are not mere stage puppets. And however melodramatic he may seem at times, there is always underlying sincerity.

The third period begins, from 1855, with *The Sicilian Vespers*, written for Paris; this is grand opera to the French taste. It is followed by three purely Italian operas, *Simone Boccanegra*, *The Masked Ball* and *The Force of Destiny*, and then another work for Paris, *Don Carlos*. In all of these there is increasing control of the medium and increasing importance is given to the orchestra. The climax of this period comes with *Aida*, a grand opera in every sense of the word. It was written to order, for the opening of the Suez Canal in 1871, at a time when the practice of commissioning operas had fallen into disuse. But Verdi, who took no small part in the shaping of the libretto, found no difficulty in providing a really great work.

Until 1887 Verdi wrote no more operas, but in that year he produced *Othello*, and in 1893 *Falstaff*, both based on the Shakespearian characters. In them a transfigured style is seen. Without imitating Wagner, though there is some use of the *leit-motif* principle, Verdi makes of *Othello* a music drama, with highly expressive declamation and a rich and subtle use of the orchestra. *Falstaff* is the apotheosis of *opera buffa*, but at the same time employs the principle of music drama as seen through the eyes of its composer.

Neither Wagner nor Verdi wrote much of importance apart from their stage works. Wagner's *Faust* overture has already been mentioned. His only other notable work is the *Siegfried Idyll*, of such beauty that we can only regret its lack of successors. Verdi's one great non-operatic work is the *Requiem Mass* which, although it may appear superficially to be rather theatrical in conception and outlook, is nevertheless of the greatest power and sincerity.

Wagner's ideas have affected, to a greater or less degree, almost every writer of operas since his day, including Englebert Humperdinck (1854 to 1921), whose one really successful work, *Hansel and Gretel*, has been described as 'Wagner for children'. Of non-Wagnerian works, Otto Nicolai's *Merry Wives of Windsor* (1849) is a delightful example of German *opera buffa*, while Peter Cornelius's *Barber of Baghdad* (1858), though never a great success, exhibits its composer's fine lyrical talent.

In Italy, Verdi's most important successors were Ruggiero Leoncavallo, Pietro Mascagni and Giacomo Puccini. The first two of these are famous chiefly for one work each, *Pagliacci* and *Cavalleria Rusticana* respectively. Both composers had a more than adequate feeling for dramatic, sometimes melodramatic effect. Their use of the orchestra is approximately that of the late Verdi, and the aria, without being obviously obtrusive, still holds its place in their work. Puccini was a greater musician, showing to some extent Wagnerian influence in the musically sustained interest of his scenes and in his modified use of the *leit-motif*. While not a 'modern' in the colloquial sense, his harmony shows some originality, and his orchestration is masterly. Although his popularity rests mainly on such operas as *La Bohème*, *Tosca* and *Madame Butterfly*, he reached perhaps his greatest heights in his last, unfinished work, *Turandot*.

In France the style of Meyerbeer's grand opera was followed by Jacques Halévy (1799 to 1862), now known only by *La Juive*. Berlioz, too, produced *Benvenuto Cellini* and *The Trojans*, of which the latter, at least, is a greater work than the rarity of its performance would suggest. The more lyrical opera is represented by Gounod's *Faust* (1859) and *Romeo and Juliet* (1867), Félicien David's *Lalla Rookh* (1862) and Ambroise Thomas's *Mignon* (1866), in all of which the accent is on lyrical melody, with a complete lack of anything Wagnerian. Rather later (1877) is Saint-Saëns's well-known *Samson and Delilah*.

Possibly the greatest French opera of the period is *Carmen* (1875) by Georges Bizet (1838 to 1875). Despite some use of a pseudo-Spanish idiom, it is typically French in its economy and deftness, while the orchestration is masterly.

Bizet, notwithstanding some limitations, was possibly the most naturally gifted French musician of his time, and in *Carmen* he produced a masterpiece.

RECORDS

Composer	Title	Catalogue No.
Weber	Overtures	STU 70568
	Freischütz and *Oberon* (excerpts)	SXL 6077
Wagner	Overtures to *Rienzi* and *Lohengrin* excerpts from *Die Walküre*	PFS 4205
	Die Meistersinger (complete)	SLS 957
	The Flying Dutchman (complete)	SLS 934
	The Flying Dutchman (excerpts)	ASD 2724
	Götterdämerung (complete)	SET 292/7
	Götterdämerung (excerpts)	SXL 6220
	Tristan und Isolde (complete)	SET 204/8
	Tristan und Isolde (excerpts)	136433
Verdi	*Il Trovatore* (complete)	SER 5586/8
	Il Trovatore (excerpts)	ASD 2395
	La Traviata (complete)	SLS 960
	La Traviata (excerpts)	SET 483
	Otello (complete)	SLS 940
	Otello (excerpts)	ASD 2690
	Falstaff (complete)	2BB104/6
	Falstaff (excerpts)	SXL 6079
Mascagni	*Cavalleria Rusticana* (complete)	SET 343/5
	Cavalleria Rusticana (excerpts)	SET 490
Puccini	*Madame Butterfly* (complete)	SLS 927
	Madame Butterfly (excerpts)	ASD 2453
	La Bohème (complete)	SLS 907
	La Bohème (excerpts)	ASD 2271
Bizet	*Carmen* (complete)	SLS 952
	Carmen (excerpts)	ASD 2282
See also	HMS Vol. 15 (Mono only)	HLP 23

CHAPTER SIXTEEN

LATE ROMANTICS
AND NATIONALISTS

IN Chapter 14 some reference was made to developments in harmony and form. We shall now deal briefly with these developments in the hands of a later generation, together with some consideration of national movements. It must be realised that not every composer has been vitally affected by all or any of the newer ideas. A nationalist, for example, may be romantic in his outlook, but not every late romantic was a nationalist. Some composers have pursued new lines of thought to a considerable degree, while others, contemporary with them, have been content to depart little if at all from traditional methods. In the past hundred years, from about the middle of the 19th century, there has been, as has so often happened in earlier ages, a good deal of overlapping of styles. In the present century, for instance, we find the late romanticism of Elgar and Strauss running parallel with the 'advanced' modernity of Schönberg and Bartók.

As we draw nearer to our own times it becomes more and more difficult to assess the value and importance of the work of composers and schools of thought, and to decide which tendencies are likely to have a lasting effect on the development of music. Our judgment of contemporary or near-contemporary art is almost inevitably coloured by personal preference, and we may, as it were, be thrown off our critical balance by the impact of new ideas. An instance of this is to be seen in the case of Alexander Scriabin (1872 to 1915). He began by writing in a kind of post-Chopin idiom, but gradually developed his own advanced and highly personal harmonic style. His later works had a startling effect in the period around the First World War,* and in many quarters he was deemed to have opened up a new path of vital importance. But he is now seen to have dealt merely in a sort of over-ripe romanticism. His new path turned out to be a *cul-de-sac*.

Properly to assess the work of a composer or the value of a trend of thought we need to be at a distance; we have to be able to look back over a period of time, so as to view things whole and to see them in perspective.† Three and a half centuries ago Gesualdo was as startling as was Scriabin between 1910 and 1925; we can now see that his experimentalism was sterile. And it is worth recalling that in their own day Telemann was considered a much greater composer than Bach. We are now far enough from the second half of the 19th century to be able to distinguish what is really important from what is less so.

The pioneers of harmonic development were, as has already been stated, Wagner and Liszt. Not every composer has been equally affected by their innovations, and we find wide differences between contemporaries. Dvořák (1841 to 1904), for example, was content with a relatively limited harmonic vocabulary and a very moderate use of chromaticism; César Franck (1822 to 1890), on the other hand, employed a great deal of high-powered chromaticism. His vocabulary was more extensive and his use of it highly personal.

The Wagnerian tendencies are marked by a broader conception of tonality (key) and an increasingly free use of discord and chromaticism. It is not merely an expansion of the range of keys used within a movement as in the

---

* He was considered so 'advanced' that the late Sir Henry Wood performed his symphonic poem *Prometheus* twice at one concert, so as to give the audience a better chance of understanding it.

† E. F. Benson puts the matter pointedly in his *As We Were*: 'Time acts on sound work much as it does on the vintages of the grape, maturing and bringing out, if the juice be noble, the fuller savour of the sunshine in which the berries ripened, while if it is thin by nature, time only reveals its weakness and age its acidity.'

Eroica symphony and comparable instances. The development lies in the use of chromaticism, sometimes to such
an extent that the tonality becomes almost, if not entirely,
obscured. This 'stretching' of tonality may be illustrated
by the 'Magic Sleep' motive in Wagner's *Valkyrie*:

Ex. 35

There are no 'new' chords here; even the combination at
(*a*) can be explained in purely academic terms. It is the
juxtaposition of the chords and the resultant vagueness of
key which are new. It should not be thought that Wagner
and his followers necessarily employed such methods to the
exclusion of anything else. Their vocabularies included
both the old and the new, and one would merge into the
other according to the expressive needs of the moment. In
Wotan's Farewell (the closing scene of the *Valkyrie*) the passage quoted above is immediately followed by a long stretch
of almost undiluted diatonic writing.

In this advanced chromaticism and the expansion of
tonality we may see a parallel with what happened to the
modal system during the late 16th and early 17th centuries.
The use of *musica ficta* gradually destroyed the individuality
of the modes and paved the way for the major-minor scale

system. The chromaticism of the late 19th century created conditions under which new technical methods could emerge, tending to the disintegration of classical tonality.* In the opinion of some the day of the major-minor system is over. It is not proposed to argue the point here, but it may perhaps be pointed out that there are still composers of international reputation who seem to find something vital to say without severing all links with tradition.

A few aspects of formal development must now be considered. We have seen how Wagner's theories of opera led him to the virtual abolition of the set number and to the greatest possible continuity of dramatic action and musical thought. We have also noted how his use of the orchestra became more and more integral in the structure of his music-dramas. Directly or indirectly, his ideas have affected almost every writer of opera since his day. Not that all have made such consistent use of the leading-theme principle, nor has the orchestra necessarily been used to provide a kind of symphonic poem concurrent with the stage action. But the principle of continuity at least has been taken for granted, together with the employment of the orchestra as something very much more than a mere accompanying instrument.

In instrumental music the developments of the earlier romantics have followed a logical course. We have referred to Berlioz's use of the *ideé fixe* as a method of binding together the movements of a symphony. This is paralleled among the later romantics by the frequent introduction of a 'motto theme'—practically another name for the same thing—announced in an introduction and brought in at dramatically appropriate points in the course of the work. Tschaikovsky (1840 to 1893) provides obvious examples in his 4th and 5th symphonies. In the former the motto reappears (in the first and last movements only) always in the

* A view of the processes as they arose in the work of one composer may be studied in *Arnold Schönberg et son œuvre* by René Leibowitz (Libraire Janin), unfortunately not available in an English translation.

same form and with the same significance as it is originally
stated.   In the latter it recurs in all the later movements,
undergoing some metamorphosis.   There is no particular
subtlety in this, though its effectiveness is undeniable.   The
Brahmsian art of concealing art by the use of a germinal
figure is more subtle and is found, for instance, in Elgar's
1st symphony, where the initial descending four notes of
the motto tend to associate themselves with later material.
We may refer also to Sibelius's 4th symphony with its almost
obsessive insistence on the interval of the augmented 4th.
The work of many composers of the last hundred years
abounds in such thematic interrelationships, though the
extent to which they are deliberate is at times debatable.
A case which we may take as intentional occurs in the 4th
symphony of Dvořák; compare the first subject of the first
movement with the theme of the variations in the *finale*:

Ex. 36

The cyclic principle exhibited in such works as Schubert's
Wanderer Fantasie and Liszt's piano sonata has been widely
adopted, in some cases whole-heartedly, in others only par-
tially.   For the former we may turn to the piano concerto
of Rimsky-Korsakov (1864 to 1908), which copies the Liszt
sonata even to the enunciation of three basic themes in an
introduction.   Partial application of the principle is seen
in Franck's violin sonata and his *Prelude, Aria and Finale*
for piano, among other works.   In his one symphony Franck
uses thematic cross-reference, material from the first two

movements recurring, metamorphosed, in the last. Dvořák takes the idea farther in his *New World* symphony, incorporating themes from the first two movements into the *development* of the *finale*.

The later romantics show further development of Beethoven's attitude to the composition of subject-matter. His treatment of the bridge-passage as part of the thematic material and his tendency to avoid any obvious indication of the beginning of the second group* has led composers to treat the exposition as one consolidated lump of subject-matter. (The way was pointed by Mozart in the last movement of the *Jupiter* symphony.) There is generally something which, from its character and possibly its key, may be labelled as the beginning of the second group, but it is, so to speak, only the first among equals. Elgar's two symphonies provide good examples, including, in the 1st, ideas which occur in both first and second groups.

Another development arising from the romantic outlook is the frequent use of an 'emotional programme' in extended works. The most obvious, and perhaps the most common, is a kind of ascent from darkness to light—(*a*) struggle, (*b*) relaxation, (*c*) triumph. The progenitor is Beethoven's 5th symphony, and among its offspring may be mentioned Franck's symphony, Elgar's 1st, Sibelius's 2nd and Tschaikovsky's 4th and 5th. In his 6th (*Pathétique*) the last-named composer effectively modified what looked like developing into the same programme, ending in the depths of despair.

While the late romantics concerned themselves largely with problems of form, one composer stands out as the inheritor of the classical outlook and the truly architectural mind, the Finn Jean Sibelius (1865 to 1957). Possibly more than any of his contemporaries he achieved an integra-

---

* An excellent example of such a 'concealed opening' occurs in the first movement of the sonata, op. 110. The reader may care to spend some little time deciding exactly where the second group begins.

tion of form and content unsurpassed since Beethoven. From the rather angular sonata form basis of his 1st symphony he progressed, *via* the tremendous compression of the first movement of No. 4 and the 'telescoping' of first movement and *scherzo* of No. 5, to the entirely original structure, in one movement, of No. 7, possibly the greatest masterpiece of musical architecture since Beethoven.* He was a master of 'economy of means', as may be seen in his symphonic poem *Tapiola*. In this, practically everything arises from a single short basic theme, metamorphosis being employed in a masterly fashion.

Development of the symphonic poem is associated largely with Richard Strauss (1864 to 1949). Far more than Liszt he allowed form to be dictated by programme, so that no real understanding of the music is possible without pre-knowledge of the literary background. Where Strauss goes farther than any of his predecessors, and this applies also in some of his operatic writing, is in his use of realism, even to the uncanny reproduction of non-musical sounds such as the bleating of sheep in the second of the *Don Quixote* variations.† The question then arises whether such procedures are musically justifiable. The point cannot be argued here, but it may be pointed out that the principle is merely an extension of that used in, for example, the 'storm' movement of Beethoven's *Pastoral* symphony.

Nationalism has two aspects, the innate and the cultivated. The national or racial characteristics of composers have always tended to show in their music; each race has produced its own interpretation of the common stock of technique and style. We may think, for example, of the earnest approach of the Germans and their frequent tendency to complexity; or of the precision and elegance of the French. No Frenchman could have written the

* Discussion of Sibelius's architecture is impossible here. The reader is referred to *Sibelius*, by Gerald Abraham (Lindsay Drummond).

† The method, for those who are interested, is 'flutter-tonguing' on muted brass.

B minor Mass or the *9th Symphony*. Equally, no German could have written *Carmen*, nor could either have composed *Aida*. But such distinctions of style are instinctive, as are the Englishness of Purcell or Elgar, or the Russianness of Tschaikovsky.

Nationalism in the commonly accepted meaning of the term implies the conscious basing of a composer's idiom on that of the folk-music of his country. Such nationalism arose in the 19th century as a revolt against the shackles of an alien style, and its effects have been as it were local. There has been no question of new basic ideas on structure arising from a nationalist outlook, nor has it given rise to notable developments in the harmonic field. Nationalist composers have followed the prevailing trends to a greater or less degree, according to personal inclination, in the same way as have non-nationalists. Although a national idiom may ultimately become instinctive, it normally begins by deliberate cultivation. This is seen, for example, in the case of Michael Glinka (1804 to 1857), the first of the Russian nationalists. His early works are in the Italian tradition, which up to his time had been considered the only acceptable style in musically educated Russia.* Glinka, having remarked to his teacher Siegfried Dehn that he was tired of the Italian style, was told to 'go home and write Russian music'. This he did in his operas *A Life for the Czar* (1836) and *Russlan and Ludmilla* (1842), and although the 'folk' influence is not so strong in them as it was to become in the work of some of his successors, it was sufficient for their composer to be accused of writing 'coachmen's music'. The libretti are based on national (Russian) stories.

The importance of nationalism lies in the breaking away from alien influence. Leaving aside France, which has

* During the 18th and early 19th centuries the prevailing taste, set by the court, was for Italian opera. Music and musicians were largely imported, such men as Galuppi, Paisiello and Cimarosa holding court positions. Russian musicians were sent to Italy for training and wrote in the Italian style.

always tended to be individualistic in matters of art, all the greatest music from the beginning of the 18th century had emanated from Germany.* No other country had produced composers of the calibre of Bach, Handel, Mozart or Beethoven, and practically all the great developments in music had arisen there. The classical sonata and symphony were of German development; Beethoven the seer was a German; the romantic movement, initiated by German poets, was furthered largely by German composers; Wagner's operatic reforms were the work of a German; and so on. It may be said that as far as Central Europe and England were concerned, 'music' meant 'German music', while in Russia it meant little but Italian opera. The German (or Italian) manner of thought and the technique bound up with it were taken for granted. The nationalist, however, began to think on his own lines, in his own language. The work of the early nationalists enabled their followers to forge a musical language, or idiom, of their own, so that to whatever extent they were affected by the work of the outstanding figures of their generation, they were no longer using the *lingua franca* of German or Italian, but wrote, as it were, in their native tongue.

Considerations of space forbid any detailed account of the work of individual composers, and little more than a mere list of the most important must suffice. In point of time the Russian school, headed by Glinka, led the way. He was followed by Alexander Dargomijsky (1813 to 1869) and the group known as the 'Five', who deliberately adopted the thesis that music should be based on national or 'folk' idiom. They were Alexander Borodin (1833 to 1887), César Cui (1835 to 1918), Mily Balakireff (1837 to 1910), Modeste Mussorgsky (1839 to 1881) and Nicholas Rimsky-Korsakov (1844 to 1908). The founder was Balakireff and the chief propagandist Cui, whose own compositions are curiously devoid of a national idiom.

* In this sense Germany, of course, includes Austria.

Immediately after the Russians came the Bohemians, Frederick Smetana (1824 to 1884), followed by Antonin Dvořák (1841 to 1904). The latter's pupil Vitezslav Novák (1870 to 1949) shows nationalist leanings in his later works. In Spain, lacking music of any particular distinction since the days of Morales and Victoria, a national school was founded by Felipe Pedrell (1841 to 1922), whose influence was asserted mainly through his writings and teaching. Notable among his followers are his pupils Enrique Granados (1867 to 1916) and Manuel de Falla (1876 to 1946); also Isaac Albeniz (1860 to 1909). A generation later are Joaquin Turina (1882 to 1949) and Joaquin Nin (1879-1949).

Of Scandinavians the best-known nationalist is Edvard Grieg (1843 to 1907), a Norwegian of Scottish descent. He was essentially a miniaturist, with a predominantly lyrical talent which served him well in small-scale works. In the larger forms his German training shows prominently, and he is less successful. In Denmark Carl Nielsen (1865 to 1931) has a high reputation.

In England, apart from the work of Arne, music suffered a rapid decline after the death of Purcell. There is a long list of mediocrities, few if any of whom contributed in any way to the development of the main stream of music. Samuel Wesley (1766 to 1837) is notable for some fine Latin motets and for his championship of Bach at a time when his name was hardly known. Wesley's natural son Samuel Sebastian (1810 to 1876) exerted an influence for good on music for the Anglican rite. William Sterndale Bennett (1816 to 1875), friend of Mendelssohn and Schumann, never fulfilled his early promise, largely owing to his professional appointments as Principal of the Royal Academy of Music and Professor of Music at Cambridge University. Arthur Seymour Sullivan (1842 to 1900), despite a varied output of oratorios, cantatas, orchestral works, etc., now lives only by his light operas, with libretti by W. S. Gilbert. They contain a wealth of good tunes and economical and sparkling orchestration. Their social and political satire is now 'dated', but their continued popularity is assured by the music, which, within its inevitable limits, is of great attractiveness.*

Three names herald the real revival of English music, Alexander Mackenzie (1847 to 1935), Hubert Parry (1848 to 1918) and Charles Villiers Stanford (1852 to 1924). While hardly of the first rank, they paved the way for the next generation, many of whom were pupils of Parry and Stanford. Stanford, of Irish birth, was perhaps the most spontaneously gifted. His work has at times an attractive Irish-folky flavour, and some of his songs are perfect gems. Parry was at his best, perhaps, in choral works, where his fine contrapuntal technique, derived from his study of Bach (his book on that composer remains a standard work), has full play.

Born in 1857, the outstanding figure of his generation was Edward Elgar, who died in 1934. Unlike the three composers mentioned above, he had no academic training, but in natural gifts he excelled them all. His early works, while often showing his great gift for melody, give little foretaste of the possibilities realised in the *Enigma Variations* of 1899 and the long list of compositions which followed. In the *Dream of Gerontius*, the two symphonies, the violin and 'cello concertos, and the symphonic study *Falstaff*, to name but a few, Elgar proved his right to be called the greatest English composer since Purcell. His mastery of the orchestra was consummate (though he rarely, if ever, indulged in Straussian 'stunting'), and *Falstaff* showed that in the sphere of illustrative music he had no need to fear competition.

* Mention must not be omitted of Johann Strauss (1825 to 1899), second of the line of great Viennese waltz-kings. His best known operetta, *Die Fledermaus* ('The Bat'), is a complete masterpiece. In view of the ultra-serious view of music which is not uncommon among students and the tendency to look down on 'light' music, it may be worth while to point out that such great artists as Lotte Lehmann and Elisabeth Schumann were quite happy to turn from *The Ring* or *The Mastersingers* and take part in *The Bat*.

The Englishness of Elgar, as of Parry, is of the instinctive, intangible kind; there is no use of a 'folk' idiom. In the work of Ralph Vaughan Williams (1872 to 1958) we find an idiom whose roots are largely in the folksong tradition, influenced by his study of the works of the early polyphonists. Dr. H. C. Colles put the matter succinctly when he remarked, in connection with Vaughan Williams's *Pastoral* symphony, that his 'creative power seems to have been set free by his converse with the folk singers.' He was in no way limited in his harmonic outlook; like Sibelius, he was prepared to use anything from the mildest consonance to the most astringent dissonance (as in his 4th symphony) to give appropriate expression to his thoughts. Vaughan Williams had a great influence on the younger generation, and helped them by his example to find their own language. In his long list of works, from the *Fantasia on a Theme of Tallis* onwards, there is none which does not bear the imprint of a strong and sincere personality.

The work of Gustav Holst (1874 to 1934), despite the frequent use of a markedly dissonant idiom, shows nationalist feeling, and so to some extent does that of Frederick Delius (1862 to 1934), together with influences from Greig and Debussy (to be considered later).

Nationalism in Hungary is represented by Zoltan Kodaly (b. 1882) and Béla Bartók (1881 to 1945). Of the latter some mention will be made in the next chapter. Kodaly's studies of Hungarian folksong have given a distinctly national flavour to such works as his *Psalmus Hungaricus*, one of the finest choral works of the present century.

We have already referred briefly to Sibelius. It may be well to mention that he was not a nationalist in the accepted sense and made no use of a folk idiom. He has been described as a 'nationalist in sentiment',* as was Elgar, but there is none of the deliberate nationalism of the Russian 'Five'.

* *Sibelius*, by Gerald Abraham, article by David Cherniavsky.

Tschaikovsky, too, might be called a nationalist in sentiment. He did occasionally make use of a Russian folk
tune, as in the last movement of his 4th symphony, but
he never adopted the methods of the 'Five'. His work is
outstanding in its free expression of emotion, sometimes
degenerating to sentimentality, and he was in the same line
of superb orchestral craftsmen as Mozart and Mendelssohn.* In the next generation are Alexander Glazounov
(1865 to 1936) and Serge Rachmaninov (1873 to 1943).
Neither was a deliberate nationalist, nor in the front rank
of composers, but both produced much work with considerable appeal. Rachmaninov's songs rank with those
of Mussorgsky, and he perhaps took the display concerto
for piano to its apotheosis.

The Germans, despite the occasional influence of the
volkslied in Brahms's songs, have yet to show interest in folk
idiom. Apart from Strauss there are the Austrian Anton
Bruckner (1824 to 1896) and the Bohemian Gustav Mahler
(1860 to 1911), Viennese by education and residence.
Both are 'classic-romantic', both absorbed Wagnerian
influences, and both tend to prolixity. Opinions vary as
to the ultimate value of their compositions; all that can
be said objectively is that they continued the tendencies of
Wagnerian romanticism.

As in Germany, so in France there have been no signs
of interest in folksong as a basis of style. The ballets of
Leo Delibes (1836 to 1891) and the operas of Jules Massenet
(1842 to 1912), André Messager (1853 to 1929), Gustave
Charpentier (1860 to 1956) and Emmanuel Chabrier
(1841 to 1894) are typically French in their elegance and
charm. Rather later was Paul Dukas (1865 to 1935), who
is known chiefly by his vivid and amusing *scherzo*, *L'apprenti
Sorcier*. The most serious-minded composer of the century
was Franck, who, although of Belgian parentage, was so long

* An example occurs at the opening of the 5th symphony. Where
another composer might have stated the motto theme on one clarinet,
Tschaikovsky uses two in unison—a quite unique effect.

resident in Paris that he is usually counted as a Frenchman.
His somewhat weighty romanticism, with its highly personal melodic idioms and at times exotically chromatic
harmony, was something new in French music. Notable
among his pupils were Vincent d'Indy (1851 to 1931),
Henri Duparc (1848 to 1933), famous for some fine songs,
and Guy Ropartz (1864 to 1956). Standing apart from
this group, Gabriel Fauré (1845 to 1924) exerted much
influence as a teacher, perhaps his most important pupil
being Maurice Ravel (1875 to 1937).

RECORDS

Composer	Title	Catalogue No.
Mussorgsky	Pictures from an Exhibition	SXL 6328
	Boris Godunov (complete)	SET 514/7
	Boris Godunov (excerpts)	ASD 2257
Borodin	Polovtsian Dances	72628
	String Quartet in D	139 423
Rimsky-Korsakov	Scheherazade ⎱ Capriccio Espagnol ⎰	6580 025
Smetana	Dance of the Comedians (Bartered Bride) ⎱ Ma Vlast (excerpts) ⎰	72461
Dvorak	Symphony in G	SXL 6169
	Symphony in E minor (New World)	138 922
	Slavonic Dances 1 and 3 Op. 46	72461
Grieg	Lyric Suite (excerpts) ⎱ Peer Gynt Suite (excerpts) ⎰	ASD 2773
	Piano Concerto	TWO 313
Granados	Song Recital	SB 6686
de Falla	Three Cornered Hat Suite, etc.	72423
Franck	Symphonic Variations	TWO 313
	Violin Sonata	ASD 2618
Tschaikovsky	Nutcracker Suite ⎱ Serenade for Strings ⎰	139 030
	Symphony No. 4	139 017
	Symphony No. 5	139 018
	Symphony No. 6	138 921
Bruckner	Symphonies Nos. 4 and 7	SLS 811
	4 Motets	ZRG 523
	(also includes vocal music by Schön-berg, Debussy and Messiaen)	
	Mass in F Minor	ST 899
Mahler	Symphony No. 1	ASD 2722
	Symphony No. 4	CFP 159
	Symphony No. 8 (Symphony of 1000)	6700 049

Composer	Title	Catalogue No.
Strauss, R.	*Till Eulenspiegel* *Death and Transfiguration* }	SDD 211
	Der Rosenkavalier (complete)	77416
	Der Rosenkavalier (excerpts)	SET 487
Elgar	Enigma Variations	ASD 2750
	Violin Concerto (conducted by the composer) (Mono)	ALP 1456
	Violin Concerto (Stereo)	ASD 2259
	Symphony No. 1 (conducted by the composer) (Mono)	HLM 7005
	Symphony No. 1	ASD 2748
	Dream of Gerontius	SLS 770
Vaughan Williams	Symphony No. 2 (*London*)	ASD 2740
	Symphony No. 5 and Tallis Fantasia	ASD 2698
Holst	*The Planets*	ASD 2301
	Hymn of Jesus	SXL 6006
Delius	On hearing the First Cuckoo in Spring Brigg Fair, etc. }	ASD 357
Sibelius	Symphony No. 1 } Karelia Suite	SXL 6084
	Symphony No. 2	ASD 2308
	Symphony No. 4 and *Tapiola*	SXL 6365
	Symphonies Nos. 6 and 7	139 032
See also	HMS Vol. 9 (Mono only)	HLP 23/24/25

CHAPTER SEVENTEEN

IMPRESSIONISM
AND THE CONTEMPORARY SCENE

ALTHOUGH the composer who is regarded as the chief exponent of Impressionism could chronologically have been dealt with in the previous chapter, as he died in 1918, consideration of his work has been deferred until now, since he brought to music a new outlook and new methods which are most logically treated in a section which is concerned with what is usually called 'modern' music.

The principles of Impressionism are seen in the work of such painters as Monet and Cézanne and such poets as Verlaine and Mallarmé. The painters concentrated on light and colour as the most important elements in a picture, largely disregarding traditional methods of 'composition' and eschewing anything that savoured of photographic realism. The poets were willing to discard prosody and even to neglect the normal rules of syntax, concerning themselves with the purely sensuous effect of words—words as sounds and symbols rather than as links in a chain of thought. Both painters and poets sought to suggest rather than to state.

Born in 1862, Claude Achille Debussy came early under the influence of the pictorial and poetical impressionists, and his style came to be based on an application to music of their underlying principles. (It is arguable that he was to some extent anticipated by Liszt in some of his latest piano works.) We have noted the romantics' interest in sound as such, leading, among other things, to developments in the use of the orchestra; Debussy's interest was in sounds as sounds, combinations of notes, whether analysable as 'chords' in the traditional sense or not, calculated, in their context, to induce certain mental or psychological reactions, rather than as links in a musical argument. Anything contrapuntal was therefore alien to his style, and he was led to experiment with such possibilities as the whole-tone scale, though not to the extent which is sometimes imagined, and the use of clusters of notes which can hardly be classified as chords in the traditional manner. (For a simple example, see the third and fourth bars from the end of the piano prelude *Le Cathédrale Engloutie*.) The traditional principle that a discord needs some kind of resolution is therefore often completely discarded, since the traditional attitude to discord no longer holds good. A ninth or thirteenth chord, for instance, is not to Debussy a discord; it is a 'sound' to be used for its particular effect—the impression it conveys—in its context. Not that he attempted to sever all links with the past or to found an entirely 'new' system of harmony. Rather he indicated the possibility of a new attitude towards its functions, retaining but expanding the traditional vocabulary. Despite the opinions held by many who have not closely studied his work, much of Debussy's harmony is more straightforwardly diatonic than that of Wagner in *Tristan* or *Parsifal*.

Debussy's aim was the capturing of a sensation or a mood, and in this he showed himself the successor of such 17th- and 18th-century clavecinists as Couperin. He 'attempted to create the musical equivalent of a literature' (and, we may add, of a pictorial art) 'permeated with ambiguity—intriguing, deceiving, yet attractive ambiguity'.* His music is illustrative in a new sense. The realism of a Strauss is not his object, though it does show clearly in such a piece as the prelude *Feux d'artifice*; he aims to suggest, to give an impression, like the painters and poets from whom he took his inspiration. In his use of the delicate tints of the orchestra —economical to the last degree—and in his highly personal style of keyboard writing, we recognise the master of suggestion. We have only to listen to the very opening of

* P. H. Lang, *Music in Western Civilisation*.

the famous *Prélude à l'Après-midi d'un Faune* (1892) to realise
his ability to create an atmosphere with, as it were, the
minimum strokes of the brush.

Debussy's one opera, *Pelléas et Mélisande*, based on the
play by Maurice Maeterlinck, is at the opposite pole from
both Wagnerian music-drama and the Italian tradition.
The singing is entirely declamatory, approaching natural
speech; the orchestra is used not as a mere accompaniment, nor does it provide a Wagnerian symphonic poem.
It suggests the atmosphere in an entirely individual manner.
Debussy influenced many composers to a greater or less
degree, but *Pelléas* stands as an isolated phenomenon,
lacking both predecessors and successors.

With his latest compositions, *e.g.* the sonatas for piano
and violin, 'cello and piano, and flute, viola and harp
(1915–17), Debussy entered a kind of 'neo-classic' phase,
nearer to traditional form and line—though harmonically
quite advanced—than his impressionist work. Nevertheless, he was perhaps more of a whole-hearted impressionist
than any other composer. Ravel and Delius were among
those who came under his influence. As a pupil of Fauré,
however, Ravel learned the value of formal stability,
clarity of outline, and precision; his musical characteristics
developed on different lines from those of Debussy, and
the influence of the 18th-century clavecinists is sometimes
apparent. Delius, at his best, perhaps, in smaller works,
cultivated a harmonic style which tends to be lush, and
lacked the *finesse* and elusiveness of the Frenchmen.

As a preliminary to some consideration of the more recent
trends in music three points must be mentioned. Firstly,
the overlapping of styles referred to in Chapter 16, post-
romantics working concurrently with the more advanced
composers. Among contemporaries we may distinguish
two main classes, though the dividing line is by no means
clearly drawn. There are those who retain strong links
with tradition, both harmonically and in their general
outlook, and those in whose work the links are wearing

more or less thin or appear to have snapped. Secondly, we must again stress the importance of the time factor. At the present day many different lines of development are being pursued, almost as many, in fact, as there are individual composers. In fifty years' time it may be possible to distinguish the geese from the swans and to decide which composers are on the main road and which are merely exploring dead-ends. All that can be done at present is to indicate what appear to be the general trends, without passing an opinion as to their potential value. Thirdly, and arising from this general rather than particular consideration of contemporary work, no attempt can be made to mention every single composer. It would be possible to give a comprehensive list of names, but to do so would be singularly uninformative. It is the music which matters most.

In the work of composers whose links with tradition are still firm their harmonic vocabulary is, logically enough, an extension of that of Liszt and Wagner, often with some influence from Debussy. It is still fundamentally based on the major-minor scale system. In matters of form, too, there is no violent break with the past, but rather a continued development of the processes of the 19th century.

In many instances nationalist traits are evident to a greater or less extent, as in the case of such British writers as John Ireland (1879–1962), Arnold Bax (1883–1953), and Herbert Howells (b. 1892). All have carried on, among other things, the English tradition of choral music, notable works including Bax's motet *Mater ora Filium* and Howells' *Hymnus Paradisi*. Arthur Bliss (1891–1975) was more eclectic and rather less traditional in his outlook. Of a younger generation William Walton (b. 1902) is to be noted, forceful and dynamic, with a highly individualised style. His *Belshazzar's Feast* may be coupled with the choral works mentioned above. Younger still is Benjamin Britten (1913–1976). His fertile imagination (especially stimulated in the setting of words) and his fluent technique, which can still find fresh resource in diatonic melody, enable him to achieve a wide range of style, from a rather steely post-romanticism to the most advanced modernity.

Among Continental composers the late romantic attitude is perhaps less common. Kodaly has been mentioned, and we may refer also to Ernest Bloch (1880–1959), born in Switzerland of Jewish parentage. He had a very original mind, and his style and idiom, often markedly dissonant but with a traditional background, are highly individual and of great dynamic power. His music has often a rhapsodic tendency and shows racial characteristics. His violin concerto is one of the finest recent works of its *genre*.

Of music in Russia it is difficult to give an opinion owing to the peculiar conditions (at least to the Western mind) under which artists are expected to work. Such composers as Serge Prokofieff (1891 to 1953) and Dmitri Shostakovich (b. 1906) have had to conform to the canons promulgated by those who dictate artistic style in the U.S.S.R. They are therefore not entirely at liberty to develop according to their natural inclinations.

In recent years a number of native-born composers have appeared in the United States of America. They cannot be regarded as a 'school' since their styles and aims vary widely. The methods of the earlier writers were naturally based on the German tradition, but more recently there has been a tendency to considerable individuality and an eagerness to absorb the most advanced methods. Many of the leading European musicians have made their home in the U.S.A., and their influence is evidently strong in shaping at any rate the language of a number of American composers. Among the more prominent of these are Samuel Barber (b. 1910), Aaron Copland (b. 1900), Roy Harris (b. 1898) and Virgil Thompson (b. 1896).

We must now deal briefly with the work of the more advanced composers. Apart from a completely free treatment of dissonance, the breaking down of the traditional distinction between concord and discord mentioned in Chapter 3, and a new attitude to form, the notable feature of such work is the disintegration of tonality. To many contemporary composers the major-minor scale system is played out; 'key' is a thing of the past. Thus, chromaticism in the true sense of the word no longer exists. Chromaticism means colouring. Notes of the diatonic scale are 'coloured' by accidentals. We see the possibilities of this taken to an advanced stage in the late Wagner and in the work of many of the contemporary post-romantics. But the true 'modern', in discarding traditional tonality, also automatically discards chromaticism. The twelve notes of what is usually called the chromatic scale all become of equal importance, so that there is nothing left to be coloured —unless we introduce intervals smaller than a semitone, as has been suggested by Alois Hába. (The result of this, interesting enough in theory, is that to the normal Western ear the music merely sounds out of tune.)

In the work of the more advanced composers we find not only new technical methods, but a new attitude to the function and meaning of music itself. The traditionalist, however startling his music may seem harmonically, still looks upon it as a means of emotional expression, even though the emotion may not always be universally palatable. The true 'modern' often tends to what is called 'cerebral' music. This implies that composition is more a matter of 'patterning' with sounds, according to a more or less definite plan. Some, indeed, seem to suggest that their music is not intended to have any 'meaning' in the usual sense of the word; it is rather a matter of an almost mathematical handling of sounds, regardless of euphony.

Such a conception of an art is new, unless we go back to the early days of polyphony when a similar attitude seems largely to have held good. It is certainly in direct opposition to the aims of composers since the 15th century, whatever variations there have been in style and method. Most notably it is opposed to the romantic spirit of the 19th century—music as a direct response to, and expression of, feeling. A reaction of some kind was to be expected.

History shows us that when a style reaches its apogee a revulsion is sooner or later inevitable. We may recall the aversion of the *Camerata* to polyphony. Non-musical factors also have influence; in the case of the *Camerata* their pre-occupation with Greek drama, for example. In the case of 20th-century music we have to allow for two world wars and a number of revolutions, together with the advent of the 'mechanical age', tending to modify man's outlook on life. This is reflected in the work of at least a proportion of artists of all kinds. Painters and sculptors produce 'abstractions', conveying no emotional message and representing nothing except some kind of visual pattern. Composers attempt to follow their lead, as Debussy followed that of the impressionist painters and poets.

The new outlook was first expressed in 'neo-classicism', of which we have signs—but not more than signs—in the late Debussy. It implied a complete turning away from the emotionalism of the late romantics and a return to many older forms—concerto grosso, suite, fugue, passacaglia, etc. —which are associated especially with Bach. The revival of contrapuntal writing, alien to the impressionists, and of the stricter contrapuntal forms, alien to the true romantics, is a feature of some contemporary music, as well as the cultivation of chamber music. The earliest neo-classicist was Ferruccio Busoni (1866 to 1924), though his popular fame rests on his prowess as a pianist. Such a work as his *Fantasia Contrappuntistica* (1912) clearly looks back to Bach's *Art of Fugue* for its inspiration. It was not, however, until Igor Stravinsky (1882–1971) produced such works as his *Octet for Wind Instruments* (1923) and *Piano Concerto* (1924) that neo-classicism began to have any widespread effect. The characteristic impersonality is seen also in many works by Paul Hindemith (1895–1963), in which he pursues a highly developed contrapuntal style. His *Ludus Tonalis* is another descendant of the *Art of Fugue*, and of the *Forty-eight*.

On the fringe, as it were, of neo-classicism lies the work of a number of composers who, while not to be considered as true exponents of this style, have nevertheless attempted to break away, in various ways, from romanticism. The band of composers in France who called themselves *Les Six* and who had a not inconsiderable vogue immediately after the First World War, are a case in point. They were Louis Durey (b. 1888), Arthur Honegger (1892–1955) of Swiss parentage, Germaine Tailleferre (b 1892), Darius Milhaud (1892–1974), Georges Auric (b. 1899) and Francis Poulenc (1899–1963). Besides being anti-romantics they also placed themselves in opposition to the impressionism of Debussy, following the leadership of Erik Satie. Honegger seems to some extent to have modified his point of view in later years, and produced works of considerable power and originality. Poulenc was an exponent of the 'witty' in music, sometimes becoming merely flippant. There is often a kind of light 'entertainment value', but seldom any great depth of meaning. With him may be mentioned the Englishman Lord Berners (1883 to 1950) and Prokofieff in his earlier years. Walton, too, indulged in this witty approach in his satirical music to Edith Sitwell's *Façade*—a masterpiece of its kind.

The desire to experiment, to explore new technical methods and possibilities, has led composers in many directions. In some cases such experiment has been systematic, but in others it seems to have been largely empirical. Of composers who have made systematic attempts to enlarge the bounds of harmony Béla Bartók is noteworthy. His curiosity regarding new aspects of sounds and their organisation, supplementary to traditional methods, led him to explore, among other things, the use of new scales, polytonality (two or more keys simultaneously) and chords built up in 4ths and other intervals instead of the customary 3rds. His *Mikrokosmos* for piano is a simple but instructive exposition of such experiments. Hindemith, too, did much to elaborate a logical, though a quite personal system of harmony. He was at one time a believer in *Gebrauchsmusik*—utility music—remarking that 'a composer should never write unless he knows of a demand for his work;

not for his own satisfaction'. In one respect, therefore, he looked back to the attitude of the 18th-century kapellmeister.

Experiment has not been confined to the harmonic side. The 'tyranny of the barline' has come under fire, in attempts to break away from the regular metrical accentuation which has been the norm for some three hundred years. Such a work as Stravinsky's ballet *Le Sacre du Printemps*, especially in its final movement, is epoch-making in this direction. Notable, too, is the tendency of some composers to discard the standard orchestral combination which has developed since the second half of the 18th century. The early years of the present century saw the apotheosis of the mammoth orchestra in the works of such men as Strauss and Mahler, but the contemporary composer often prefers not merely to reduce the number of players but to use entirely new combinations of instruments. Schönberg's works of his early post-Wagnerian phase—the *Gurrelieder* and *Pelleas and Melisande*—utilise enormous forces, but his *Chamber Symphony* of 1906 goes to the other extreme, requiring only fifteen solo instruments. Stravinsky's *Sacre du Printemps* (1913) needs a huge orchestra, but his *Histoire du Soldat* (1918) is scored for one each of violin, double-bass, clarinet, bassoon, cornet and trombone, with eight percussion instruments. The tendency generally is to employ only those instruments which are felt to be actually needed, rather than to write automatically for a full normal orchestra. Economic factors have also to be considered. It is useless to demand an orchestra of a hundred-odd players when nobody can afford to pay them.

We have mentioned the wide variations of style to be found in the work of some contemporary composers. In some cases we can trace a clear and continuous line of development onwards from a post-romantic idiom to more or less advanced modernity. In others, as in the case of Bartók, a peak of modernity is followed by some relaxation,* some return to a more 'human' style. In the case of

* Compare the remark on Schütz's *Cantiones Sacrae* in Chapter 8.

Stravinsky there has been a kind of vacillation, almost from work to work. In his opera *The Rake's Progress*, he made a return, in structural method if not in harmony, to the 18th century, while latterly in the ballet *Agon* and the choral work *Canticum Sacrum*, he has made use of Serial technique developed from Schönberg's Twelve-note System. Stravinsky, whose influence on the younger generation has been not inconsiderable, has been described as a master of styles rather than of style. He has never limited himself to a single style, but varies his mode of expression from work to work.

Possibly the most consistent line of development is found in the work of Arnold Schönberg (1874 to 1951). Beginning as a post-Wagnerian romantic, as in such works as *Pelleas and Melisande* and *Verklärte Nacht*, he moved farther and farther towards intense use of discord and away from traditional tonality, ultimately arriving at a highly organised system of atonality (absence of key) based on a scale of twelve semitones, in which every note is of equal importance. The twelve notes of the "chromatic" scale are arranged in an order chosen by the composer, this forming the 'series' or 'tone row'. The whole composition is based on this, the basic principle being, very broadly, that no note of the series should be repeated until the whole row has been used up, either horizontally or vertically, *i.e.* in chordal combinations.* This method is called Serialism.

The urge behind Schönberg's development was, according to one writer,† a desire to increase the emotionally expressive power of music, 'to express an excessive degree of emotional tension, at the same time following his emotions down to their deep-seated subconscious roots'. The system involves a use of dissonance which at times reaches the limit of intensity. Schönberg's pupil Alban Berg (1885 to 1935)

* There are various complications and modifications, too complex to be dealt with here. Elucidation may be found in *Studies in Counterpoint* by Ernst Křenek (Schirmer) and *Twentieth Century Counterpoint* by Humphrey Searle (Williams and Norgate).

† Mosco Carner, article in *The Concerto* by Ralph Hill (Pelican Books).

proved in his violin concerto, among other works, the great
expressive possibilities of his master's methods, though he
was by no means inflexible in his application of them.. Another pupil, Anton Webern (1883 to 1945) took the purely
cerebral aspect towards its extreme, in patterns of pure
sound.

The serial idea has also been applied to both rhythm and
dynamics, notably by Oliver Messiaen (b. 1908) in his
Mode de valeurs et d'intensités (1949) and *Cantéyodjayâ* (1953).
Analysis of such works as these may give the impression that
they are conceived entirely mechanically.   For example, in
one section of the *Cantéyodjayâ* the rhythm of one 7½ bar
passage is exactly reversed in the next 7½; in another section
the duration of the notes in the bass decreases progressively
from 23 demisemiquavers to 1 while the treble does the
opposite, increasing from 1 to 23.   Such procedures are
obviously worked out mechanically, but what ultimately
matters is not so much the composer's method of working as
the eventual effect in sound, *i.e.* what the listener actually
hears. If it is meaningful (whether or not the average
listener can grasp the meaning), then its object is achieved.
It is perhaps permissible to suggest that some of Bach's
complex uses of fugal devices—stretto, etc.—and such
things as the canons in his *Musical Offering* must also have
been worked out mechanically, but the purely musical
results can at times be overwhelming.

Younger composers such as Pierre Boulez (b. 1925)
though elaborating Messiaen's serial treatment of rhythm
and applying the idea to dynamics, tempo and timbre as
well, have been even more strongly influenced by Webern's
fragmented treatment of texture.*

Although the works of such composers as those just
considered may seem more or less incomprehensible to the
musical man-in-the-street, they nevertheless retain a
traditional attitude with regard to the basic factors which

* On this and other relevant matters the reader is again referred to
Searle's *Twentieth Century Counterpoint.*

constitute music—sounds of definite pitch and duration, melody and harmony (interpreted in the widest possible sense).   They still employ the normal apparatus of musical instruments, often, however, in unusual combinations and requiring from them effects which are far from traditional. The strings of a piano, for example, may be plucked by the fingers; or the fingers may execute a glissando up and down the strings themselves; or a whole row of keys may be depressed simultaneously by the side of the forearm, giving a 'cluster of notes'.   This kind of thing may come under the heading of 'exploiting new sonorities' but it can be taken to extremes.   (In his notice of a performance of a work of this nature a critic wrote that 'Mr. . . . . . . did everything he could to the piano except kick it'.)

Of those concerned with such experiments, particularly with percussion, the earliest was Edgar Varèse (1885 to 1965) who anticipated in the 1920s many of the novel sound effects which present-day composers are using.

The most advanced of the *avant garde* schools have at times entirely discarded any links with traditional methods or *media*, preferring to indulge in experiments in sound as such. This approach was first developed in the *Musique Concrète* of Pierre Schaeffer (b. 1910).   It involves the use of tape recordings and tapes of natural sounds, mixed or super-imposed and at times distorted in whatever way the composer chooses.   A possibility, for example, could be a few lines of Hamlet's Soliloquy played backwards at twice normal speed combined with the sound of low notes on the piano with the tape reversed so that the tone swells instead of diminishing, punctuated by thumps on the bass drum. (This is not claimed to be an actual instance; it merely shows the kind of procedure which may be employed).

Whether this can be legitimately called 'music' is a matter of personal opinion; it certainly has no traditional basis.   At the same time, and without expressing any opinion as to the value or otherwise of *Musique Concrète*, one may recall that somebody once remarked that if Palestrina could have heard the *Meistersinger* overture, he would not have considered it to be music at all.

The work of Karlheinz Stockhausen (b. 1928) and his followers involves the use of sounds generated from an electronic oscillator, but does sometimes retain some tenuous links with tradition in the use of accepted musical instruments and the human voice, in however untraditional a manner.

There are also experiments in "chance music". In this the various performers are left free to interpret their parts (which themselves only *suggest* by means of mystic symbols what is to be done) more or less as they themselves may choose. This was pioneered by John Cage (b. 1912) with his music for 'prepared' piano, and in one way or another has since become an ingredient in the works of numerous composers, along with serial and electronic techniques. To single out composers is perhaps invidious, but in England the music of Peter Maxwell Davies (b. 1934) gains coherence through the medieval aspect taken on by his use of chance and serial methods; while in America Milton Babbitt (b. 1916) brings his training as a mathematician to bear on electronic music and on the more esoteric forms of serialism. As one writer* puts it, the composers of the most advanced schools have forsaken 'an accepted musical vocabulary and syntax in favour of something varying from a total serialization of the elements of pitch, duration, tempo, dynamics and timbre in musical construction to their haphazard interaction through aleatory (*i.e.* chance) contrivances'.

At the present time it is, of course, impossible to express any definite opinion as to the intrinsic, or even potential value of all this experimentation; we are too close to it to be able to get it in perspective. But the view may be hazarded that Luigi Nono (b. 1924) in a work such as *Il Canto Sospeso* and Krzystof Penderecki (b. 1933) in his *St. Luke Passion* and *Stabat Mater* have managed to humanise these methods,

---

* Ian Spink—*An Historical Approach to Musical Form* (Bell).

bending new techniques to a recognisable expression of feeling which may be communicable, at least to some small extent, to the uninitiated.   The problem which arises from contemporary *avant garde* writing is that of communication with the listener.   To his limited circle of admirers and devotees, such a composer as Stockhausen is, to use a convenient colloquialism, 'the last word'.   To the ordinary listener, whether professional or amateur, his works are apt to sound meaningless and incomprehensible.   Yet we cannot on that account dismiss them as simply wild and worthless experiments.   Only time will enable us to sift the good from the bad, the worthwhile from the valueless.

With this we must conclude our all-too-brief discussion of 20th-century trends.   The question remains: Whither are they leading?   It would seem that we are living in a period of transition, comparable in a way to the 17th century. As then, new ideas are in the air, experiment is widespread. We cannot say which ideas or experiments may be really fruitful or which may turn out to be valueless. All we know is that music will not, and cannot, stand still.

RECORDS

Composer	Title	Catalogue No.
Debussy	*La Mer* *L'après-midi d'un faune* }	72533
	Nocturnes Printemps } Rhapsodie	72785
	Preludes, Book I	SLS 803
	String Quartet } String Quartet	HQS 1231
Ravel	*La Valse* } Bolero	SXL 6065
Walton	Symphony No. 1	SB 6691
	Belshazzar's Feast	SAX 2319
	Façade (Entertainment)	STL 5449
Britten	Young Person's Guide to the Orchestra } Variations on a Theme of Frank Bridge	SXL 6450
	Spring Symphony	SXL 2264
	War Requiem	SET 252/3

Composer	Title	Catalogue No
Stravinsky	The Firebird ⎱ Petrouchka ⎰	ASD 2614
	Symphony in 3 Movements ⎱ Symphony of Psalms ⎰	SDD 238
	Rite of Spring	72054
Honegger	Pacific 231	6065
	Symphony No. 2 ⎱ Christmas Cantata ⎰	SDD 189
Bartok	Concerto for Orchestra	6580 036
	Piano Concerti 1 and 3	ASD 2476
	String Quartets 3 and 4	61119
Prokofieff	Piano Concerto No. 3	ASD 2411
	Symphony No. 1 (Classical) and No. 7	ASD 2410
Shostakovitch	Symphony No. 12	ASD 2598
Webern	5 Pieces, Op. 10 ⎱	
Berg	3 Pieces, Op. 6 ⎰	SAL 3539
	Violin Concerto	72070
Schönberg	Piano Concerto ⎱ Violin Concerto ⎰	72642
	5 Pieces from Op. 16	SAL 3539
	Variations for Orchestra ⎱ Chamber Symphony ⎰	SXL 6390
	Pierrot Lunaire	SLPX 11385
Varèse	Offrandes (1922) ⎱ Octandre (1924) ⎱ Ionisation (1931) ⎰ Intégrales (1925) ⎰ Density 21·5	STGBY 643
Messiaen	Chronochromie (1960)	ASD 639
	Et expecto resurrectionem mortuorum ⎱ Couleurs de la cité celeste ⎰	72471
Stockhausen	Kontakte ⎱ Gesang der Junglinge ⎰	138 811
Boulez	Pli selon Pli	72770
	Soleil des eaux	ASD 639
Penderecki	St. Luke Passion	6700 022

INDEX

INDEX